SOCIALISM

PRAISE FOR *SOCIALISM*
AND MICHAEL HARRINGTON

"Mr. Harrington is a sensitive, compassionate advocate of a just, humane, and civilized future. . . . [*Socialism*] has a lively air of optimism and boldly challenges traditional ideas."

—*The New York Times*

"Magnificent . . . More than anything, this is a book about hope."

—*Los Angeles Time Book Review*

"Harrington is a nondogmatic thinker, and this succinct, readable synthesis of the various strands of his thought conveys a sense of urgency deepened by his struggle with inoperable cancer. His blueprint for a 'visionary gradualism' deserves a reading."

—*Publishers Weekly*

"Harrington is a lucid writer, able to say plainly and exactly what he means . . . A scholar of extraordinary diligence and depth."

—John Kenneth Galbraith

"In this lively book, the late Michael Harrington draws on a lifetime of thinking and politicking to reject much that has passed for socialism and to define the new forms that will make it the only 'hope for human freedom and justice' in the twenty-first century. The new socialism, he says, has to be truly international (unlike most socialism in past practice) and must be democratic in more than a political sense, providing real participation in economic decisions. Scarcely any past socialists meet Harrington's standards, but he makes his 'visionary gradualism' sound pragmatic."

—*Foreign Affairs*

"In a time when America and the world were moving rightwards, Harrington kept the socialist flame burning, and fitted the socialist idea to the global challenges of the twenty-first century."

—Harold Meyerson, editor-at-large
of *American Prospect*

"Harrington has done us a great service by challenging us to roll up our sleeves to begin the struggle anew."

—*Philadelphia Inquirer*

SOCIALISM

PAST
and
FUTURE

The Classic Text on the Role of
Socialism in Modern Society

MICHAEL HARRINGTON

ARCADE PUBLISHING • NEW YORK

First Arcade Paperback edition 2011

Arcade Publishing books may be purchased in bulk at special discounts
for sales promotion, corporate gifts, fund-raising, or educational purposes.
Special editions can also be created to specifications. For details, contact
the Special Sales Department, Arcade Publishing, 307 West 36th Street,
11th Floor, New York, NY 10018 or arcade@skyhorsepublishing.com.

Arcade Publishing® is a registered trademark of Skyhorse Publishing, Inc.®,
a Delaware corporation.

Visit our website at www.arcadepub.com.

10 9 8 7 6 5 4 3

Designed by Virginia Evans

Library of Congress Cataloging-in-Publication Data is available on file.

ISBN: 978-1-950691-51-7
Ebook ISBN: 978-1-62872-221-5

Printed in the United States of America

For Willy Brandt and
the Socialist International

Editor's Note to the 2011 Edition:

Socialism: Past and Future was Michael Harrington's last book. Published by Arcade Publishing in 1989, this text was literally Harrington's last word on the subject—a cause he had dedicated his life to understanding. It has since become the definitive book on socialism and it is our pleasure to bring this classic back into print in 2011. We have preserved Harrington's original text and we believe his vision for socialism as "the hope for human freedom and justice" is as relevant and informative today as it was upon its first publication.

Contents

Contents

Acknowledgments

This book was begun the day I was told that I had inoperable cancer and a limited time to live. I asked my doctors to keep me alive long enough to complete a summary statement on themes I had thought of throughout an activist life. They did. I therefore want to thank Doctors Nemetallah Amin Ghossein, Juden Reed, and Gerald Fleischner, their assistants Jeannie Nusbaum, Patricia Stacey, Joan Mullen, and Peggy Costigan, and the nurses and staff of Eight South at Einstein Hospital who showed that even chemotherapy can be carried out with humanity.

I have no idea of what is now in store for me, but if these fine people will keep on in their work, perhaps there will be time for another book. Or two. Or three.

Under these trying circumstances, Irving Howe showed himself to be, as I knew he would, a perfect friend. He read the manuscript in both its first and second drafts and was of enormous moral importance to me.

My editor, Dick Seaver, who responded magnificently to my first encounter with cancer, was just as supportive this time. He is a friend and a comrade as well as a colleague.

SOCIALISM

SOCIALISM

1

Hypotheses

I

Socialism, I want to propose, is the hope for human freedom and justice under the unprecedented conditions of life that humanity will face in the twenty-first century.

Socialism? The hollow memory of a passionate youth, a youth that took place a hundred years ago? How can a nostalgic irrelevance be the precondition of anything?

Once upon a time, to be precise, on July 14, 1889, when the nascent socialist parties of the world came together in Paris on the centenary of the Bastille, it was reasonable to take socialism seriously. It confidently announced itself as the inheritor of the great bourgeois revolutions, the movement that would redeem a promise of *liberté, égalité et fraternité* that could not possibly be fulfilled within capitalist limits. Parties were being created everywhere in Europe — and in Australia, New Zealand, Latin America, Canada, and the United States. Some of them were so sure of the future that they organized in countries in which the workers had not yet even won the right to vote. The movement may have lacked funds and the least shred of political power, yet it was rich in hope and vision. It felt the winds of history in its sails, and more than a few thoughtful capitalists feared that it was right to do so.

A century later, the democratic-socialist parties of Europe, Latin America, Canada, and the Pacific are a major political force, either in government or in the opposition. Yet none of them has a precise sense of what socialism means, even if they have often proved to be more humane and efficient trustees of capitalism than the capitalists themselves. The idea of a triumphant working class transforming society from the bottom up has not survived the fragmentation of class structure in every advanced nation. Indeed, "the" working class — homogeneous and united by revolutionary class solidarity — never really existed. And there is now the enormous new social complexity as the world economy and its multinational corporations begin to dictate politics and economics to once sovereign national states. The outcast socialists of a hundred years ago have become men and women of partial power and decent values, but also profoundly uncertain about how to apply their ideals to a world never dreamed of in their philosophy. Werner Sombart, who later became a dedicated foe of socialism, wrote in 1909 that one of the most striking things about the socialist congresses was the way they sang the "Internationale" in unison. "The heads may now and then sway apart," he wrote, "the hearts after all beat in common." At the 1969 Congress of the Socialist International in England, the organizers had to telex to London to get the text of their anthem because a good number of delegates no longer knew the words. But then, neither did the organizers.*

At the same time, there are societies resolutely dedicated to the suppression of freedom as a precondition of their continued existence — class societies stratified according to principles of inequality — that proclaim themselves to be socialist. And that is an even more decisive rejection of any necessary link between socialism and freedom and justice than the inability of the Western socialists to conceptualize — not to mention achieve — their goals in an environment light-years removed from July 14, 1889.

And yet it is the central hypothesis of this book that *the political impulse and movement represented by those bewildered, half-exhausted democratic-socialist parties continue to be the major hope for freedom and justice.* Even now there are tentative attempts within those parties to define a new socialism. If there

---

*The endnotes, which contain the references for quotations and other factual material, cover entire sections of the text and are indicated at the end of each section.

were not, this book would be impossible, the mere imaginings of an isolated individual.

In thus basing my hopes on the existing socialist movements, I am not going back to the absurd dogma that socialism is the wave of the future, the inevitable mode of social organization in the twenty-first century. There is no guarantee that socialism will triumph — or that freedom and justice, even to the limited degree that they have been achieved until now, will survive the next century. All I claim here is that, if they are to survive, the socialist movement will be a critical factor.[1]

II

MY SECOND HYPOTHESIS is that *the fate of human freedom and justice depends upon social and economic structures.*

That radical proposition about the future is in some way based on a conservative cliché about the past. More precisely, it relates to an insight that was shared historically by John Locke, Adam Smith, and Karl Marx.* For all the celebrants of the magnificent accomplishments of capitalism — most emphatically including the socialist celebrants, like Marx — understood that there was a connection between social structure, freedom, and justice.

Prior to capitalism, one or another kind of authoritarianism was pervasive. Then capitalism created, not the full reality of freedom — and certainly not of justice — but a space in which men and women could fight for and win democratic rights and even make advances toward justice. In precapitalist societies economic exploitation — the ability of a tiny minority to appropriate all the wealth not needed for the immediate subsistence of those who produced it — was ultimately based on political power. A democratic feudalism was impossible, for it was unthinkable that the

---

*This is not one more study of Karl Marx or of Marxism. I have already written two volumes showing that the unknown Karl Marx was a revolutionary, *democratic* socialist, and that his methodology has been caricatured to the point of absurdity by so-called Marxists almost as much as by anti-Marxists. But I do not want to go into these matters again. I will, of course, refer often to Marx and his tradition, particularly in the first part of this book. An analysis of socialism that ignored him would be like the proverbial interpretation of Hamlet without the prince.

serfs would freely vote to perform unpaid labor to create an aristocratic standard of living for the lords. They performed that unpaid labor because their religion told them it was their duty and because they would be crushed by armed men if they refused. In Athens, there was, of course, a democracy long before the rise of capitalism, but on the condition that the majority of the people — slaves and women — be excluded from participation. They had to do the work so that free men would have the leisure to be democrats.

Capitalism was a radical new innovation, the greatest achievement of humankind in history, a culture and a civilization as well as an economy. As a rule, the direct producer was no longer coerced to surrender a surplus by soldiers acting in the name of God. Discipline was now economic, not political. One worked at the prevailing wage in obedience to an impersonal market and with the option of starving to death instead. It seemed that everyone — labor, capital, landlords — was paid his or her just, contractual due even though the result was, at first, that a few became quite rich and the overwhelming majority merely survived. But political power no longer *had* to be authoritarian, for it had ceased to be the principal instrument of economic coercion. The worker was "free" in the double sense that he or she was no longer tied to a given manor and had the right to choose between work and death.

A scientific, and then a technological, revolution formed part of this process. Reason itself — with its sovereign disrespect for the traditions that had been so important to precapitalist societies — had become a powerful economic and social force. An objectivity that had been accepted as a given, as an immutable fact from the beginning of historic time, was now to be taken and shaped by human beings. Immanuel Kant announced the "Copernican revolution": that truth was not dictated to our minds by the world, but imposed upon the world by our minds. In such a universe, Napoleon's astronomer said, God himself was no longer necessary as a hypothesis.

There were, as a result, new women and men, new kinds of lives. There were now *social* classes, rather than juridical estates and orders in which one was born and died, and one of them, the capitalists, began routinely to engage in unprecedented activities like building private rooms, marrying for love, and making money as a career. The novel, with its richness of social detail and focus on marriages and money, was the art form that refracted this reality most clearly. And there was the painting of the Flemish Renaissance, in which household goods became the subjects of serene meditations.

There is, however, an important qualifying complexity in this capitalist idyll: the shifts in social structure opened up *possibilities* of freedom and justice, not inevitabilities. After all, the rulers of the system were, more often than not, horrified by the unintended potential of their own magnificent accomplishment. They were terrified that civil rights for the people — or, as the Enlightenment *philosophes* indelicately and habitually referred to them, the rabble, *la canaille, der Poebel* — would mean an end of property rights for the elite. Not so incidentally, that oversimplification was shared by the radicals who spoke on behalf of that "rabble." The young Karl Marx was naively convinced that universal suffrage in a Britain with a proletarian majority would automatically produce socialism. It was, however, the *Realpolitik* of capitalist power that prevailed, not the democratic illusions of revolutionaries like Marx.

In the spring of 1791, during the radical phase of the French Revolution, workers in Paris organized, the carpenters in particular. In response, there was the Chapelier law of June 1791. It forbade the workers to come together "to deliberate on, or take decisions about, their common interests." The strike did not become legal until 1864, and union organization was not recognized until 1884, almost a century after the Revolution proclaimed its goal of liberty. The rationale was that allowing workers to organize interfered with the freedom of labor in the society. Economic liberalism was, for the upper classes, much more precious than political liberalism, that is, democracy. The latter was to be the work of the "rabble" and, in Europe, of the socialists.

All this was theorized with stunning clarity in the Tenth Federalist Paper of James Madison, in one of the greatest defenses of human manipulation in the history of political theory. In an inverted, pre-Marxist Marxism, Madison argued that social classes based on "the various and unequal distribution of property" gave rise to factions. "The regulation of these various and interfering interests" — creditors, debtors, landlords, manufacturers, financiers — "forms the principal task of modern legislation." The danger, Madison continued, was that the majority of the people would create their own faction. At that point, "the form of popular government . . . enables it [the majority!] to sacrifice to its ruling passion or interest, both the public goods and the rights of other citizens. To secure the public good, and private rights against the dangers of such a faction, and at the same time to preserve the spirit and the form of popular government, is then the great object to which our inquiries are directed."

This was the source of the famous distinction between a democracy, the direct rule of the people, which threatened property rights, and a republic, "the delegation of the government to a small number of citizens elected by the rest." Later, Madison went on to point out that the separation of powers, a senate not based on democratic representation, indirect elections, and other features of the new constitution all made it possible to forestall the great danger, which was that the majority would not only organize, but act, in its own interest. All in all, Madison's analysis was a clearheaded, candid statement of how the new freedom was to be kept within proper bounds.

The political socialism of the first half of the nineteenth century — and the feminism and abolitionism — might be described as a militant disenchantment with such profoundly bourgeois limitations that were placed on the universal claims of the French and American revolutions. The initial impulse was "the struggle for democracy," the achievement of that political freedom that capitalism had made structurally possible and then had fought tooth and nail. The first great workers' mobilization, British Chartism, was a class-based movement for civil rights, not for bread, even though it peaked in "the hungry forties."

In most democratic countries, universal democratic rights were not won — for workers, women, for blacks in the United States — until well into the twentieth century (in America, 1965!). Established power did everything it could to frustrate the possibilities it had opened up, while the "rabble," often with middle-class allies, became the civilizing force.

My second hypothesis, then, has become slightly more nuanced, focusing on the *possible* political outcomes of economic and social structural change, but it has still not departed from the great consensus of the Western Right and Left on the way in which capitalism was an essential element in the growth of freedom and justice.

The only unusual aspect of this cliché is that I suggest that it may well apply to the future as well as to the past. That is clearly a critical distinction. Most people who repeat the standard history I have just recited do not ask themselves whether the same kind of relationship between social, economic, and political structure might apply in the midst of the present transition, a moment more radical with regard to the conditions of human life than anything that occurred in the seventeenth and eighteenth centuries.

All of which brings me to my third hypothesis: *the revolution we are now living through is creating a social and political environment that, if it is not subjected to democratic control from below, will subvert the possibilities of freedom and justice that capitalism did so much — if reluctantly — to foster.*

III

IT IS WELL KNOWN that, in a passage that ended with an unfortunate Hegelian flourish, Marx predicted that capitalism would be nothing less than "the negation of the negation," that, having destroyed feudalism, it would then do away with itself.

Free competition would inexorably turn into monopoly, which would fetter the one great economic excuse for the system's being: its single-minded expansion of productivity. But the very process that led to this contradictory outcome also had created a proletariat, centralized and organized, which now understood that its tormentors had lost their social usefulness to society. Forced to revolution by the stagnation of what had once been a truly revolutionary system, the workers would sound the death knell of that system in the name of a progressive humanity committed to developing real wealth in freedom and justice rather than monopoly profits. Capitalism, that awesome negation of traditional society, would itself be negated by its own implacable logic and the angry proletariat it had produced.

Unfortunately, the metaphysics and the metaphors of this analysis, which have not exactly stood the test of time, have been immortalized, not the least in the Erfurt Program of the German social democracy in 1891, one of the most influential definitions of socialism ever made. So most people have not noticed that the profound analysis that preceded the rhetoric has proved true, but not in the way Marx imagined. The capitalist — and antisocial — socialization of the world is indeed subverting its most priceless accomplishment, the creation of the possibility of freedom and justice. And there must be a genuine — and social — socialization if the precious gains of the capitalist era are to be retained and deepened.

There is an unfortunate, but inevitable, ambiguity in posing the issue in these terms. One and the same word, *socialization*, is used to describe counterposed phenomena: the growing centralization and interdependence of capitalist society under the control of an elite; and the possibility of a democratic, bottom-up control by the majority. I had thought of escaping from this confusion by referring to capitalist "collectivization" and contrasting it with socialist "socialization." I had to abandon that attempt, for collectivization asserts, at a minimum, state control and even ownership, but capitalist socialization is often much more subtle than that. Ronald Reagan, as we will see, used the power of the state for a class-based, discriminatory *reduction* of taxes as a way of subsidizing the tiny minority of the rich. That was clearly a use of social power on behalf of an elite, but it would be hard to call it "collectivization."*

On the other hand, if one refers to socialism as "collectivization," that, too, implies that *state* ownership and control is the defining characteristic of the new system. And that, as this book will make clear in innumerable ways, is not the point at all.

So I have reluctantly decided to live with the ambiguity of Marx's formulation but want to warn the reader at the outset that "socialization" describes two very different ways in which society

---

*Marx, in the quotation summarized in the text, talks of capitalist property as both "social" [*gesellschaftliche*] and "collective" [*kollective*]. More often than not, he and Engels wrote of a capitalist "socialization" [*Vergesellschaftung*] that would be turned into its opposite by socialist "socialization." I am concerned by the use of a single word to refer to two radically different processes, in part because Joseph Stalin rationalized a totalitarian antisocialism in the name of socialism precisely by equating them. Explaining why Marx and Engels invited confusion by their language would lead us too far afield to explore here. Let me simply, and cryptically, say that it probably had something to do with the Hegelian notion of *Aufhebung* in which a revolutionary change does not simply destroy, but also maintains, that which led up to it.

can become more social: under capitalism, there is a trend toward a growing centralization and planning that is eventually global, but it takes place *from the top down;* under socialism, that process is *subjected to democratic control from below by the people and their communities.*

The reality behind these terms is relatively easy to grasp. In precapitalist society, and above all in the late feudalism that preceded the capitalist revolution, one encountered workers who owned or controlled their own means of production. They were artisans with their own tools, peasants with the use of their own plots of land. The resulting mode of production was based upon atomized, isolated property, and consequently was characterized by low levels of productivity. Capitalism begins, Marx argues, with the "expropriation . . . of that private property which is based upon the labor of the individual." The peasants are driven from their land, the artisans "deskilled" by the process that leads to the capitalist enterprise.

In the place of that individualistic form of private property, capitalism, Marx holds, creates a "social, collective property." The new system, which regularly defended its legitimacy on the grounds that the laborer deserved title to the property he or she transformed through hard work, began precisely by expropriating such property and develops as a dynamic contradiction in terms, as a *private collectivism.*

The new order began not with technological change — the industrial revolution occurred long after capitalism was already in motion — but with the social organization of work. On the basis of the old tools and methods, ten artisans laboring under the direction of a single capitalist were much more productive than if they worked alone. That was, Marx rightly commented, "the secret of social labor," the foundation of capitalism's unprecedented output of wealth and, after a century or so of class struggle, even of higher living standards for many of the people. Initially it involved only the "formal" subjugation of the producers to the rule of capital, and the substance of the work process did not change.

That happened as capitalist socialization proceeded apace. The artisans in small shops gave way to less skilled workers who tended the machines of large factories; the medium-sized capitalists took over their small competitors and in turn were taken over by the larger capitalist. Science, the social form of knowledge, achieved prodigies as it was utilized in the new system of manufacture. For the first time in human history, the world was created as a political and economic unity. Life became more centralized, more organized, more interconnected in every aspect; it was socialized. By the end of the nineteenth century, *laisser-faire* — where entrepreneurs obeyed the "invisible hand" of the market — turned into corporate capitalism, where the "visible hand" of professional executives sought, with assistance from the government, to dictate to markets rather than to follow them.

This capitalist socialization process was in the main antisocial. The costs were imposed on the most vulnerable individuals and communities; the benefits, particularly before the rise of the labor and socialist movements, were monopolized by a tiny minority. Traditional society was destroyed; peasants and artisans were uprooted; and the evil, fetid cities depicted by Dickens and Hugo came into being. There were alcoholism — gin was the first hard liquor for the masses, and it dulled the agony of the rise of British capitalism — wife and child abuse, and new kinds of plagues and epidemics that sometimes threatened a biological crisis of the entire society. For the first time in human history, there was a bewildering poverty, the product of growth rather than scarcity, of a perverse abundance rather than of famine.

And competition, just as Marx predicted, did lead to monopoly, particularly in the quarter of a century or so prior to World War I. By 1914, free enterprise, an argument pretending to be a definition, had largely lost its real content. A once innovative, decentralized system that more or less heeded the signals of supply and demand turned into its opposite. Had there not been countervailing political and economic movements, the system might well have "negated itself," as Marx had suggested. But the classes did not polarize as they were supposed to, the middle did not disappear, even if it became subject to the power of the monopolies. Moreover, the socialist movements falsified their own worst predictions. They imposed a minimum of social responsibility upon a system that, left to its own devices, would have become increasingly powerful, antisocial, and centralized.

But even with those countertendencies, there is a red thread running through the social, economic, and political history of well over a century. No matter who was in power, Left or Right, or where, North or South, every society on the face of the earth has more and more socialized itself and the world in the bargain. There was indeed an invisible hand at work, but it did not automatically maximize human happiness and economic efficiency, as Adam Smith thought. Rather, as Marx predicted, it socialized the world in an unsocial way.

It is, I suspect, clear to every thoughtful person that this trend is far from over. If humankind does not, in the most dramatic display of creativity since Genesis, annihilate itself, we can be certain that the further socialization of life in the twenty-first century will make my little history a mere prelude to much more profound transformations. An example or two should make this obvious.

The internationalization of the world economy took a quantum leap in the years after World War II, above all with the emergence of the multinational corporation. In the crisis of capitalist financial markets in October 1987, it turned out that the twenty-four-hour trading day, which began in Tokyo and proceeded to New York with only the merest of electronic pauses, could be a high-tech device for the proliferation of panic. In the huge accumulation of Third World debt, the rich countries discovered that interdependence had become almost perverse. Repayment might be a disaster, depriving them of huge markets as the poor countries used their hard cash to pay off banks rather than to buy goods.

So there were tentative attempts to try to coordinate a system which had always proclaimed that its supreme glory was that it was not coordinated. But nothing like the Bretton Woods system, which ruled the capitalist world from 1944 to 1971, came into being. The surging forces of international socialization were simply too imperious to submit to such a moderate discipline. Indeed, after international capitalist summits at the Plaza Hotel in New York and the Louvre Museum in Paris in 1986–87, the *London Economist* wryly suggested that the next conference be held at a church in Rome since it would mainly offer an act of faith.

Yet, it would be fair to say that conservative capitalists were being forced by the imperatives of a socialized planet to move, not simply in the direction of some kind of world government, but toward international economic planning as well. They would, to be sure, reject my way of generalizing their pathetically inadequate improvisations. But the trend is there. There is no question that, as Scott Lash and John Urry have argued, the conscious planning of nationally based "organized capitalisms" — the Keynesian welfare states — has been partially subverted by the internationalization of the world economy in recent years. But that trend, with its intense and seemingly old-fashioned competition, is, as we shall see, only the prelude to new forms of planetary integration. The issue is not whether there is going to be a global economic order, but what kind of an order it will be. The essential question is: Will this one world further, or frustrate, the freedom and justice of individuals and their communities?

At the same time, there is a basic change in the way the advanced countries produce. It is almost as momentous as the original capitalist discovery of the social power of labor.

The United States had been the trailblazer in the years before World War I, innovating a mass-production system in which semiskilled workers used single-purpose machines to turn out huge batches of standard products. Many analysts, including this writer, call this innovation "Fordism," because Henry Ford did not simply perfect the assembly line but also understood that its unprecedented output would swamp the economy unless there was mass consumption as well. In the 1930s, and then after World War II in all the countries of the advanced world, that Fordist approach was legislated into law in ways that Henry Ford himself despised.* A legal floor was put under consumption by means of the welfare state, and that laid the basis for the enormous increase in production and productivity that took place after World War II. The government now guaranteed that the people would be able to "buy back" their own output.

The welfare state was thus not simply the result of socialist and liberal conscience and working-class struggle. It was also a functional imperative of the capitalist socialization process itself, a way of allowing the system to absorb the enormous productivity of the new forms of collective labor. It was no accident that the Great Depression came at the end of a decade of capitalist technological revolution. Output, as Henry Ford had feared, had far exceeded consumption, and a modest increment in social justice had become a precondition of the system's survival. Once again,

---

*I have gone into these matters in considerable detail in *The Next Left.*

the capitalists did not recognize this fact — Ford himself was bitterly opposed to a legislated, unionized mass-consumption floor — but were forced into a modicum of rationality by those at the bottom of the society.

But even in the glory years of Fordist achievement — roughly the period of rising production and real living standards in the West that started in 1945 in the United States and around 1950 in Europe and lasted into the early seventies — there were new trends, which had to do with the very process of production itself. Computers and robots, and workers who were encouraged to use their intelligence and creativity — and not to join "alien" unions — became the basis of a microelectronic manufacture that could shift to new products in the twinkling of an eye. The laborious, time-consuming "model changes" on Henry Ford's assembly lines could now be carried out by programs of computer-assisted design. Unions, which had been based on the stable structures of Fordist factories, now came under bitter attack as roadblocks to a new industrial flexibility.

At the same time, the Fordist culture, with its Keynesian imperative to consume, its new universities, and an occupational structure in which the percentage of professionals grew rapidly and that of assembly-line workers declined gradually, undermined many of the verities of traditional capitalist development. Once again, a process of unthinking socialization, of accidental radical transformations, could not be contained within the welfare-state structures that had saved the system from its previous blundering revolution.

"During the next two decades," the Office of Technology Assessment of the U.S. Congress reported in 1988, "new technologies, rapid increases in foreign trade, and the tastes and values of a new generation of Americans are likely to reshape virtually every product, every service, and every job in the United States." And in a remarkable study of existing computerized enterprises, *In the Age of the Smart Machine*, Shoshana Zuboff told how management introduced a technology that made the old hierarchies unnecessary — and regularly did everything in its power to maintain those hierarchies. The habits of the obsolete past dominate the possibility of a radically humane future.

That is because, like the internal-combustion machine, capitalism — sophisticated, late-twentieth-century capitalism —

moves by means of explosions. The new technology and occupational structure are accompanied by stagnation, increased chronic unemployment, and poverty. These eminently typical outcomes of capitalist change are then blamed on the welfare state, which had alleviated the problems of the Great Depression. And the transition is facilitated by austere social and economic policies that strike at the most vulnerable people and lay the foundations for a new crisis in the system as a whole.

It is unclear whether this process will result in a breakdown as deep and wrenching as the Great Depression. But it is quite clear that, whether the crisis is explosive or cumulative, it will be resolved by a further increase in capitalist socialization — or in steps toward genuine socialization. The sophisticated capitalist option could well take the form of simply providing custodial care for large numbers of people who are already being marginalized and for many more who will quite likely follow them. Will they, like the "proles" in Orwell's 1984, simply be left to eke out meaningless lives? Or could these new human prodigies of production actually serve the needs — including the need for freedom — of the people?

These are, so to speak, obvious and possible futures — the choice between top-down and bottom-up socialization — that are already at work in the present. But we can hardly guess the full social and political implications of microbiology or the new science of light. Having broken the genetic code, human beings have taken the first steps to rewrite it to their liking. This technology, like so much of what is happening, has a "natural" tendency to be elitist. With photonics there are openings that we can only imagine. Both, and the ongoing scientific-technical revolution, are the work of trained and brilliant experts, like those nuclear engineers who, so innocently and wrongly, proclaimed that their mode of power was so clean and safe that there would be no need to monitor it and little need to meter it.

In 1988, the worst drought in half a century hit the heartland of American agriculture. In June of that year, a climatologist from the National Aeronautics and Space Administration (NASA), James E. Hansen, suggested that this tragedy could well be the work of humans rather than of nature, the result of the greenhouse effect, a warming trend that results from pollution and the destruction of rain forests, which can no longer absorb industry's carbon dioxide. Whether or not this theory turns out to be correct, it is clear that there are radical and dangerous new possibilities already in existence. In June 1988, the Norwegian and Canadian delegates to an international governmental meeting in Toronto called for a global Law of the Atmosphere treaty to deal with such trends.

These dramatic events are just cases in point of a much larger issue: How does one democratically control the revolutionary consequences of our increasingly social human genius?[2]

IV

SOCIALISM WAS THE first movement to pose that question. More than one hundred years later, its answer is still quite relevant. It sought, precisely, the democratic socialization of the process of elitist, irresponsible, and destructive socialization of capitalism — a process that is very much at work today as revolutionary new modes of producing wealth are being introduced in ways that increase poverty and unemployment and widen the gap between the affluent and hungry areas of the world.

At the beginning of the movement, socialism was largely an attempt to hold back the collectivist future of capitalism. We will deal with that fascinating complexity later on. But the definition of socialism as the movement seeking democratic socialization holds from the last quarter of the nineteenth century to the present. Even more to the point, it defines the ongoing relevance of socialism to the twenty-first century.

The first mass social basis of the movement was, of course, the working class created by capitalism. It was the inevitable result of the first truly social mode of production in history. It was itself a collectivity in a way that no previous lower stratum had ever been: concentrated in huge masses in gigantic, originally urban, factories. It was also the human victim of the capitalist socialization process, and the socialists organized its anger and energy in a remarkable way. The extraordinary success of the social-democratic parties in Europe and Australia in the twenty-five years before World War I was the result of an inspired exercise in the practice of a theory that might have seemed quite dubious in the 1870s: that the impoverished, and often degraded, mass created by capitalism would be the source of the most idealistic movement in human history.

It was in this context that socialism defined itself.

Marx and Engels were quite succinct in *The Communist Manifesto:*

> Capital is a communal [*gemeinschaftliches*] product and can only be set in motion by the common activity of many, and in the last instance of all, members of society. Thus capital is not a personal, but a societal power. When capital is transformed into communal property which belongs to all the members of the society, personal property is not transformed into societal property. Only the way in which property is societal changes. It loses its class character.

Or, as Engels was to put it later on in a very popular formulation, socialism is the conscious recognition of the social nature of the modern forces of production, the social form of socialization.

At the same time, Engels, who lived through the Bismarckian reforms of the 1880s, caught the beginning of another historic trend even if he did not realize where it would lead. The capitalist nationalizations of Bismarck, he wrote in 1885, had given rise to a "certain false socialism" that saw every government takeover of an economic function as a step toward socialism. If that were true, Engels said wryly, then Napoleon and Metternich were among the founders of the movement, and the conservative proposal to nationalize the bordellos in Prussia in the 1830s was socialistic. It was terribly wrong, Engels wrote in an 1881 letter, for socialists *"to accept what the capitalists themselves only pretend to believe, that state ownership is socialist [Staat sei = Sozialismus]."* (emphasis added)

After World War I, and particularly with the rise of Stalin, those comments on Bismarckian "socialism" took on a relevance that Engels never imagined. There was a new claimant to the socialist name: a system of antidemocratic, and anticapitalist, socialization.

It was no accident that this tendency spread from the most backward capitalist society, Tsarist Russia, and then, in one form or another, to many nations of the colonial revolution after World War II. Now the struggle was not to achieve the democratic production and distribution of the wealth of a successful capitalism. Rather, it was the desperate attempt of emergent elites in poor countries to catch up, to modernize. Those elites were neither bourgeois nor proletarian — in Africa, they sometimes led nations that were not even nations — and to them "socialism" meant a forced modernization, the substitute for, rather than the transcending of, capitalism. This came to be a new variant of antisocial socialization that, though it often mobilized masses, was based on the exclusion of the people from the decision-making process even more than capitalism. That is, it was a form of antisocialist "socialism": public property and planning as a means of subjugation rather than of liberation.

But even this brutal deviation from the socialist vision confirms a part of the socialist analysis. The dictatorial collectivism of communism, the statification of almost every Third World society, whether capitalist or communist, is a powerful example of the ubiquity of the invisible hand of socialization that Marx first defined as the central tendency of capitalism. Socialization, in one form or another, is the imperative of every society in the late twentieth century, including those most given to free-market incantations; it is the fate of the entire world in the twenty-first century.

None of the conservative ideologies of the late twentieth century — be they nostalgic for Adam Smith's markets or Edmund Burke's organic society — can cope, intellectually or politically, with these developments, which destroy the historical basis of conservatism. As the contemporary German social democrat Oskar Lafontaine wrote, the conservatives who speak in the name of maintaining values, of safety and security, fail to realize that "security arises only through the avoidance of risk. But the crises of modernization in the world today can only be avoided when the traditional economic, social and political power structure is refashioned through a progressive democratization on the basis of a new ethic of responsibility." That, not so incidentally, is why conservative governments, like those of Margaret Thatcher and Ronald Reagan, their rhetoric notwithstanding, were incapable of actually turning back to *laisser-faire* and simply socialized, in the Bismarckian manner, on behalf of the rich rather than the poor.

The dictatorial collectivization that calls itself communism is in an even deeper crisis than capitalism, and, unless (as one fervently hopes) it is basically reformed, it acts as the antithesis of freedom and justice. But democratic socialism is precisely the analysis and strategy based on the drive to create political institutions that will make the inexorable socialization of these times responsive to the freely expressed will of the people.

But now let me admit: the argument of this chapter thus far is characterized by the quintessential socialist flaw.

I have demonstrated by means of sweeping historical analysis that something called "socialism" is the logical response to the predicament of freedom and justice on the eve of the twenty-first century. At the same time, I have acknowledged that the real-world socialist movement is not now ready to carry out the task to which that logic assigns it. That contrast dramatizes the embarrassing fact that, contrary to the bold unity of theory and praxis announced by Marx, the socialists have understood the world — but not fundamentally changed it.

And yet, I am not simply making the academic claim that socialism provides the best analytic paradigm for dissecting the contemporary plight; I am asserting that the democratic socialist *movement*, with its baggage of historic failure, is the political hope of freedom and justice in the twenty-first century. If that assertion is to be anything more than utopian, socialism must understand why, with all its tremendous insight, it has thus far failed in its basic task.

Ironically, then, this book, while ultimately optimistic about the future of socialism, will first be concerned with clearing away the deadwood of the socialist past. It will try to understand why socialism stumbled so often in the twentieth century in order to prepare it to walk more boldly in the twenty-first.

V

ONE AMBIGUITY HAS to be clarified at the outset.

Suppose that the perspective of a revitalized socialism turns out to be a chimera. Neither I nor any present reader of this book will know whether this is the case, since the verdict will doubtless not be in our own lifetime. But let us assume that everything goes badly — even that the possibilities of freedom and justice turn out to have been a capitalist interlude in an authoritarian history. *Under those conditions, I would still argue that the democratic-socialist movement of that last hundred or so years has done more for humanity — spiritually as well as materially — than any other social or political movement.*

At the risk of repetition: capitalism created enormously important new possibilities of freedom and justice, which capitalists then resisted with all their might. Insofar as those possibilities were partially realized, it was the movements of the working people, of women, of minorities, of the colonized, of middle-class reformers — and above all, the socialist movement in its broadest definition — that were responsible.

In 1913 in the Cathedral of Basel, socialists from Europe — from France and Germany in particular — sang their secular hymns and solemnly pledged, in the name of working-class solidarity, that they would not fight against one another in a capitalist war. One year later they were at each other's throats in the most cruel and senseless conflict of modern times. In October 1917, the Russian Revolution seemed to have created a new institution of truly popular participation: the workshop democracy of the Soviet. That led to the most bureaucratic and centralized social system in human history. In 1931, in the midst of the greatest crisis capitalism had ever known, German trade unionists demanded that the venerable Marxist leader Rudolf Hilferding support measures no more radical than those soon to be instituted by the capitalist Franklin Roosevelt. To take such measures, Hilferding told them, was impermissible. Either the crisis would be resolved by capitalism, in which case there would be no such relief; or else it would lead to socialism and there would be no need for it.

In 1945, the British Labour Party marched into parliament with a huge majority and a very specific program. The new socialist government proceeded to redeem every single one of its election promises, and the resulting welfare state was then taken over by the Conservatives in 1951. In 1981, the French Socialists, under François Mitterrand, achieved a presidential and legislative majority for a program to "change the way of life" of France, above all by enriching the daily existence of the most vulnerable. Admirable reforms followed, but within less than two years the

Socialists were engaged in administering a regime of "rigor," otherwise known as capitalist austerity.

Is there any theory that can account for these spectacular failures to act upon the socialist vision even when the conditions seemed favorable? Of course not. To deal with each one of these events, it is necessary to go into national histories, the world political and economic conjuncture, the circumstances of time and place. However, some patterns seem to have been at work in each one of these cases.

First, the idea of "socialization" as the key to the modern world was both an inspired insight and the basis of enormous political and economic vagueness. It was remarkable that the socialists were the first to understand that the logic of free enterprise led toward monopoly, centralization, and even statism. It was of critical importance to counterpose an ideal of democratic socialization to the actual, and irresponsible, socialization of the triumphant capitalist system. But what exactly did that democratic socialization mean? That was a key term, and the socialists were inexcusably confused about its content.

Marx, as Alec Nove shows, often simply assumed that "society" would take over the direction of the economy from the capitalists. But there is no unitary subject of historic action called "society" any more than there is a *volunte generale*. Society could be a representative government, a federation of workers' councils or of communes, or something in between. More ominously, particularly when one talked of "society" in the singular and implicitly suppressed all the vital differences and conflicts within actual social life, this mode of speaking could be an argument for centralization and even dictatorship. Marx, on those rare occasions when he permitted himself to glimpse the socialist future, talked of an economy run by the "associated producers," which is the language of direct and participatory democracy. To the very end of his life he insisted that the state would eventually "wither away," a utopian formulation if there ever was one. And when he once tried actually to describe the "dictatorship of the proletariat," Marx saw it prefigured in the Paris Commune, a quasi-anarchist body that provided for the immediate recall of all elected officials.

So much for textual gloss. The fact is, the central socialist proposal was to "socialize," and the socialists were woefully imprecise about what it meant, much less as to how to put it into practice. One might say from 1883 (when Marx died and the social democracy was about to enter its golden age) to 1945 the socialists attempted, with notable lack of success, to figure out precisely what they meant by socialism. Then in the postwar age, it seemed that John Maynard Keynes had miraculously provided the answer that Marx had neglected: socialization was the socialist administration of an expanding capitalist economy whose surplus was then partly directed to the work of justice and freedom. When, sometime in the seventies, that Keynesian era came to an end, the socialists were once more thrown into confusion. Which is where we are now.

Second, the early socialists made a fundamental error of analysis that they then corrected in theory but never eliminated from their emotions, myths, and expectations. The young Marx had thought that a proletarian majority in a democratic society would automatically mean socialism. But that assumed, first, a proletarian majority, and second, that such a majority would be homogeneous, seamless, united for a single purpose. In fact, as Marx recognized, the "simplification" of social class structure into a gigantic proletariat, a tiny bourgeoisie, and little else in between, as it was proclaimed in the opening pages of *The Communist Manifesto,* never took place. The problem was, he made that self-critical and utterly basic revision of his own ideas in manuscripts that were not published until after his death as the *Theories of Surplus Value,* a three-volume book read by only the most dedicated of Marxologues. Meanwhile, in the real world the working class itself rather quickly divided on the basis of skill, gender, religion, and the like. Some of the most bitter conflicts within the new movement were those that pitted trade unionists against socialist politicians. To complicate matters further, each of those strata within the working class acquired its own bureaucracy with a stake in institutionalizing the differences.

The socialists, of course, were aware of this reality; it was a fact of their daily lives. In a private letter written before World War I, Karl Kautsky, the dean of the first generation of post-Marx Marxists, wrote that it had become impossible to get anyone in the movement to do anything as a volunteer. The outcast revolutionaries, as Michels vividly showed in his famous study of German socialism, had turned into staffers.

But that did not change the movement's own myth of itself — a myth in which it passionately half-believed. One of the functions of Marxism, Antonio Gramsci perceptively wrote, was to give the "aroma" of necessity to individual, and sometimes hopeless, struggles. So even in the days dominated by bureaucratic routine, and all the more so in the times of upheaval, there was a belief in a *deus ex machina*, "the" working class, which would finally impose its unitary will upon a reluctant history. Alas, that working class never existed.

In the post–World War II period, when the shift toward the professionals and the service sector became blatantly evident, the socialists were forced to confront the fact that their historic ideal had been shorn of its supposed agency. The Marxists had always derided the utopians, who prated of the just society without specifying the class forces that would be driven to realize it. But now practical socialist politicians, leading mass movements and heading governments, found themselves in something like that utopian position.

All this is not to say for a moment that social classes and their politics have disappeared, or worse, that they never existed. It is absurd that there are late-twentieth-century Candides asserting that "everyone is middle class" even as a new working class and a new poverty are appearing in every advanced society. It is also true that, if the socialist *myth* of class was wrong from the start, the practical socialist politics of class were the basis for the rise of the most important mass movement in Western history. All that is urged here is that the united, revolutionary working class which would act as History's right arm for the creation of socialism did not, and does not, exist.

That reality — or rather, that absent reality — was a main cause of socialist failure in the first half of the twentieth century. The socialists had known and acted upon the truth in their daily practice for years. But when, after World War II, the fact became so unmistakable that only a handful of sectarian true believers could deny it, the loss of the myth was a blow to socialist emotion, and socialist identity as well.

Third — and most complex — what is the historical "space" that lies between capitalism and socialism? Once the early, chiliastic notions of a revolutionary leap into the socialist future were abandoned — above all, once the social-democratic political

strategy was adopted — that question became of decisive importance. The answer became one of the most difficult and ironic
complications that socialism had ever faced. The period between
capitalism and socialism would be dominated by . . . capitalism.

But, after all, didn't capitalism develop within feudalism? Why
couldn't socialism develop within capitalism? (Edward Bernstein,
one of the first German social-democratic revisionists of Marx,
said that it would do precisely that.)

It is true that markets and money exchange did subvert feudalism from within. But there the essential change was economic,
not political. It was capital, not men and women, that had to
become free. Indeed, the bourgeoisie did not lead the bourgeois
revolution. In England, modernizing landowners were in the vanguard, and the new manufacturing class did not even get the vote
until 1832; in Germany the transition was carried out by plantation owners (Junkers). But a socialist transformation required
nothing less than a conscious political and democratic reshaping
of the system from within the system.

In such a perspective, it might be argued, the obvious contradictions should have convinced the socialists that sudden insurrection was the only way out. But even assuming there was a
majority political will for such a course — in fact, none has ever
existed within a Western society — it still would not resolve the
problem. Karl Kautsky formulated the issue just after the turn of
the century. "A socialist revolution," he wrote, "can at a simple
stroke transfer a factory from capitalist to socialist property. But
it is only gradually, through a course of slow evolution, that one
then transforms a factory from a place of monotonous, repulsive
forced labor into an attractive spot for the joyful activity of happy
human beings." One can seize power — but then it is necessary
to run an entire, complex economy, and that cannot be done at
the point of a gun. The day after the revolution, there would still
be capitalist structures staring the revolutionaries in the face.
What, exactly, were they supposed to do with them?

More broadly, the capitalism that the socialists proposed to
transform was unlike any social-economic formation that had
ever existed. It was, as Marx had emphasized in the *Manifesto*,
something unheard-of in human history, a dynamic status quo
that had to expand in order to survive. Moreover, by the time the
socialists organized, capitalism was no longer an uncoordinated

system that somehow blundered into coherence by the workings of an invisible hand. Now it was corporate, monopolistic, more and more intertwined with the government. It had achieved a level of complexity and range unknown in human history.

In short, "capital" had ceased to be a fairly simple thing, an accumulation of money or the control of a single factory. It was an increasingly broad array of functions — investment, technological innovation, pricing, distribution, and the like — often run by nonowning managers. Marx had in fact commented on this development in *Das Kapital;* he was one of the first analysts to see that competition led, not simply to monopoly, but to the separation of ownership and management, in effect to the elimination of entrepreneurs. Naively, he thought that the socialists would be able to take over a corporate capitalism more easily than the free-market variant because it would have collectivized itself. What he did not realize was that this would happen in such a way as to make it much more difficult to "take it over."

Where, for instance, were the workers capable of carrying out those complex managerial functions in a radically new way? Capitalism hardly specialized in preparing factory "hands" — who were in any case even less skilled than the artisans of the system's infancy — to learn such things. The capitalist version of the market economy was indeed a mechanism for maximizing profits rather than human needs, just as the socialists maintained. But those markets did in fact function to coordinate an extraordinary range of human desires. Was there a socialist substitute for those markets, either a plan or a new kind of market? Thus, even if one could, at least in theory, solve the political difficulties by projecting a sudden and decisive socialist takeover, that would simply postpone all the other problems to the next morning — as happened, catastrophically, with the Bolsheviks after the Revolution. In any case, the masses did not want that sudden seizure of power, and the socialists, as a matter of principle, were stuck with gradualism and all its attendant problems.

The British Fabians thought that was fine. They proposed to have socialists "permeate" the society from top to bottom. That overlooked one of capitalism's most surprising characteristics: its ability to co-opt the reforms, and even radical changes, of the opponents of the system. Not that the capitalists themselves were, in the main, shrewd enough to maneuver in this way. The American corporate rich fought Roosevelt's functional equivalent of social democracy with a passionate scorn for the "traitor to his class" who was President. Yet these same reactionaries benefited from the changes that the New Deal introduced far more than did the workers and the poor who actively struggled for them. The structures of capitalist society successfully assimilated the socialist reforms even if the capitalists did not want that to happen.

Thus, one of the main consequences of the socialist movement has been not socialism but a more humane, rational, and intelligent capitalism, usually in spite of the capitalists. That tendency is compounded by a further irony. In "ordinary" times, when the system was working on its own terms, the socialists never had the political power to make decisive changes and were thus fated to make marginal adjustments of a basically unfair structure. In the extraordinary times when the socialists did come to power, after wars or in the midst of economic crises, they had a broader mandate, but never a support for "revolution," and they inherited almost insoluble problems from their capitalist predecessors.

The basic dilemma underlying all these trends can be rather simply put: How does a political movement make basic change gradually when at the same time it must observe the constraints of the system it seeks to transform? That was a problem light-years distant from the militant visions of 1889. It was, however, the reality the movement had to face, and it makes the failure to radically alter the system in the course of a century of struggle all the more understandable.

Fourth, the socialist movement was utterly unprepared for the internationalization of politics and economics that has been one of the decisive trends of the twentieth century.

There is a historic irony to this point. It was one of Marx's most spectacular errors to have underestimated the power of nationalism and to have overestimated the instinctive internationalism of the proletariat. But even then, his internationalism was primarily focused on the *European* working class. In their few comments on what is now called the Third World, Marx and Engels were uncertain whether socialism would triumph prior to colonial liberation or after. And they were even vaguer about how socialism in advanced countries would relate to the underdeveloped areas than they were about that advanced socialism itself.

When social democrats did get those frustrating installments of partial power in capitalist parliaments, their dilemmas were international as well as national. They now had a voice — but only a voice — in the policy of imperial countries engaged in the exploitation of subject peoples, and they were loud in their condemnation of this latest capitalist crime. But when the German socialists refused to vote in support of a military campaign against the people of Southwest Africa in 1906, they went on to suffer, in the campaign of 1907, their first electoral setback since 1884. And the Belgian socialists had the problem of deciding between a Congo that was the personal property of the king or a Congo that was under the imperial rule of the nation. Each alternative was, of course, intolerable.

After World War II, it might have seemed that these problems were resolved. The British Labour government of 1945 played an important role in making India independent, a policy Winston Churchill opposed. To be sure, the majority French socialists, after some vacillation, supported the continuation of French colonialism in North Africa and Indochina, but there was a significant minority, which would provide many of the cadres of François Mitterrand's Socialist Party in the 1970s, who courageously fought for an anticolonialist politics. And with the wave of decolonization, it seemed that most of the newly independent nations were themselves committed to "socialism."

The problem was that Third World "socialism," particularly in Africa, turned out to be either naively utopian or, worse, a cover for new authoritarian, exploitative, and inefficient regimes. Further, the process of political decolonization was accompanied by the rise of an economic neocolonialism, in which the Third World as a whole remained in a structurally inferior position while there was a further increase in global inequality, with the rich richer and the poor poorer. To the credit of Willy Brandt and the Socialist International, which he rejuvenated in 1976, the European socialists did reach out to Asia, Africa, and Latin America (particularly Latin America and the Caribbean). Programs were elaborated — under the direction of Brandt, Olof Palme of Sweden, and Michael Manley of Jamaica — for global economic policies that would create employment and growth in both the advanced and underdeveloped economies. But, as Manley often ruefully remarked, the resolutions were much better than the actual policies of socialist governments in power.

At the same time, capitalism, by means of the multinational corporation, was engaged in an unprecedented internationalization of production, turning the whole world into a "global factory." Now any movement that claimed to stand for freedom, justice, and solidarity had to propose nothing less than a reorganization of the politics and economics of the planet. That was not just an imperative of international morality. Bankers and other very practical people in power understood this point — as various ineffectual attempts at worldwide capitalist coordination clearly demonstrated. And the failure of the bold plans of the Mitterrand government in 1981–82 were caused, above all, by an open economy that had to bow to the discipline of capitalist world markets rather than follow a program that had been democratically voted by the French people.

So it was that socialists, who had yet to resolve their century-old problems of identity and program in individual nation states, were now confronted with the additional responsibility of formulating a serious program for the entire world.[3]

2

Socialisms

PEOPLE SPEAK OF socialism. We should speak of socialisms.

There is an amnesia about the socialist tradition that abandons entire definitions of that ideal made by serious mass movements. There are dictionary definitions — socialism is the public ownership of the means of production and distribution — which are faded abstractions of one fragment of a rich conceptual heritage. There are Marxist statements, often Delphic in their vagueness but always suffused with a sense of history, which are turned into transhistorical truths and chiseled into stone. And there are simplistic assumptions that the antisocialist practice of states calling themselves socialist describes something called "really-existing" socialism.

What is needed, if socialism is to find a new relevance for the twenty-first century, is some sense of its enormous diversity and complexity. This chapter and the next will survey socialisms, the various and conflicting ways that the movement tried to give specific meaning to its profound and imprecise demand for democratic socialization. This history is far from linear: it opens with the recent rediscovery of the earliest "utopian" socialist tradition and its relevance to the future. And it attempts to learn from the terrible socialisms — the antisocialist "socialisms" — as well.

All of this is not an act of piety toward the past and certainly not an attempt to write, even in outline, a survey of socialist thought. It is thematic, focusing on a few particularly revealing moments. It frankly and knowingly concentrates on that part of the past that might be usable — as either a good or a horrible example — in building the future. That is fully apparent in the very first socialism to be discussed, that of the "utopians."

It was no accident that utopian socialism was rediscovered in the 1960s and had a significant impact on important political movements in the West a century and a half after it began. Suddenly, ideas that had been given an elegant, somewhat respectful burial by Marx and Engels seemed to speak to significant numbers of the post–World War II generation in the advanced capitalist countries. Utopian socialism also took on a new incarnation in "African" socialism. And it pointed toward a new history of the nineteenth-century past in which the long-forgotten struggles of artisans suddenly came to life because scholars now lived in the age of the computer.

I

IT IS, MARTIN BUBER wrote, "the goal of Utopian socialism ... to substitute society for State to the greatest degree possible, moreover a society that is 'genuine' and not a State in disguise." That is as good a definition as you will find — even though it is more complex than it might at first seem. For though utopia exalted society as against the state, it led to technocracy as well as anarchism, to Stalinism as well as the Israeli *kibbutz*. And it may well be relevant to the twenty-first century in ways that its nineteenth-century progenitors, for all of their talent for the imaginary and even the fantastic, would never have imagined.

This early socialism was concerned with morality, community, and feminism. None of its founders — Henri de Saint-Simon, Charles Fourier, and Robert Owen — was a democrat, but the movements they inspired were profoundly democratic. Saint-Simon tried to win both Napoleon and Louis XVIII to his ideas, and some of his followers reached out to Metternich; Fourier waited for some wealthy philanthropist to make his proposals possible; and Robert Owen tried to convince both the lords and bishops of his native Britain and the Congress of the United States. So one has to look, not simply at the ideas that the utopian thinkers put down on paper, but at the shrewd readings made of them by people without much formal education.

In most histories, the first modern socialist is Gracchus Babeuf, the leader of the Conspiracy of Equals during the French Revolution, a man who tried to carry Jacobinism to its ultimate and radical conclusion. In contrast, these utopians tended to be anti-Jacobin, decentralist and social rather than centralist and political, and two of them, Fourier and Saint-Simon, had unhappy personal experiences with the upheaval in France. They wrote as the industrial revolution was taking off. Owen was a factory owner, and Saint-Simon might be said to have been the first philosopher of industrialism and, for that matter, the first "historical materialist," with his emphasis on the underlying importance of the economic in social and political history. Both of them greeted the new technological world as a means to their utopian ends. Fourier is the exception, the one of the three who was not that enthusiastic about industrial progress. Yet he was far ahead of his time as a thinker who made an almost Freudian definition of what socialism would be.

These are all familiar facts. But there are ambivalences and ambiguities concealed within them that are not so obvious and yet had a profound impact upon subsequent history. Above all, there was a strange mix of the technocratic and the decentralist in Saint-Simon and in some ways in Robert Owen. It was a major source of that dangerous imprecision in Karl Marx and most of the socialists of the twentieth century about the meaning of socialization.

Saint-Simon was a champion of industrial progress and saw the concentration of industry and, above all, of finance as a precondition of his most radical hopes. At the same time, he was caught up in the Romantic fascination with the organic as opposed to the artificial and saw the high point of medieval society — with its ordered, functional hierarchies — as one of the great positive accomplishments of humanity. That attitude was, of course, a staple of the reactionaries and conservatives, of Maistre, Bonald, and Edmund Burke, and all the others who fulminated against those who would try to plan the future on the basis of some kind of a rational model. Yet Saint-Simon, who was explicitly influenced by the French variant of that conservative school, was one of the first to formulate the concept of economic planning.

This celebrant of industrial centralization was also the first major theorist to proclaim the "withering away of the state." In the past, Saint-Simon argued, government had been imposed upon society from the top down; it was not organic. But now society was becoming industrial, the economic and the technological were the critical determinants of everything else, and there would be no need of politics. The functional organization of production was all the leadership and direction that was needed. To be sure, there had to be leaders — Saint-Simon, like the other utopians, was appalled by the ugly competitive anarchy of *laisserfaire* — but now they would be defined organically, by their role in the economy, and not by an extraneous state.

In his initial version of this theory, the leaders were to be the wise men, the scholars and engineers. Later, Saint-Simon saw them as the captains of industry — *les industriels* — and counterposed them, and everyone else who worked, to the parasitic bourgeois who simply lived off of capital. Ultimately, Saint-Simon and his followers looked to bankers to take a pride of place among the *industriels,* seeing them as planners who, by their rational criteria for investment, overcame the wasteful competition sponsored by the lazy bourgeoisie. As a result, this utopian socialist was recognized as a mentor by some of the most successful financiers in France.

But how can one man inspire both the banking industry and the socialist movement? In a profound sense, Saint-Simon himself did not effect that paradox. He remained true to the obvious technocratic implications of his analysis — although in 1819 he did propose in his *Parabole* that it was possible to dispense with the entire ecclesiastical and bureaucratic apparatus of the French state, a suggestion that got him into trouble with his more conservative supporters. It was the Saint-Simonians who squared the circle. If government was now to be replaced by society as defined functionally, then the critical question became: What is society and who are its functional leaders? For Saint-Simon, the answer was industrialists and bankers — but bankers and industrialists who were viewed as workers in contrast to the coupon-clipping bourgeois. Saint-Simon died in 1825 under the Restoration, and that was his mature view.

But the men and women who elaborated *The Doctrine of Saint-Simon,* in an enormously influential book of that name, lived and worked immediately before and after the Revolution of 1830 and, in the name of an orthodox "exposition" of the master's thoughts, radically changed it. The state, they said, would turn into "the *ASSOCIATION OF WORKERS*." Saint-Simon could have agreed with the verbal formula, since he thought of a banker as a worker — but that was not what the new interpretation had in mind. It referred to the new class of proletarians. Moreover, a striking word had come into play, one that echoes throughout the history of French socialism: *association*. Saint-Simon himself had never used it, and, as read by workers and revolutionaries, it came to mean that *socialism was a society controlled from the bottom up by associations of workers*. That notion was to be key to the syndicalist socialism of Proudhon and to the utopianism of the arch anti-utopian, Karl Marx.

At the same time, the Saint-Simonians defined both the class struggle and the concept of exploitation. Chapter 6 of *The Doctrine* was headed, "The successive transformation of the exploitation of man by man and of the right of property: Master-Slave — Patrician-Plebian — Lord-Serf — Parasite-Worker." That formulation anticipates, but is transformed in, the first line of *The Communist Manifesto*. The chapter went on to show that a "fair" contract between a rich parasite and a poor worker was inherently unfair and brought wealth to the former and poverty to the latter. And that, of course, is a central theme of *Das Kapital*.

These ideas did not remain the property of a small sect of true believers. Particularly after the disillusionment with the Revolution of 1830, Saint-Simonianism became a major movement in France, in large part because one of the central themes of the utopian socialists was feminism. Indeed, it can be argued that the cultural and social radicalism of the Saint-Simonian movement was decisive in transforming a technocratic theory into a socialist and democratic vision.

All three of the great utopians placed a major emphasis upon the role of women. "The change in an historical epoch," Fourier had written, "can always be determined by the progress of woman toward freedom, because in the relation of woman to man, of the weak to the strong, the victory of human nature over brutality is most evident. The degree of feminine emancipation is the natural measure of general emancipation." Indeed, Fourier's basic definition of community was that it would put an end to instinctual repression, allow the human passions to become the mainspring of social life, and lead to erotic, as well as economic, liberation.

"Too many restraints have been imposed on the passion of love," Fourier wrote. "This is proved by the fact that no man wishes to obey the legal injunction to practice continence outside of marriage. The infractions of men have inspired those of women, and love in civilized society is nothing but universal anarchy and secret insurrection." People with exotic sexual tastes would, so long as their activity was consensual and did not do bodily harm, "meet regularly at international convocations which would be pilgrimages as sacred to them 'as the journey to Mecca for Muslims.' "

Some of the Owenites had a similar view. "If you love one another," one of them told the young people, "go together at any time without any law or ceremony." One of the reasons for this attitude was a feeling that the bourgeoisie bought and sold wives and even encouraged prostitution. Sex, these utopian movements said, had to be freed in every way from commercialization. In the case of the Saint-Simonians, feminism was probably a decisive factor in turning the movement toward the Left and democracy. That is how the Saint-Simonian *movement*, which was Romantic where the master was technological, became a significant force in France in the 1830s, with a nationwide network of "temples of humanity" and some 40,000 adherents and intellectual sympathizers, including George Sand, Heinrich Heine, Goethe (the ending of *Faust* is Saint-Simonian), and Franz Liszt. Flora Tristan, a fascinating and influential woman from an extraordinary family — her brother became president of Peru, her grandson was the painter Paul Gauguin — combined two of the central Saint-Simonian themes: she saw the "equality of rights between men and women as the sole means of establishing Human Unity"; and she believed that the democratic organization of the working people would become a self-governing estate of the realm.

As George Lichtheim summarized the Saint-Simonians:

> Here, all of a sudden, there was a new vision of man no longer dull and rationalistic, but sentimental and passionate. The synthesis operated at every level: intellectual, moral, political, metaphysical. Socialism was a *faith* — that was

the great discovery the Saint-Simonians had made! It was
the "new Christianity," and it would emancipate those
whom the old religion had left in chains — above all woman
and the proletariat!

Owen's ideas went through a similar metamorphosis, with the
difference that the master himself participated in both the conservative and radical interpretations of his thought. In the first
phase, which lasted from the turn of the century into the 1820s,
Owen was an imaginative industrialist who discovered that acting
decently toward his workers changed their moral conduct and
increased productivity at the same time. He then tried to convince the British and American elite that social justice was a
pragmatic investment. During the very hard times after the Napo-
leonic Wars, there were widespread misery, unemployment, and,
as a result, fear of revolution. The cost of caring for the poor —
outlays that had been undertaken in considerable measure as an
insurance policy against a French-style revolution in Britain —
rose even as the wartime prosperity ended.

As E. P. Thompson put it, "The poor were unsightly, a source
of guilt, a heavy charge on the country, and a danger." In this
setting, Owen proposed that the poor be put into "Villages of
Cooperation" where, after initial public funding, they would pay
their own way and engage in useful work that would make them
disciplined and temperate. Cobbett wrote of the scheme: "Mr.
Owen's object appears to me to be to cover the face of the country
with workhouses, to rear up a community of slaves, and consequently to render the labouring part of the People absolutely
dependent upon men of property." The Fourierists, with their
Romantic values, were suspicious of Owen all along; but some of
the Saint-Simonians, with their scientific emphasis, were at-
tracted by his hardheadedness.

But then a number of things happened, and not only Owenism
but Owen himself moved from humane elitism to a kind of
working-class radicalism. One factor was that Owen's atheism
became widely known and he was effectively shut out of polite
society. Even more important, the Anti-Combination acts, which
had been passed in 1799 and 1800 at the height of anti-Jacobin
sentiment and which had done so much to frustrate organizing
among the workers, were repealed in 1824–25. Trade-union and

cooperative activity began to grow, and when Owen returned from his trip to the United States in 1829, he found himself in contact with a mass movement of unionists and cooperators. The sophisticated elitist became a tribune of the people.

Owenism was thus transformed from a philanthropic, top-down scheme for evading the class struggle through cooperation into a bottom-up insurgency of working people who were determined to rely on their own strength. At the same time, the cultural radicalism that had inspired Owen to denounce all religions as "a mass of iniquitous error" now asserted itself in his attack on marriage as "a Satanic device of the Priesthood to place and keep mankind within their slavish superstitions." In the new world, he said, "there will be no marriages of the priest or giving in marriage." This trend was reinforced, Barbara Taylor documents, when the Saint-Simonians came to propagandize the English in 1832 and advocated "moral marriage," that is, free unions based on affection and without the sanction of official ceremony. The French and British socialists, one hostile observer said, address themselves "to the weaker sex, upon whom they hope to make a fatal impression, as the serpent succeeded with Eve."

As Owenism developed in this fashion, it also converged with some of Fourier's communitarian ideas. Fourier was not simply an isolated — and sometimes half-mad — proponent of fascinating utopias, although he was certainly that. He answered the standard conservative challenge, Who will do the dirty work?, with the proposition that "small hordes" of children, who love to play in the mud, would exercise that function. More seriously, he looked to the transformation of the very nature of work: in his commune (the *phalanstere*), there would be two thousand people, none of whom would work more than two hours at the same job, all of whom would freely choose the task they liked best and become masters of it.

These utopian ideas — if not the "anti-lion," a gentle version of that animal capable of lying down with lambs, that he imagined would come to exist in the utopian era — had a significant impact upon the Saint-Simonians, particularly when they talked of "associations" as the key to the future, reached out to the Transcendentalists at Brook Farm in the United States, and found echoes in the cooperative movement in Britain. There was a reason why such notions found a surprising resonance among ordinary people, and it is most visible in E. P. Thompson's description of the Owenites.

A good number of them were artisans. They could become cooperators in part because they had confidence in their own skill and the value of their work. They, like most of the early socialists, believed in some variant of the labor theory of value — that honest work is the source of wealth, and therefore it is the honest worker who should be the recipient of that wealth. This view coincided with their own personal experience. And they were often political radicals who believed in a "republican" ideology in which no citizen should ever have to bow down to any other citizen. America, which seethed with utopian experiments during the nineteenth century, had the same tendencies. We know that the Left — republican — wing of the revolution in this country was, more often than not, supported by artisans.

So were the radical and trade-union movements of the early nineteenth century. The first labor parties in world history were formed in 1828 and 1829 in Philadelphia and New York, and the feminist and interracialist, Frances Wright, found appreciative artisan audiences in the process. This was a stratum hungry for ideas, which met to discuss books, and which often reinterpreted the programs of their "betters" — as they did so dramatically in the case of Owen and Saint-Simon. They were joined by outcasts from the unskilled and deracinated poor, and by middle-class reformers.

The utopians failed. In Europe, their high-water mark was the 1830s, and they were not really an organized force by the time of the upheavals of 1848. But that is not quite precise. There was a second definition of socialism that came very much to the fore in Paris in 1848, and it is associated with the name of Louis Blanc. Socialism, this tendency said in an anticipation of the Keynesian social democracy of the 1960s, is *full employment, the right of every worker to a job*. Blanc, who had a brief moment of power in the February revolution, wanted to fulfill that promise by national work shops. But — and here this progenitor of an early democratic socialism acknowledged a debt to the utopians in general and Fourier in particular — the workers were to elect the directors and were to become part of local communes sharing housing and social services.

Moreover, the struggle of artisans throughout the nineteenth century against a centralized, machine-run technology, which changed the nature of work and robbed them of the value of their acquired skills, was clearly connected to the utopian insistence on the creativity and dignity of work. In the United States, the historian David Montgomery has described a long war of attrition between those skilled workers and management about who would control the workplace itself. In that down-to-earth history, one hears the ongoing relevance of Fourier and Owen.

Utopian socialism, then, was not the preserve of scholars in their studies. It was a movement that gave the first serious definition of socialism as communitarian, moral, feminist, committed to the transformation of work. That tradition came to be regarded as an immature first step, a prelude, rather than as something of enduring value. If there is to be a twenty-first-century socialism worthy of the name, it will, among other things, have to go two hundred years into the past to recover the practical and theoretical ideals of the utopians.[1]

II

UTOPIAN SOCIALISM WAS given a decent burial by Karl Marx. That is ironic since Marx himself, to the very end of his life, was in many ways a utopian — but also an anti-utopian. What he did, and it was to be one of his greatest accomplishments as well as a source of ambiguity, was to *democratize* the idea of utopia.

Martin Buber, who did so much to show the twentieth-century relevance of the utopian tradition in his *Paths in Utopia*, shrewdly understood this paradox. Marx, he wrote, remained utopian with regard to his ultimate definition of socialism. What separated him from the utopians had to do with the political means of achieving those goals. Since, Buber argued, that involved him in advocating a centralist tactic for reaching a decentralist goal, Marx thereby introduced a dangerous ambiguity into his perspective, one seized upon by both Lenin and Stalin.*

---

*Edward Bernstein, the "revisionist" critic of Marxist orthodoxy, made the same point long before Buber but for utterly different reasons. For him, Marx's error was not to root out the utopianism that subverted his scientific work; for Buber, the problem was that Marx became so "scientistic," so un-utopian, that his writings could be appropriated by dictators.

What is the evidence for Buber's claim that Marx remained true to the utopian ideal? To the end of his life he insisted upon the "withering away of the state" — that is, the notion that socialism is the transformation of society, not of the government. In the *Grundrisse* he envisioned an automated economy in which the necessity of work itself would disappear, and in *Das Kapital* he argued that the "kingdom of freedom" began when creative free time became more important than necessary work. And he insisted in a famous critique of the German social democrats that the goal of the movement was not equality but the far more radical concept of "from each according to his ability, to each according to his need," that is, that the goods of the world would no longer be rationed by money or individual performance but apportioned on the basis of human need. In that same document — which was not only a product of Marx's maturity (1875) but a calculated political act — Marx opposed "state" education of children and took the American community school as his model.

In one of the most important of his brief references to what socialism would be — it occurs just before the comment on the "kingdom of freedom" and the radical reduction of the working day in Volume III of *Das Kapital* — Marx equated "socialized man" with the "associated producers." That is, the mature Marx used the classic phrase of French utopianism for the worker-managed enterprise to explain his ideal.

Indeed, as both Ernst Bloch and Paul Ricoeur have stressed, there is a sense in which Marx's fundamental methodology is based upon a utopian vision. In order to define the fact of alienation in the early writings, or to document the crippling of the human capacity in the analysis of factory work in *Das Kapital*, Marx had to have a notion of what humans should and could become. Men and women were alienated from that futuristic potential — that possibility of "human nature" — that no one had ever seen and that had never existed. It was only in terms of that radical — utopian — notion of what people could become that Marx could so clearly define their present degradation.

The radical break with the utopians came, then, on the question of how to achieve the ends that Marx shared with them. But Marx, the student of Hegel, knew perfectly well that the means are themselves the end in the process of becoming. By changing the definition of how one gets to socialism, you change the definition of socialism itself. The issue was no longer the desirability of socialization, where Marx agreed with the utopians, but how it was going to take place and therefore what it was.

The first step in the socialization process, Marx and Engels wrote in *The Communist Manifesto*, is to win the battle of democracy, to get universal suffrage. Since Marx wrongly argued in the *Manifesto* that the proletariat would inevitably be "the independent movement of the overwhelming majority in the interest of that overwhelming majority," the democratic state would, *ipso facto*, be "the proletariat organized as a ruling class." It would gradually make "despotic inroads" upon private property by expropriating landed property, abolishing inheritance, instituting progressive taxes, creating a central bank, organizing national factories on the base of a community plan, providing free education, and the like. This socialization process, Marx stressed, would be a way of facilitating "the fastest possible expansion of productivity."

This perspective, it must be understood, did not simply counterpose Marx to some of his more visionary and less political predecessors. It brought him into conflict with his own comrades in the League of the Just and the Communist League, people whom he had to deal with as internal opponents. And that explains both the vehemence of his respectful denunciation of utopianism and a concession or two that he made to that tendency in the *Manifesto* itself.

The utopians who were Marx's adversaries in the German emigration in Paris and London in the 1840s were artisans, but quite unlike those who had played such a critical role in the Owenite movement. Capitalism was now almost half a century older, and its new methods of production had relentlessly begun to devalue and destroy the skills of shoemakers and tailors and bakers. The victims of this process wanted to hold back productivity, not increase it. Their backs were against the wall and they wanted an instant revolutionary end to the work of the hated bourgeoisie. That made them open to the appeals of "proletarian messiahs," such as Wilhelm Weitling, who believed in sexual communism and the organization of forty thousand thieves to bring the system down.

Marx's target, then, was a feverish, messianic utopianism, not the Saint-Simonian or Owenite movements of the 1830s. And he

therefore argued, in the *Manifesto* and elsewhere, that the utopian phase of socialism was a product of immaturity, of a time
when neither the working class nor capitalism had come into full
being. For political as well as intellectual reasons he had to stress
the irrelevance of that tradition — even though he himself still
participated in it. He had to insist, he later recalled, "that our
task was not that of trying to bring any kind of utopian system into
being but . . . that of consciously participating in a historical
revolutionary process by which society was being transformed
before our eyes."

One part of that realism, which emerged with striking clarity in
Marx's 1847 polemic with Proudhon, was an insistence upon the
importance of an emergent trade-union movement to socialism.
In one of his most audacious insights, Marx understood that the
unions, even when focused on immediate demands, were potentially the school of socialism, the point of contact between the
movement's idealism and the practicality of the masses. That led
him to make an even more explicit commitment to democracy
when he helped to bring trade unionists together in the International Workingmen's Association in 1864 and asserted that the
reform limiting the working day to ten hours, even though won by
a coalition that included conservatives as well as proletarians,
was a "victory of the political economy of the workingclass." And
that, in turn, pointed to the strategy adopted in the 1870s in the
IWA of building working-class political parties as a means toward the socialist end.

Did this mean that Marx had abjured the idea of the violent
overthrow of capitalism? Yes and no. In those societies where
democratic rights were repressed, he and Engels insisted that the
violent option had to be kept open (and, to the embarrassment of
the German social democrats, who were harassed by the police,
Engels made it clear that he included Germany in that category).
But in countries like France, Britain, and the United States, Engels wrote in 1891, there was a very real possibility of a peaceful
and democratic transition to the new society. It was a historic
tragedy that, on a very few occasions, Marx and Engels referred
to the democratic and nonviolent alternative as the "dictatorship
of the proletariat." Clearing up that confusion would lead us into
a lengthy detour, so I will simply note that Engels believed a
"democratic Republic" — of the type then existing in the United

States — is "the specific form of the dictatorship of the proletariat," a comment that makes no sense whatsoever if you understand dictatorship as meaning the suppression of democratic liberties.*

Finally in his 1895 Preface to a new edition of Marx's *Class Struggles in France*, Engels summarized the democratic strategy in sweeping historical terms.† The German socialists, Engels writes in making use of a famous French formulation, have transformed the right to vote "from the means of duping people, which it has been up until now, into an instrument of emancipation." Now, universal suffrage, which had been an institution for organizing the state power of the bourgeoisie, is being used by the workers to attack that state power. At the same time, barricade struggles and violent revolution have become problematic, if not obsolete, as the power of the army has increased in comparison to 1848 (the German social democrats had edited out the reference to the nonobsolescence of violent revolution).

By the end of the century, continued Engels in an unrealistically optimistic mood, the socialists will have won the greater part of the middle strata of society, the peasants and petty bourgeoisie, and this power will simply become too much for the present government. The only power that could set back this trend for a while would be armed repression, as in Paris in 1871. But even that would not work in the long run, for a party that counts its adherents in the millions cannot be put down by guns.

"Thus," Engels concludes,

> the irony of world history stands everything on its head. We, the "revolutionaries", the "subversives" [*Umstürzler*] thrive on legal means much more than on the illegal means and

---

*Stalin agreed with the interpretation made here! In *The History of the Communist Party of the Soviet Union*, which the Russian dictator personally edited, Engels is attacked for his statement that the "democratic Republic" was the form of the "dictatorship of the proletariat" and Lenin is praised for having revised Engels to make dictatorship mean dictatorship pure and simple. I discussed some of these matters in my book *Socialism*; Hal Draper documents my point in the volume, *The "Dictatorship of the Proletariat,"* which is part of his larger work, *Karl Marx's Theory of Revolution.*

†The Marxist Left as well as the Communists correctly note that the Engels text was edited by the German social democrats to remove some formulations that might have brought repression from the German government of 1891. I have used the restored version of the manuscript.

violent overthrow [*Umsturz*]. The party of order, as it calls itself, is defeated by the very legal situation which it created. . . . And if *we* are not so crazy as to let them drive us into street fights, then in the last instance, all they can do is to break the laws which are so deadly for them.

At the end of this essay, Engels draws an almost utopian picture of the socialist triumph. The proletarian movement, he writes, is like the early Christians. Over the first three centuries, the Christians expanded their numbers and their power throughout the Roman society, winning over entire legions to the cause. Diocletian responded with "anti-Christian" laws, not unlike the antisocialist legislation of Bismarck in the 1880s. But the law was a dead letter, for the social power of the Christians was too great, and a mere seventeen years later, Constantine proclaimed Christianity as the state religion of Rome. Engels's scenario is, in contemporary terms, Gandhian, and in the nineteenth-century context, utopian, that is, it presents socialism as the triumph of society over the state.

Yet that utopian echo is really part of the ambiguity of the new definition of socialism. Now *the utopian goal is to be achieved by democratic, parliamentary means wherever possible.*

Marx and Engels's turn toward what can only be called democratic socialism was a critically important deepening of the idea of socialism itself. The utopians had not been democrats, even if their followers were, and their projections of the future, with their vision of an "organic" and nonpolitical transition to the new society, thus omitted the essential: the democratic socialization of a more and more complex economy from below. Now that basic omission had been corrected. At the same time, the gain in clarity was also the means of making socialism a mass force by the end of the nineteenth century. Above all, Marx's inspired linking of his ideal and the nascent working class and trade-union movement, even when it was "only" reformist or democratic and not socialist, turned that ideal into a political power.

Yet, there were ambiguities that, as a result of this transition, became even more profound than before. The democratic state was to be the instrument of socialization. But how? By what measures? That was still left vague and unspecified. Second, by turning so decisively against the utopians, Marx made undeniable progress but also prepared the way for a restricted definition of socialism. In the United States, for instance, the Marxists of the 1880s found themselves in a united front with the more conservative trade unionists and in opposition to the sometimes irresponsible reformers who were raising basic issues about race and gender. Granted that the American utopians were often dilettantes and even strikebreakers, was it an unalloyed gain for the Marxists to have become the effective champions of a "pure and simple" trade unionism?

Even more serious, radical utopian goals were now going to be achieved by means of a parliamentary system whose genius was incremental and coalitional. Wasn't that a contradiction in terms — and a contradiction that invited a rhetorical solution whereby one repeated the visionary slogans on May Day but followed the practical dictates of the moment the rest of the time?

In broader compass, the schizophrenia in Marx's attitude toward utopianism and power politics was only one expression of an ambivalence found in his thought from beginning to end. It was not, as Ernst Bloch argued, that the visions of human emancipation of the "warm" Marx were complemented by the impersonal deduction of the inevitability of socialism by the "cold" Marx. Rather, as contemporary scholars like Jean Cohen and Thomas Meyer have suggested, in Marx's most profound theories there were *both* an "objective" account of a socialist future preordained by the evolution of the capitalist economy *and* a sober analysis of how socialism must be the work of human freedom. They coexist and they contradict one another.

Both of these incompatible concepts are found at every level of Marx's development, that is, they are not, as some have claimed, successive stages in Marx's intellectual life, a transition from a libertarian youth to a mature authoritarianism. Moreover, Marx never resolved this conflict and there is no dialectic that can do so. This is one of the reasons why his disciples were often at each other's throats with conflicting interpretations of the master, all of which had a certain plausibility.

Karl Kautsky is a case in point. He did more to define socialism for the first half of the twentieth century than any other individual and influenced even those, like Lenin, who came to detest him. What he did was to reduce Marx's ambivalence to just one of its contradictory terms. He, with help from Friedrich Engels and others, was the creator of Karl Marx, the scientist of revolution, the Darwin of the social world, the prophet of the inexorable socialist triumph. It was not just that the utopian vision was lost in the process; so was Marx's lifelong stress on utopian values such as decentralism, cooperation, and, above all, women and men creating the new society as an act of human freedom.[2]

III

KAUTSKY WAS A COMPLEX political figure and socialist theorist. A man of real talent, if not of genius, the founder and longtime editor of what was probably the most brilliant of all Marxist journals, the *Neue Zeit*, he was not the "renegade" from Marxism denounced by Lenin. His stubborn insistence on the democratic character of socialism was true to the Marxist vision and Lenin himself was the deviant. But then Kautsky wasn't simply a cautious centrist, either, the man of the middle ground between Edward Bernstein's right-wing revisionism and Rosa Luxemburg's left-wing commitment to revolution. At critical moments, he and Luxemburg had a *de facto* alliance, and in 1905 Kautsky defended her against the official party press, which, he said, was controlled by "ignoramuses and intriguers."

At the risk of simplifying the intellectual biography of a man and the political evolution of a movement, I will focus almost exclusively on Kautsky's fateful definition of socialism (and of socialization). There is, however, a crucial irony in all of this that will require some reference to the historical background of the German social democracy: Kautsky's concept of socialism was elaborated under the influence of exceptional German conditions but widely adopted by foreign socialists who did not live under those conditions. Even more to the point, Kautsky's notion of "socialization," which came to be accepted around the world, was very much the product of special German conditions.

Germany was exceptional in that, in the midst of modern capitalists and workers, there were, as Engels put it, "the most marvelous, antediluvian fossils alive and wandering around." The fossils, to make matters even more confusing, were modernizing Junkers (aristocratic plantation owners) who, following Bismarck, were bent on making a capitalist transformation from above, without the intervention of the masses and with the capitalists themselves playing only a supporting role.

But how does a socialist labor movement relate to the struggle between bourgeois liberals, who are antisocialist, and the feudal forces supporting Bismarck's authoritarian modernization? Throughout their lives, Marx and Engels gave the same answer: by uniting with the liberals, *so long as they remained true to their liberalism*, in the fight for democratic liberties, which were the very air the workers' movement needed if it was to breathe.

In the Revolution of 1848, Marx and Engels were so committed to an alliance with the left-wing liberals that, as Marx ruefully admitted, they purposely played down economic and working-class issues in their paper, the *Neue Rheinische Zeitung*. Even in a temporary mood of intransigence, when the treachery of the German bourgeoisie made them insist on the independent, armed organization of the proletariat, they argued that the workers would still have to fight alongside the liberals.

In the 1860s, the tactical questions came to the fore again. Marx and Engels's disciples tried to coalesce with the liberals in the People's Party. But Ferdinand Lassalle, an enormously talented organizer — Marx was to say of him that he did the "immortal service" of waking the German working class from a "fifteen-year slumber" — took a completely different tack. He fought the liberals and looked to Bismarck and the Prussian royal house to grant the universal suffrage and state aid to cooperatives that were his immediate goals. "The working classes," Lassalle wrote to Bismarck, "are instinctively inclined to dictatorship, if they can be justly convinced that this dictatorship is in their interest."

Marx and Engels were furious that Lassalle attacked the liberals' capitalist sins while remaining quiet about the Junker exploitation of agricultural labor in Prussia, and they disdained his "royal Prussian regime socialism." Engels put the Marxist attitude most forcefully. Even if the bourgeoisie would give up the struggle for bourgeois liberties — for the freedom of press, assembly, organization, and all the rest — the labor party would have to go on fighting for them.

On the principled issue, Marx and Engels were right, Lassalle wrong. Bismarck's revolution from above left reactionary social and ideological structures intact and prepared the way for Adolf

Hitler. But Lassalle was prescient about *Realpolitik*. By 1870, German liberalism had indeed turned its back on its onetime working-class allies, and the socialists were pushed into a proletarian ghetto. The resulting political and social isolation of the German socialist movement was to be refracted in Karl Kautsky's theories about the very nature of socialism.

The German constitution of 1871 created a Reichstag elected by universal suffrage — but it could only debate, not initiate legislation. It could not even refuse taxes to the government, which was financed by permanent fixed duties. In Prussia, the dominant federal state, the Diet was chosen, not on the basis of universal suffrage, but by a class-based electoral system (in 1908, for instance, 600,000 votes elected 6 Social Democrats and 418,000 votes returned 212 conservatives to office). The Junkers, the Prussian landowning aristocracy, controlled the Diet, the army, and the bureaucracy, and thereby the nation. And this establishment hounded the socialists, outlawing the party in 1878 for a period of twelve years.

Political reality, in short, coincided with the most simplistic definition of the "democratic" state as a mere facade for the class rule of capital. That was not a theory. It was a fact of daily German experience.

This was true even though Bismarck offered carrots as well as wielding the stick. When he illegalized the socialist party — but not socialist candidates — he proceeded to co-opt a good part of its program and created the first social-insurance welfare state in world history. But the people understood that it was socialist strength, and not Bismarck's kindness, that led to this result, so the socialist vote grew even when the party was illegal — except the socialist deputies were in a situation in which their growing numbers did not increase their power one iota. Their increased vote did not change their basic and inferior *position* in the society; their strength mocked them.

As for the conservatives, they gave a standing ovation in the parliament to a leader who declared, "The King of Prussia and the German Emperor must always be in a position to say to any lieutenant: 'Take ten men and shoot the Reichstag.'"

The workers' isolation was not simply political. It was social as well. Guenther Roth described this reality as the "negative integration" of the German workers into the system. Despite the growth of the socialist movement, they felt that they had no stake, no lever, in the politics of the society. As a result, they created a countersociety of their own, their "negative" form of integration: there were the party, the unions, cooperatives, socialist schools, sports organizations, even quasi-religious institutions for agnostics and atheists. The political and economic ghetto created an enclosed proletarian culture, and it was possible to be born, to live, and to die within the movement. There, to revert to Engels's analogy between socialism and early Christianity, the catechumens awaited the fullness of time.

These very German political experiences coincided with the tremendous wave of recessions and depressions that swept the capitalist world from the mid-1870s to the mid-1890s. So it was that, in 1891 when the Social Democratic Party adopted the Erfurt Program, it seemed that the Marxist predictions of a final conflict between the workers and capitalists were a prosaic description of the imminent future. But by one of those ironies of history of which Hegel was so fond, within a few years a revived capitalism made real gains possible for the unions. And a party that had become Marxist because of police persecution and economic crisis now thrived because of relative prosperity.

An even more significant irony from our point of view is that in practically every other country in Europe, the emergent labor and socialist movements did not follow the German path. They made alliances with the middle classes and/or the small peasants, above all in the struggle for the vote. Yet the German social-democratic theories, which were a response to a unique history, became dominant in countries in which they were alien to the national experience. Jean Jaurès, the great French socialist, understood this point well and argued, against Kautsky's political mentor, August Bebel, at the 1904 Congress of the Socialist International that there could be no supranational model for socialism. In particular, Jaures said, Germany, where parliamentary decisions simply vanished into emptiness like a wind, could not define the tactics of a country like France, where the socialists could have a real impact on governmental priorities.

But these very German experiences did not simply have to do with questions of political strategy. They also shaped the way in which Kautsky and the party defined socialism itself. The new society would benefit the overwhelming majority, including many who were not workers — but it would be brought about by the working class alone, the Erfurt Program proclaimed, "since all other classes, despite their conflict of interest among themselves, exist on the basis of private property and have the common goal of maintaining the existing society." This theory arose naturally out of the isolation of the party and its policy — which made a positive virtue out of the German necessity — of refusing lasting alliances with other forces. This view, though it has gone down into history as "orthodox" Marxism, is a profound revision of Marx and Engels's coalition tactic for dealing with the exceptional German reality. In 1895, only six months before his death, Engels wrote enthusiastically of how the social democrats would, in five years, win over "the largest part of the middle strata of the society, the petty bourgeoisie as well as the smaller peasants."

Kautsky had a different perspective. While capitalism prevailed, the movement would propagandize and organize for socialism; when history turned a corner, the workers would then create socialism. That abrupt, even apocalyptic, conception of the socialist road to power meant that socialism itself was, of necessity, a society on the far side of a historic rupture that could not possibly be defined in the present. Ending unemployment, Kautsky said, was a key goal "the day after the revolution" but "in just what manner this problem . . . would be solved we shall not here try to investigate."

To be sure, *tactical* coalitions with left-wing liberals in Prussia on the question of political democracy were desirable and permissible, and Kautsky was contemptuous of the British sectarian socialists who told the workers that there was "no difference" between the Tories and the Liberals. Still, for Kautsky the state was purely and simply the instrument of the ruling class — which was certainly the case in Germany — and one could not ask it to undertake any reform program, since it was concerned only with the needs of capital. Therefore, he said, "the program must show what we *demand* from the present society or the present state, and not what we *expect* from it." Indeed, in 1891 Engels had to point out that the first draft of the Erfurt Program was wrong to assert that the poverty of the workers was growing. Proletarian *insecurity* was increasing, Engels said, but precisely because of the organization of the workers, poverty was not.

Kautsky accepted Engels's correction, but he remained basically hostile to any notion of democratic reforms leading toward socialism. In that same critique, Engels reiterated his thesis that democratic countries, like Britain, France, and the United States, could make a peaceful transition to socialism, which was not possible in authoritarian societies like Germany.

Kautsky did not make that crucial distinction. For him, propositions that accurately described the particular problems of the movement under German conditions revealed the basic truth about socialism itself. There was capitalism on the one side of a chasm and socialism on the other. The daily politics of the socialist movement were therefore fated to be without real effect and were primarily a means of developing consciousness of the need for a once-and-for-all change. How, then, was that change to take place if it could not possibly be the result of the normal struggles of the movement?

In a justly famous statement, Kautsky answered, "Our task is not to organize the revolution, but to organize ourselves *for* the revolution; it is not to *make* the revolution, but *to take advantage of it*." It was history that was proceeding inexorably toward the rendezvous with socialism, and the workers, who were unable to effect much under capitalism, would not "make" their own revolution.

Capitalist society, the Erfurt Program said, developed with the necessity of a natural process to destroy the small shops and create monopolies of enormous productivity. Meanwhile, the number of proletarians inevitably increases as a result of the same imperious necessity, the class struggle becomes sharper, and society divides into two camps. Crises and growing insecurity then prove that the forces of production have become incompatible with private property in the means of production. And this is true for all industrialized countries.

Thus the German socialists, in large measure because of their isolation and the continuing powerlessness that attended their every success, were passive revolutionaries, waiting for an apocalypse that would not be their own doing, a revolution *ex machina*. And this faith in history acted as an integrating ideology, a messianic promise that all of their present suffering would be made good in the future. At the Erfurt Congress, August Bebel had said, "Yes, I am convinced that there are only a few people in this hall who will not experience the great day." And, Rosa Luxemburg reported, "a warm, electric stream of life, of idealism, of security in *joyful action* went from Bebel through that assemblage."

That religious mood was one of the reasons why there was such an emotional reaction to Edward Bernstein when he contested some of the facts behind this vision — that the proletariat was inexorably growing and the middle class declining — and indeed questioned the messianic end itself. As the socialist historian Jules Braunthal put it, Bernstein's critique was an attack on "one of the sources of enthusiasm of the socialist movement because it [the inevitability of socialism] was the base of the workers' faith in their triumph." This belief in an ordained socialist triumph, Antonio Gramsci was to say some years later, was the "ideological 'aroma' of Marxism, a form of religion."

But then, it was not just that historic necessity would place the revolution on the agenda. Kautsky, like Marx and Engels, was aware that the conditions of working-class life, and above all the denial of access to high culture, meant that the average worker, who understood the need for unions, would not immediately grasp the doctrines of "scientific" socialism, which were, for the most part, the work of left-wing defectors from the bourgeoisie (like Marx, Engels, and Kautsky), that is, of the "intelligentsia." A proletarian elite, Kautsky wrote, would take the lead of the entire class. When Lenin first presented his notion of a vanguard party in *What Is To Be Done* (1902), he cited Kautsky on his own behalf. And once again, the workers themselves were to play only a supporting role in their own revolution.

This view of *how* socialism would come about had much to do with *what* socialism would be understood to be. Now, after about a half century of debates about "socialization," an authoritative voice defined the term. Socialization, Kautsky said, *is the ownership by the democratic state of the large-scale industry, which is the inevitable outcome of capitalist development.* That definition was in some ways a deduction from the German experiences and tactics we have just outlined, but its impact was global.

Capitalism, Kautsky wrote in his commentary on the Erfurt Program, is becoming more and more concentrated, creating gigantic national factories. Therefore, all of the cooperative and decentralist versions of socialization — not simply those of the utopians like Fourier, but the ones introduced at the congresses of the International Workingmen's Association in the late 1860s as well — had been rendered obsolete.

As a result, a cooperative [*Genossenschaft*] which will meet all of its own needs and embrace all of the factories which are necessary to them, must have dimensions completely different from the *Phalansteres* [Fourier's communes] and socialist colonies at the beginning of the nineteenth century. Given the current organization of society, there is only *one* cooperative which can be used as a framework in which to develop the socialist system, and that is *the modern state.*

This is *not*, however, a simple equation of socialism and statism. As we saw earlier, Marx, Engels, and Kautsky were perfectly aware that Bismarckian nationalizations were a way to further exploit the workers, not to liberate them. Indeed, Kautsky's first polemics in the *Neue Zeit* were directed against that theory and planned with the active cooperation of Engels himself. Java under Dutch imperialism, Engels wrote him in 1884, is a fine example of state socialism. The Dutch have organized state production on the basis of communal traditions, "guaranteed the people a quite comfortable existence according to their standards," and made an enormous profit in the doing. In that same spirit, Kautsky warned in his book on the Erfurt Program — with a prescience he would fully understand only when he confronted Stalinism — that "the state is, as an exploiter, more effective than the private capitalists, for it can use governmental power against the exploited as well as the economic coercion employed by the capitalists."

So the German socialist definition of socialism was not state ownership of the means of production, but *democratic* state ownership of the means of production. Still, it was a vision of a society as a gigantic factory, and it held that the trend toward concentration that had begun under capitalism would continue under socialism. The cooperative character of the society would be maintained, though, because all of the workers would be united by a common interest. And since the economy would be planned, those workers would not be able freely to change their jobs since the point was not "the *freedom of labor* but *freedom from labor.*"

This vision flowed logically from the theories and strategies that refracted the unique conditions of German socialist life. Since it was history and its laws of inevitable economic concentration that created the necessity and inevitability of socialism, since the workers were seen as lacking the culture to elaborate their own idea of the good society, one did not have to bother too much about the details of the society-factory that would be run by the democratic state. Socialism was the culmination of capitalism as well as its transformation, and it was defined by that fact rather than by the socialists themselves.* "Socialization" was now light-years away from any notion of the "associated producers" running the system from the workshop floor.

As time went on — and long before the socialists betrayed their messianic faith by supporting their own capitalists in World War I — Kautsky and every other sensitive observer realized that the historic scenario was not working. The proletariat, just as Bernstein said, was not inexorably increasing, and the middle strata were proliferating rather than being proletarianized. Worse, the unions were focused on fairly narrow material issues, and the working class itself was often apathetic, the party leadership involved in endless bureaucratic detail. At this point, Kautskyan Marxism ceased to be a projection of visible tendencies of the present into a socialist future, and the keepers of the doctrine had to argue that, despite this enormous detour, history would *eventually* get back on track. There were, to be sure, socialists who rejected this definition of socialism. The British Fabians had the same sense of inevitable collectivism as Kautsky but hoped that the trend could be socialized by a multiclass and gradualist movement led by socialist intellectuals and based on municipalities as well as the central government. More profoundly, Jean Jaurès responded to the statism of the German definition: "Delivering men to the state, conferring upon the government the effective direction of the nation's work, giving it the right to direct all the functions of labor, would be to give to a few men a power com-

---

*Students of Hegel and the young Marx will recognize the famous notion of *"Aufhebung,"* in which a revolution is both the culmination and transformation of the past.

pared to which that of the Asiatic despots is nothing, since their power stops at the surface of society and does not regulate economic life."

But Kautsky's definition of socialism had enormous influence, even in countries like Sweden in which the socialists made alliances with the liberals almost from the very beginning of the movement. In the United States, rural socialists at their political revival meetings greeted the progress of monopolies and trusts on the grounds that it was moving the country toward socialism. And Kautsky's conception also became the standard *antisocialist* statement of what socialism was, not the least because in making socialism statist it also made it all the easier to refute.

What Kautsky had done, with the best will in the world and considerable ingenuity, was to have reduced Marx to the "objective" strand in his thought and to have suppressed, not simply his residual utopianism, but his profound commitment to the notion of socialism as the creation of men and women in struggle as well.[3]

IV

AFTER WORLD WAR I, power was thrust upon the socialists in Germany, and they could no longer postpone all the fundamental questions about the relation of socialism to a postrevolutionary future. In a sense, the revolution had happened, but not in the way anyone had imagined. It came not through the internal evolution of capitalism but in the wake of military defeat; it was led by the conservative wing of the party; and, above all, it was now clear that reality was not going to leap from capitalism to socialism, as Kautsky had said, but would pass through an ambiguous period of neither/nor that was not quite capitalist and not quite socialist.

But if that was true, how do you radically reform a system while working within it? That problem was first discovered by timid socialists who had no intention of radically changing anything, which obscured the fact that, even had they been revolutionaries, the very same difficulties would have existed.

With the Central European power structure in ruins and socialists in positions of strength, the issue of socialization had become a question for government policy. As the Austro Marxist Otto Bauer put it, the interest in socialization was now so intense that even bourgeois economists, like Joseph Schumpeter, were debating it. But that meant that the socialists now had to become specific about their central demand under conditions they had never imagined.

Bauer gave a poignant description of what that meant to Austria in the wake of the war.

> Socializing was the slogan of the day. But that slogan meant one thing in the mouth of a worker and another in the mouth of a bureaucrat. The bureaucrats educated in the school of the war economy saw socialization as the statist organization and direction of the economy. To the workers it meant something quite different. The workers didn't want to be the living tools of the enterprise any more. They wanted to share control where they shared work.

The representatives of the workers, Bauer continued, spoke "of the needs of the Republic, of its dependence upon foreign powers and the dangers of conflict with much stronger capitalist countries. *Hunger, despair, passion in the audience; insights into economic possibilities, knowledge of the international limits upon the revolution, admonitions of prudence and responsibility from the speaker's podium.*" (emphasis added)

In Germany, Kautsky was on the multiparty "socialization commission" established by the government. But the party leadership took a most cautious attitude toward these discussions. The commission, the official party organ said in December 1918, would have "to act from the outset with such prudence that no fear of irrational experiments need arise and no one [among the industrialists] could suffer for resuming activity that had been interrupted by the war."

The government wanted order, and it felt that radical measures of socialization would disrupt the economy, create unemployment — and encourage the revolutionary tendencies that were already quite powerful in the society. But even if the government had been much more to the left, it would have faced the same un-Kautskyan problem: How can you have a system that is half capitalist and half socialist? And since there is no way of going immediately from capitalism to socialism, what alternative is there to this contradiction in terms? This difficulty is compounded, as Bauer discovered in postwar Austria and Kautsky in Germany, when a socialist-led society attempts to experiment within a world market still dominated by capitalist powers (a problem faced by François Mitterrand and the French socialists as recently as 1981).

The immediate tragedy of the cautious social-democratic policy in Germany was that the leading socialists, in the midst of a revolutionary situation in which the old order was reeling, did not make even a minimal attack on the reactionary economic and social structures of the society. They carried out a democratic revolution, no more and no less. But within that political democracy, they left the underlying power of reaction — an undemocratic army, Junker economic power, concentrated heavy industry — intact. To be sure, they could not solve all of the questions of socialization quickly, not the least because they had never really thought them through. But they could have nationalized some key industries, broken up huge estates . . . They did not. They left a Bismarckian social structure that was to play into the hands of Adolf Hitler a mere fifteen years later.

That failure could be charged to the bureaucratic conservatism of right-wing social democrats. But then the members of the socialization commission found out that their cherished goal itself was much more problematic than they had thought. Karl Korsch, then a leftist social democrat (later one of the most imaginative of the dissident Communists), pointed out that if you socialized from the standpoint of the producer — "the mines to the miners, the factories to the workers!" — that would set the producer, who wanted the highest possible wage, against the consumer, who wanted the lowest possible price. But if you socialized from the perspective of the consumer, you had the opposite problem: prices against wages. And there were the issues of scale that the "revisionist" Marxist Edward Bernstein had raised years before. How, exactly, did you socialize a gigantic, impersonal, hierarchical plant? And even before Bernstein, a sympathetic critic of the social democracy, F. A. Lange, had spoken of the enormous problems in creating a "republican factory."

There were vague revolutionary ideas in this debate about a government by workers' councils ("Soviets" in Russian). Rudolf

Wissell was much more specific and moderate. He argued for compulsory cartels with worker and consumer participation with the aim of increasing the GNP. For the socialists had now run into another unhappy truth. As Carl Landauer summarized it,

> mere nationalization could not fundamentally improve the standard of living of the masses and might actually reduce it temporarily. The share of the rich in the social product is not large enough to make it possible to increase substantially the share of the underprivileged by mere redistribution. . . . Consequently, the raising of the lower stratum of society depends on the enlargement of the social product.

That was an intimation of the growth-oriented, Keynesian social democracy that was to come.

In the 1920s, however, the socialization commission came to no practical conclusions and simply went out of existence. But now that the party had been thrust into a nether-nether world of a capitalist economy sometimes under socialist political control, what was it to do? The new answer came from Rudolf Hilferding, one of the most brilliant Marxists of the century, and it left the party totally unprepared for the greatest collapse that capitalism had ever known and all but guaranteed that, at this supreme moment of crisis, it would be impotent to intervene.

The fact that Hilferding erred in the twenties by an incredible optimism is ironic in the extreme. His great book of 1910, *Das Finanzkapital*, was extremely somber and pessimistic, and one might have thought it a perfect text to ready the socialists for a coming crisis (Lenin borrowed from it very heavily in writing his famous, and very radical, pamphlet, *Imperialism*). Capitalism, Hilferding wrote, was now becoming more centralized as banks took on a planning role. At the same time, the state was entering into the economy on the side of capital, and one confronted not *laisser-faire* but organized capitalism. Now that the system was dominated by trusts and cartels controlled by financial institutions, it had matured to the point that it could not sufficiently realize profits within national boundaries. Therefore, capital had to export itself in order to survive, and a conflict between the various capitalist powers, all of them driven by the same imperative, became inevitable. The age of imperialism was at hand.

Capital in its early phase, Hilferding argued, had been peaceful and humanitarian, concerned with free trade and progress. Now, it had turned bellicose, and "in place of the idea of humanity there came the idea of the strength and power of the state." This meant that the internal struggle over this utterly collectivized but still capitalist system became all the more bitter. The way to socialism was prepared, but now the way to that end was that "the dictatorship of the magnates of capital would turn into the dictatorship of the proletariat." That was, clearly, a new and extremely sophisticated rationale for the either/or strategy proposed by Kautsky: either organized capitalism and cult of the state, or socialism itself.

In the 1920s, Hilferding made his rather apocalyptic theory of organized capitalism the basis of a gradualist tactic of the slow democratization of the economy, that is, into the exact opposite of the Kautskyan perspective. Now, he focused on the idea that a more socialized capitalism was ripe for socialism, that it made it easier to make the transition to the new order, not more difficult. "Organized capitalism," he told the Party Congress in 1927, is nothing less than *the replacement of the capitalist principle of free competition by the socialist principle of planned production.*" Therefore, "the problem is posed to our generation: with the help of the state, with the help of conscious social direction, to transform the economy organized and led by *capitalists* into an economy directed by the *democratic state.*" It was no longer a question of a shift from one class dictatorship to another, but of a peaceful transformation of the system by means of democracy.

Socialism was now the gradual self-socialization of a capitalist democracy under the control of the parliament. The Kautskyan thesis of the inexorable evolution of capitalism into socialism was retained — but tamed. The state, which had been the chosen instrument of bourgeois domination, was now the means of socialist transformation.

In the process, Hilferding in effect assumed that capitalism had, by becoming organized, overcome its crisis tendencies, that there could be a long period of gradual, peaceful socialization under the aegis of the democratic state. So it was that 1929 came as a shattering event, a resurgence of the most basic, unsocialized, and old-fashioned capitalist crisis, which totally subverted that perspective. But Hilferding, for all of his brilliance, could not face up to the new reality. Even more to the point, for all of his revisions of *Das Kapital,* he had now returned to a kind of Kautskyan fundamentalism. Either the economy was capitalist — and under those circumstances, socialists had to run it in a capitalist way — or it was socialist. The problem was, no one knew what that socialist state of grace was.

In 1932 on the eve of Hitler's triumph, Hilferding made his famous response to trade-union demands for immediate relief from the Depression: "Depressions result from the anarchy of the capitalist system. Either they come to an end or they must lead to the collapse of the system." Capitalism was now once again anarchic, not organized. The resulting politics of either/or had reduced a mass workers' movement to impotence. There were no immediate proposals of how to deal with the agony of the unemployed — and no ultimate proposals for a "socialism," which remained, after more than a century, a concept rather than a program.

Nor was this simply a German problem. That mindset, in some measure due to the pervasive influence of Kautsky's either/or, was to be found in practically every European socialist movement in 1933 (the Swedes, and to a certain extent the French, were exceptions). In Britain, for instance, the country least influenced by Marxist theory, the Labour governments of the 1920s followed conservative capitalist orthodoxy on the grounds that they were administering capitalism, not socialism. At one point, the Liberal John Maynard Keynes became so exasperated with this attitude that, in a meeting with Labour Party leaders, he snorted that he was the only socialist in the room, that is, the only person there willing to actually make a few "despotic inroads" upon the system in order to deal with its immediate problems.

There is a terrible irony in this sorry socialist history. In the process of failing to define their central purpose, the socialists achieved more than any mass movement in human history.

An outcast social class, created in poverty and haunted by disease, had, in what was the historical twinkling of an eye, organized itself into a disciplined political force in almost every capitalist nation. Its utterly imprecise vision of a socialized future had captured the souls of women and men who were forced, by those very conditions of life, to struggle for their daily bread, not utopia. And even as the movement was often disdainful of mere reform, it forced major concessions from the powers that be, unwittingly civilizing capitalism in the name of a socialism it could not define.

In Germany, for instance, a focus on the conceptual weakness of the Social Democrats is misleading. It omits the fact that an organization with a confused theory that contradicted its actual practice and operating under intolerable limitations upon democracy was a major factor in forcing Bismarck from power in 1890. Or that, for all the compromises with imperialism on its Right wing, the Social Democratic Party had been a prescient mobilizer of mass sentiment against the militarism that was an integral part of German capitalism and a major cause of World War I. Kautsky, to his eternal credit, was among those who broke with the official leadership on the issue of the war. When an antiwar movement did begin in 1916 and 1917, it started precisely among those who had been politically formed by that same Social Democratic Party that had supported the army in 1914.

But history is not determined by relative success. The fact that the socialists did not know what to do when power suddenly came to them in 1918, or when capitalism all but collapsed in 1929, was decisive. In Germany, it did not simply give capitalism a new lease on life — it led to the most monstrous variant of that system.

In 1933, then, the socialists of Europe (with the exception of the Swedes and, to a certain extent, the French), after about one hundred thirty years of struggle and agitation, could not seriously define socialism as an operational ideal. But meanwhile, in the Soviet Union, socialism, it was claimed, existed as a reality.[4]

3

Authoritarian Collectivisms

THE RISE OF Communist states — dictatorships with centrally planned, nationalized economies — did more to distort and confuse the meaning of socialism than any other event in history.

In the post–World War II period, these societies dominated one third of the world and ceaselessly proclaimed their dedication to socialism — even if, after the Titoist and Maoist breaks with Moscow, they sometimes denounced one another in revealing ways. They spoke in the name of Marxism, they flew red flags, and they were, unquestionably, not capitalist. Small wonder that many in the West took them at their word and that, in the Third World, even non-Communists borrowed from the Communist pattern. Small wonder, too, that by the 1980s the overwhelming majority of the people in the capitalist democracies and a growing number in the Third World rejected these unfree and inefficient systems as any kind of model for the future.

It is an intolerable irony that societies that are anything but socialist should thus define what socialism is in the eyes of so many. It is an irony that has to be undone.

But isn't it an exercise in political metaphysics to dismiss an existing reality that defines itself as "socialist" and to claim that an ideal, not yet found anywhere in the world, "really" represents the meaning of the word?* Long before they had seen Bismarck-

---

*The notion that the Soviet model, with all of its manifest imperfections, is to be defended as "real" or "actually existing" socialism dates from the Brezhnev

ian "state socialism" in action, Karl Marx and Friedrich Engels denounced what might be called antisocialist socialisms. In *The Communist Manifesto*, they defined no less than four basic types of fraudulent "socialism": feudal, petty bourgeois, abstract intellectual ("true" socialism), and conservative-bourgeois. All of these ideologies, they argued, utilized socialist phrasing to conceal antisocialist purposes.

These pseudosocialisms, Marx said in a telling phrase in 1859, were the "false brothers" of the real movement. And his analysis of them always focused on the same criteria that I will employ in this chapter. Does a movement or society claiming to be socialist in fact institutionalize the power of the people over the means of production? Or does it rationalize the power of a dominant class or stratum over the people? The existing Communist states themselves admit that this is the proper basis for judgment — the Soviet Union asserts its socialist legitimacy by arguing that the working people are in command — but they are organized contradictions of their own proclaimed ideal.

But if the Communist societies are not socialist, what are they? They are collectivist, but not socialist. The means of production are indeed nationalized, but the people have no control over the economy they theoretically own. The state that possesses those means of production is virtually the private property of a bureaucracy that manages them in the name of the people. Power is thus determined by the position of an individual, or a class, in the dictatorial political structure rather than, as under capitalism, in the economic and social structure. I call this system bureaucratic collectivism and argue that it is neither capitalist nor socialist.

This analysis has the potential of demystifying Communist dictatorships. They are not the creation of conspiratorial devils, but the historic product of societies trying to achieve rapid economic development under conditions that do not permit the classic Western road to modernity. There were two or three centuries of colonial robbery and rape, internal civil wars, mass immiseration

---

era. It marks a revival of the old, right-wing Hegelian argument that whatever *is* must be rational. It is also a sign, as Lubomir Sochor has pointed out, of a very conservative reinterpretation of the bureaucratic revolutionary ideology of Marxism-Leninism (which, as we will see, was itself a significant departure from the Leninism of Lenin).

and disease that prepared the way for the capitalist triumph of the nineteenth century. An antidemocratic collectivization planned by the state is one way to try to compress the brutalities of that process of "primitive accumulation" so as to allow the creation of independent national economies in a matter of decades.

Given this analysis, this chapter will not simply deal with the origins of the Communist "socialisms" of the Soviet Union, China, or even with the Third World countries, like Cuba and Angola, that followed — for a time at least — those models. It will also confront the relevance of authoritarian collectivism and democratic socialism to that majority of the human race that cannot follow the traditional capitalist path of private socialization but has been forced to take a planned and political road to the modern world.

At this point, I will approach these complex trends from one, and only one, angle: How do they affect our understanding of the very meaning of socialism itself? In particular, I will focus on the notion, present in one way or another in all of these societies, that *socialism is a "temporary" dictatorship of a party-state based on nationalized heavy industry as a means of overcoming economic backwardness.*

The conservative glee over the failure of Third World "socialisms" — so convenient in proving the superiority of First World capitalisms — requires one more preliminary comment. Those failures are the result of deeply flawed attempts to deal with a human agony of poverty and underdevelopment imposed upon these societies by an amoral Western capitalism, which rationalized its crimes in the name of a "civilizing mission." If it is critically important to understand Third World defeats in their historical and structural context, one should never lose sight of the fact that the men and women who suffered them were often initially motivated by a completely understandable rage against injustice and frustrated by conditions not of their own making.

I

IN THE YEARS BETWEEN the October Revolution in 1917 and his death in January 1924, Vladimir Ilyich Lenin acted first upon the most utopian, antistatist definition of socialism, then moved abruptly to a statist, anti-utopian model and, in the last months of his active life, turned toward Asia for the solution to difficulties he found all but insuperable. The second and third of those strategies were to have an immense influence upon the conception of socialism, and their effects are felt to this day.

But wasn't Lenin only a power-seeking, proto-totalitarian who used socialist models cynically in order to forward his — or his party's — goals? Wasn't he, as is widely believed in the West, merely a Communist Machiavellian who believed that his ends justified any means, so that there is no point in taking his political transitions seriously?

That is much too simplistic. Lenin did indeed create the precedents that led to Stalinism, but he was no Stalinist himself. A leader with a profound, if dogmatic, knowledge of Marxism, he most certainly deployed quotations from the master in order to promote his immediate political purposes. But he was also a man of substance, of daring political imagination, and, as his onetime mentor and then implacable critic, Karl Kautsky, admitted, he won political power by persuading masses of people to rally to his cause. Lenin is, in fact, an ambivalent figure, and the mix of libertarianism and authoritarianism in his writings is an honest contradiction, not a pose.

In this perspective, Lenin, in the period leading up to and right after the October Revolution, was dead serious about his utopian plan to begin the "withering away of the state" immediately.

That strategy was based on a euphoric attempt to make the dynamic — and very democratic — energy of the Soviets at the height of the revolutionary upheaval a principle of everyday life. The Soviets — the word is Russian for "council" — had first appeared during the Revolution of 1905 as face-to-face, continuous assemblages based on the workplace. All of the workers in a given factory would constitute themselves as a Soviet (a workers' council), and then the various Soviets would ally themselves in citywide groupings. During the events of 1917, that organizational form became one of the principal sources of revolutionary vitality, and there were Soviets of Soldiers' and Sailors' Deputies as well as factory and peasant Soviets that eventually joined in a nationwide federation. These were the institutions in which Lenin's Bolshevik Party eventually achieved a majority — through democratic means.

In the standard Western (and particularly conservative) version of the Russian Revolution, it was the work of a disciplined and monolithic party, a *coup d'etat* behind the backs of the people. Again, an extreme simplification. Lenin had indeed tried to create a centralized and tightly controlled party, but in 1917 the Bolsheviks seethed with debate and disagreement, and he repeatedly had to fight against internal opposition for his point of view. In October on the eve of the Revolution itself, Kamenev and Zinoviev, two of the prominent Bolsheviks who thought that an insurrection would be adventurist, publicly revealed the plans for an uprising in the press. Lenin could not even win an expulsion vote for this egregious breach of discipline.

The idea of the Soviet was not simply a Russian invention. It had its intellectual origins in Saint-Simon's vision of a society that would be ruled by functional, industry-based groups. There had been anarcho-syndicalists in Spain, members of the Industrial Workers of the World and followers of Daniel De Leon in the United States, and Guild Socialists in Britain who had developed very similar concepts. The Guild Socialists were, for instance, quite consciously opposed to Kautsky's statist version of nationalized property and counterposed the democracy of the immediate producers to the indirect rule of the parliamentary republic. The goal was a nonbureaucratic form of social ownership run from the bottom up, an ideal that, as we will see, is quite relevant to the twenty-first century.

In September 1917, when Lenin formulated his critical demand of "All Power to the Soviets," his opponents had a clear majority in the Soviets. The Bolsheviks won control by the time of the October Revolution because their policies — above all, their opposition to the continuation of Russian participation in World War I and their slogan of giving land, that is, private property, to the peasants — had received the support of the revolutionary people. And in the first period of the Revolution, Lenin argued that the immediate democracy of the Soviets would become the institutional basis of the new society.

There would be no need for a bureaucracy since ten or twenty million citizens would not simply make the decisions but carry them out themselves. If housing needed to be rationed, one would not send an official to carry out the order but a group of revolutionaries in which the poor were overrepresented. There would be no standing army but a people in arms. And all those elected by the Soviets would be subject to the immediate democratic recall by the rank and file. There would be no "state" above the people, no parliament that, once elected, would acquire a life of its own. The masses in their workplaces and villages would be the executive and the legislature all in one. The model was Marx's idealized version of the actual practice of the Paris Commune of 1870–71.

These utopian hopes were quickly and rudely shattered.

When the Bolsheviks took power, they knew that Tsarist Russia, an economically backward society with a tiny, if highly organized, working class and a huge peasantry, possessed neither the wealth nor the political movements capable of creating socialism. The socialization of poverty, as the young Marx put it pungently in *The German Ideology*, leads not to socialism but to "the old crap in new form." This knowledge of the profound limits on the Russian Revolution, Lenin was to say at the very end of his life, was "an incontrovertible proposition." But capitalism, at least in its classic form, was not an option either, a point on which, in the years before the Revolution, Kautsky, Luxemburg, Lenin, and Trotsky agreed. The Russian bourgeoisie was too weak and dependent on foreign capital to take the leadership of the transformation; the peasants were dispersed and disorganized; and the workers, although a small minority, were concentrated in huge factories, militant, and therefore possessed a social and political weight disproportionate to their numbers.

Lenin and the Bolsheviks had assumed that the European revolution would quickly save the Soviets from the contradictions that made a socialist revolution possible in a country not yet ready for socialism. So Lenin wrote in 1920, "soon after the victory of the proletarian revolution in at least one of the advanced countries, a sharp change will probably come about: Russia will cease to be the model and will once again become a backward country (in the 'Soviet' and the socialist sense)." But the European revolution did not come, and Lenin was now reduced to maneuvering within constraints that damaged his basic purposes.

At the same time, there was civil war from internal minorities financed by foreign capital and aided by foreign military intervention. Under siege, the Bolsheviks defended themselves by a regime of "War Communism," which involved confiscating the surplus of the peasants to feed cities and the army. Meanwhile, the militant workers were decimated on the front lines of the war — the proletariat, Lenin said, was "declassed" — and those who stayed behind proved incapable of managing industries that had been nationalized out of euphoria rather than on the basis of a plan. By the time the foreign invaders had been driven from Soviet soil, the economy was in a shambles, and it was clear that Lenin no longer had a majority, or anything like it. Yet he continued to rule, as the "dictatorship of the proletariat" turned into the dictatorship of the majority of the Bolshevik Party.

There was now a momentous new rationale for the Bolsheviks to retain power. The leader and the party no longer represented the masses as they actually were, but rather the masses as they should be.

The resulting idea of a "temporary" dictatorship over the people in the name of the people was a radical, and tragic, redefinition of the meaning of socialism. It is, alas, alive and well today, not simply in those societies where it has been institutionalized as the basis of an antisocialist "socialism," but in revolutionary movements that are genuinely struggling for emancipation, but in ways that lead to new tyrannies.

In a famous prophecy, which embarrassed him when he later presented himself as more Leninist than Lenin, Trotsky had anticipated this development in a critique of the Bolsheviks. Lenin, Trotsky said in 1905, was embarked on a logic of "substitutionism," where the party was substituted for the proletariat, the party organization for the party, the central committee for the party organization, and finally, the leader for the Central Committee. This now happened — with Trotsky's approval.

This was made quite clear in a speech that Lenin gave on trade unions in the Soviet system at the end of 1920:

> The dictatorship of the proletariat cannot be exercised through an organization embracing the whole of that class, because in all capitalist countries (*and not only over here, in one of the most backward*), the proletariat is still so divided, so degraded, and so corrupted in parts (by imperialism in some countries) that an organization taking in the whole proletariat cannot directly exercise proletariat dictatorship. It can be exercised only by *a vanguard that has absorbed the revolutionary energy of the class.* . . . It cannot work without

a number of "transmission belts" running from the vanguard to the advanced class, and from the latter to the mass of the working people. *In Russia, this mass is a peasant one.* There is no such mass anywhere else, but even in the most advanced countries there is a non-proletarian, or a not entirely proletarian, mass. [emphasis added]

Earlier, Lenin had been even more explicit. It was a petty-bourgeois, social-democratic illusion, he said, "to imagine that the working people are capable, under capitalism, of achieving the high degree of class consciousness . . . that will enable them to decide, *merely by voting*, or at all events, *to decide in advance*, without long experience of struggles, that they will follow a particular class or a particular party."

The workers' and peasants' revolution, then, is not made by the actual workers and peasants, who are too backward to know their true objective interest, but by the party vanguard. That remarkable revision of socialist principle was legitimated through the disastrous Bolshevik theory of "bourgeois democracy."

The Marxists had long pointed out that democracy under capitalism was less than fully democratic. It was not just that the capitalists had resisted giving the people the right to vote, or that electoral structures were often rigged, as the Tenth Federalist Paper made so clear, to frustrate majorities. Basically, there could never be genuine political equality so long as there was fundamental social and economic inequality. The point of this critique was not to denigrate democracy but to demonstrate that it could exist in its fullness only under socialism.

Now Lenin equated democracy itself with bourgeois democracy. Therefore, all of the critics of the revolution who assailed its repression in the name of democracy were said to want simply to restore capitalism. But, Lenin continued, the Soviets knew that the "dictatorship of the proletariat" meant the rule of the proletariat "unrestricted by any laws." Was this a barbaric notion? Well, then, it was necessary to fight tsarist barbarism with a counterbarbarism. For Lenin — and after him, for revolutionaries around the world — democracy, defined as a reactionary concession to the restoration of capitalism, was to be rejected on principle during the socialist transition.

Rosa Luxemburg, a luminous Marxist and principal founder of

the German Communist Party, had been alert to the authoritarian trends in Leninism as early as 1904–05. Lenin, she wrote then, was trying to keep the Bolsheviks pure by simply not allowing the actual life of the working class — the retreats and hesitations that grew out of the conditions of working-class life and were in no way an insidious plot by the capitalists — to intrude on doctrine. He believed, she said, in the tutelage of "an all-knowing and omnipresent central committee," which proclaimed itself the voice "of a non-existent peoples' will" and presumed to dictate to history itself.

Despite these profound misgivings, she supported the Bolsheviks after 1917 — but privately worked out a devastating critique of their theory of bourgeois democracy. She wrote:

Lenin says the bourgeois state is an instrument for the repression of the working class, the socialist state an instrument for the repression of the bourgeoisie. In a way, for him the socialist state is the capitalist state stood on its head. But this simplification ignores the essential. Bourgeois class rule does not need the political schooling and education of the entire mass of the people beyond very narrow limits. For the proletarian dictatorship, that schooling and education is the life-giving element, the air without which it cannot live.

The implicit assumption of the theory of dictatorship in the Leninist-Trotskyist sense is that there is a complete recipe for the socialist transformation in the pocket of the revolutionary party, which then only needs to be implemented with great energy.

Then she turned to the charge that the critics of the Bolsheviks were simply partisans of formal — bourgeois — democracy.

We always differentiate the social essence of *bourgeois* democracy from its political form, we unmask the harsh core of social inequality and unfreedom which exists under the sweet husk of formal freedom and equality. But we do so not to reject freedom and equality, but to spur on the working class so that it is not satisfied with the husk but rather conquers political power in order to give that husk a new social content. It is the historic task of the proletariat, when it

comes to power, to replace bourgeois democracy with socialist democracy, not to abolish democracy itself.

Socialist democracy begins not in that blessed land in
which the basis of the socialist economy is already in existence. It is not a Christmas gift for the brave people who
have for a long while supported a handful of socialist dictators. . . . It begins with the very moment of the taking of
power by the socialist party.

One can argue — wrongly — that Luxemburg's view is utopian or
naive. What cannot be disputed is that it represents the central
Marxist tradition of more than half a century, a tradition that
Lenin radically, and tragically, revised in his attempt to provide a
rationale for a minority dictatorship.[1]

II

THIS POLITICAL SHIFT from Soviet power as the rule of the
democratic people to Soviet power as the dictatorship of the Bolshevik Party — and eventually to the total domination of the
society by Stalin — was accompanied by a momentous change in
economic policy. Socialism itself was now defined as a factory
society with capitalist technology and rules, but under the control
of Marxists.

In thus pushing Kautsky's theory of socialism as the logical
outcome of capitalist centralization to the extreme, Lenin made
an important distinction. Confiscating or nationalizing industry,
he said, was easy enough, but socializing it — getting real control
of its operation — was something much more complex. That is a
central truth that has been often ignored by socialists who have
made nationalization per se a fetish. The point, Lenin understood, is not to transfer legal title of any enterprise from a private
owner to the public. It is to get real control of that enterprise's
decisions and operations. To which I would add that fascists,
Stalinists, liberals, sophisticated capitalists, and many others can
"nationalize" — but real socialization is a question of the workers
and the society transforming the hierarchical and authoritarian
organization of work.

Lenin was blunt in 1918: Russian conditions made such socialization impossible. Therefore, he said, it was now necessary to bring capitalists — even capitalists who had tried to sabotage the revolution itself — into the industries now controlled by the state. For in this period of transition, which "contains elements, particles, fragments of *both* capitalism and socialism," moving directly to socialism was an impossibility and creating a system of state capitalism would be a triumph. With that rationale, Lenin now turned from a semi-utopian model to ultrarealism. What is the quintessence of that state capitalism he advocated?

It is Germany. Here we have the "last word" in modern large-scale capitalist engineering and planned organization, *subordinated to Junker-bourgeois imperialism.* Cross out the words in italics, and in place of the militarist, Junker, bourgeois, imperialist *state* put *also a state,* but of a different social type, of a different class content — a *Soviet* state, that is, a proletarian state, and you will have the *sum total* of conditions necessary for socialism.

This made the remarkable assumption that the state could be utterly independent of the way in which the economy was organized. One was to take the Soviet mode of rule — the immediate involvement of ten or twenty million rank and filers in the execution as well as the determination of policy — and impose it on the most bureaucratic and antidemocratic capitalist structure then in existence.

Lenin did not flinch from carrying this logic to its extreme conclusion. Taylorism was named after the American founder of "scientific management," of capital expropriating the skills of the workers by rationally calculating every move they would make — the kind of shovel to be used, how far to stand from the furnace, how many shovelfuls per hour — and imposing that discipline on the direct producers. It was anathema to every trade unionist in the United States, the very symbol of the dehumanizing tendencies of capitalism. Lenin wrote, "We must organize in Russia the study and teaching of the Taylor system and systematically adapt it to our ends." But how, in liberating workers, can one "adapt" a philosophy that tries to wipe out their autonomy?

Lenin wrote about these concessions to capitalism in May 1918. But by June the imperatives of War Communism took over as the chief guide of policy. These necessities were then turned into virtues — even images of socialism — by some of the Soviet leaders, most notably by Bukharin and Trotsky, who wanted to reorganize the trade unions on the model of an army.

By 1921, the discontent provoked by War Communism had brought the economy to a standstill and led to an opposition within the Bolshevik Party that demanded a return to the Soviet democracy of 1917. In the midst of the Tenth Congress of the Party in 1921, the sailors at Kronstadt — who had been heroes of the Revolution — revolted in the name of Soviet power, and delegates from the Congress joined in crushing the insurrection. Lenin responded to these pressures by returning to the pragmatic ideas of May 1918, legalizing capitalism in the countryside, *and* by "temporarily" tightening up discipline in the Party by banning internal factions. That last move meant that even the Bolshevik minorities no longer had the right of organized disagreement with the Central Committee.

There were those, like Bukharin, who, in a dramatic shift from his glorification of War Communism, now thought that the New Economic Policy of allowing peasant capitalism but taxing it moderately in order to finance heavy industrial investment could open up a gradualist path to a new society. "Socialism at a snail's pace," he called it. But Lenin, who became ill in the spring of 1923 and died in early 1924, was not so optimistic. In a series of articles, the dying leader was amazingly frank about the failure of his hopes.

Yes, he admitted, Russia was not "ripe for socialism" in 1917. But the Revolution *was* possible, and who could blame a people "influenced by the hopelessness of its situation" for flinging itself "into a struggle that would offer it at least some chance of securing conditions for the further development of civilization that were somewhat unusual?" Perhaps they had found, if not socialism, then a way of creating "the fundamental requisites of civilization in a different way from that of the West-European countries." So now the claim was that the Soviet Union had found a new way of doing what capitalism had achieved in the West.

But the Soviets, Lenin shrewdly understood, were not alone. They were on the border of Europe and Asia, the bridge between two worlds. So even "in our present state of ruin" and given the absence of a revolution in Europe, Asia was in motion; World

War I had jolted India and China out of their rut. This meant, Lenin continued, that the majority of the people of the world had now been drawn into the struggle and that ultimate socialist victory was therefore assured. But in the meantime, the Soviet Union could not proceed to socialism because it lacked the "civilization" to do that. The Party had to keep the confidence of the peasants and industrialize "by exercising the greatest possible thrift in the economic life of our state."

Lenin defended the Revolution in these essays, of course, but his justification was now light-years removed from the claim that it had discovered a new, and democratic, form of the state — or indeed that the state had actually begun to "wither away." Now he argued that the Soviet Union was pioneering not socialism itself but a noncapitalist road to industrialization that would lay the material foundations for an eventual socialism. But the reality was that the Asian revolution — which now took the place of the European revolution as the *deus ex machina* that would save the Soviets from backwardness — could not possibly play the role Lenin assigned it. For India and China were even poorer and more backward than Tsarist Russia, and if they followed Lenin's lead they could only encounter even worse contradictions than he had faced.

And yet, in a sense Lenin was right about how Asia's future — and that of the entire colonial world of the 1920s — was to be bound up with the fate of the Russian Revolution. Only he could not have imagined the form in which his own prophecy would come true. He had taken power in the conviction that he was creating a necessarily backward, if progressive, variant of the most advanced revolution in human history. In fact, his actions led to the most advanced variant of the revolution of the backward countries. That gave Communism a global resonance that lasted for about a half a century and gave rise to a whole new, and confusing, family of socialisms.

Nikolai Bukharin, one of the leading theorists of Bolshevism until he was defeated by Stalin, grasped this point as early as 1923. England and America, he said, represented the "world city" and the agrarian colonies were the "world countryside." Now the proletariat of the world city would link up with the rural poor of the world countryside in a socialist alliance against the capitalist elite. Peasants, of whom Marx had once remarked that they had the organizational vitality of potatoes in a sack, were now seen as coauthors of the coming revolution.[2]

III

I STRESS THIS Third World relevance of the Russian Revolution for a purpose. In understanding Soviet developments as a response to economic backwardness, one sees the rise of Stalin not as the work of diabolical conspirators but as a historical process. That is not to rationalize the attendant crimes in the name of necessity. It is simply to place them in the context in which they must be judged, and this, not so incidentally, helps explain why the exploitation of workers and peasants could come to be widely accepted as socialism, particularly in the post–World War II Third World.

The fundamental change in the Soviet Union — the one that gave such a distinctive, and disastrous, meaning to "socialism" — did not occur until 1929. It resolved the bitter quarrels that took place between Lenin's death in January 1924 and Stalin's "revolution from above" in 1929, and was an answer to fundamental economic and political issues that were also to be posed by the struggle of many of the newly independent countries for genuine autonomy after World War II. That fact, and not Communist Machiavellianism, is why Marxism-Leninism had such an appeal to the revolutionary elites of the Third World.

How, the Bolsheviks asked, does an underdeveloped nation undertake its own industrialization? Who staffs the emergent institutions of the new society? How can a poor country resist the relentless pressures of a world capitalist market to subordinate itself to an international division of labor organized according to the priorities of the rich economies? In a society with a rural majority and a city-based revolutionary government, what is the relationship between the peasantry and urban power? And what is the political form — democratic, dictatorial, totalitarian — of this transition?

During the five years in which these questions were argued, the Soviet Union was a political dictatorship with a considerable amount of social and economic pluralism. In framing his New Economic Policy (NEP), Lenin did not relent in his defense of one-party rule. But he insisted that the Soviets had to pay attention and make concessions to popular unrest even though the people were not allowed to participate in the political decision making. In dramatic contrast to Stalin, as Hannah Arendt has noted, he "had a passion for public admission and analysis of his own errors, which is against the rules of even ordinary demagogy." And while his survivors battled for his mantle, they more or less pursued the NEP policy he had decreed in 1921.

So much of the economic activity of the society was in private hands. Peasants produced for a market and bought industrial goods from the cities. The government, rather than requisitioning their surplus at the point of a gun, collected a fixed tax in commodity form (a tax "in kind"), which left room for profits. In 1925 and 1926, Moscow even tried to revive the rural Soviets, and a considerable number of nonparty people took part in their administration. There were middlemen — the NEP men — who facilitated this exchange and thus formed a petty-capitalist stratum in the cities themselves. The industrial sector was under state control, to be sure, but until 1926 its official goal was the modest one of putting existing capacity to work, not rapid expansion. While there was no relaxation of political repression, poets and playwrights and even philosophers were allowed a certain limited freedom.

What was the next step? In the first phase of the New Economic Policy, it was relatively easy to achieve rapid growth since all that was required was to put that existing, and unused, capacity back to work. But after those gains had been made, further expansion demanded a new approach.

There were two basic points of view in the Bolshevik Party on this issue, and neither of them prevailed in the end. The Center-Right, led by Stalin (a "moderate" at this point) and Bukharin, was for continuing the NEP perspective of riding to socialism, in Bukharin's words, on a "peasant nag." The nationalized industries were to grow in tandem with prosperity in the fields and to be financed by that nonconfiscatory tax. The Left, led by Trotsky and backed up by a brilliant theorist, Evgeny Preobrazhensky, warned that capitalism was growing within the interstices of the society. In the first period of NEP, they said, there was room in a devastated economy for both the private and state sectors. But eventually, either one or the other would have to dominate. And unless there were measures to build up industry, financed by getting more of the peasant surplus, capitalism would triumph and the Soviet Union would be incapable of defending itself against imperialist attack.

The polemics of this era made it seem that Bukharin and Trotsky-Preobrazhensky were diametrically opposed to one another. That, as Alexander Erlich suggested in one of the clearest summaries of the debate, was not the case. Bukharin understood that there had to be investment, if only to make it possible for industry to provide sufficient goods for the peasants. And Trotsky and Preobrazhensky were in favor of raising peasant living standards and against the notion of forced collectivization. The policy that did in fact prevail — Stalin's "revolution from above," which began in 1929 — was not mentioned during the factional debates by anyone, including Stalin.

It was Preobrazhensky who raised the most fundamental question, one that faces every underdeveloped society bent on modernization. In Marx's analysis of capitalism, the system's takeoff had been preceded by a brutal period of "primitive accumulation." Peasants were driven from their fields, the colonies were plundered, the artisans were ruined. And that was followed by the early days of industrialization itself, in which men, women, and children were subjected to a fourteen-hour day and working conditions that literally threatened the biological existence of people in the new cities. That cruelty, Marx was always careful to note, was functional as well as criminal, that is, it laid the material base for the greatest economic and social advance humanity had ever made.

But how is a poor country, desperately short of capital, to create the foundations of industry without using those outrageous capitalist methods? Above all, how is a socialist government to accomplish this buildup when the capitalism it expropriates is almost as impoverished as the country itself? Marx never asked such questions since it never occurred to him that it would be possible to carry out socialist policies under these conditions. He had always assumed that a just social order could only be erected on the basis of a wealth-producing system that had passed far beyond the period of "primitive accumulation." That was why he celebrated the accomplishments of capitalism even as he thundered like a prophet against their human cost.

But once the Bolsheviks had decided to retain power in spite of their minority status in the society, and revolution in Europe failed to rescue them from these contradictions, they had to try to square this circle. Preobrazhensky's solution was that "primitive socialist accumulation" would take place by the "exploitation" of the peasants. But this would be done in considerable measure through pricing policy — making the terms of trade between the city and countryside unfair so that the peasants paid more for industrial goods than they received for their own agricultural produce. Even then, Preobrazhensky said in the last article in which he could freely express himself — he later capitulated to Stalin and denounced his own ideas — it was doubtful that the Soviet Union could succeed without aid from a triumphant European revolution.

Preobrazhensky's theories were much too probing and straightforward in a power struggle in which intellectual honesty was extremely dangerous. Stalin, Bukharin, and all of Trotsky's foes could now argue that Trotsky had broken with Lenin's insistence on making concessions to the peasants in order to maintain them in an alliance with the workers.

Having made a bloc with Bukharin and defeated Trotsky in the name of a Leninist defense of peasant interests, Stalin soon adopted a policy of exploiting those peasants that made the Trotskyist policies seem humane and moderate. He had indeed found a way to carry out a remarkable industrialization in the course of a decade by bringing totalitarian force to bear on the peasants and workers, on the social classes that supposedly dominated the society. As a book written under Stalin's personal direction was later to say with surprising candor, this was a "revolution from above." In the process, he would not simply define, but create the reality of, a "socialism" whose basic structures persist to this day even if they are no longer as grossly cruel as in his era.*

Between 1929 and 1934, the Soviet peasantry was forced into

---

*There is a scholarly debate, quite significant in other respects, that I will simply note here since it does not impinge directly on the Stalinist definition of *socialism*. Was Stalin's move to forced collectivization in 1929 premeditated, or was it an improvised response to peasant resistance to deliver grain to the state? Did that collectivization of agriculture actually yield substantial profits that were then invested in industrialization, or was it an economic fiasco that actually retarded the development of the Soviet Union?

collective farms. There was a civil war against the people of the countryside that Stalin himself, in a conversation with Churchill, was later to compare with the devastation of the fight against the Nazi invasion. At the height of this process, Stalin announced that the rich peasants who had cooperated with NEP were to be "liquidated as a class"; individuals could be executed for pilfering small amounts of food from the collective farms; grain was exported to get hard currency to buy capital goods abroad even though people were starving; and angry peasants destroyed livestock in retaliation. The famine of 1932–33, which was a direct consequence of these policies, took five million lives, and another five million were lost before and after that tragedy; more than half of the horses and two thirds of the sheep and goats in the country were slaughtered.

There was a grim rationality in all of this and it was Stalin's resolution of the debates of the twenties. The peasants were forced to deliver their grain to the state at prices that sometimes did not even cover the cost of production. The government then sold that grain to its own nationalized industries at a much higher price and with a large "turnover tax" on the transaction. The profits made in this way were then supposed to fund a good part of the industrialization effort. However one resolves the scholarly debate over the economic effectiveness of this policy, the labor and hunger of Soviet peasants were indeed a major source of "primitive accumulation" to a degree that Trotsky found shocking.

The peasants were not alone in their suffering, even if it was extreme. As they flooded into the cities to become workers in the new factories, there was not enough housing or other basic urban amenities. These new entrants to the work force then changed their jobs so frequently — the average worker in the coal industry left his work three times in a year — that Stalin decreed that they were tied to their factories, unable to move without official permission. For the entire working class, old and new, money wages rose as a result of a labor shortage, but inflation increased at a much faster rate. At the same time, the system began to use forced labor — prisoners and deportees — on its projects. The result was, as Alec Nove summarizes the evidence, that "1933 was the culmination of the most precipitous peacetime decline in living standards known in recorded history."

In 1934, most historians think, there was a secret session at the Seventeenth Congress of the Party at which the delegates demanded that this forced march to industrialization be slowed down. And between 1934 and 1937, life became somewhat less brutal, at least for the workers, as some of the investments of the early period began to pay off. The "revolution from above" had worked; the hyperexploitation of the people had provided the basis for a gigantic economic leap.

It would be wrong to see the resulting industrialization as the result of force and force alone. There were, Nove comments, workers who were genuinely enthusiastic about the socialist slogans, and there were foreigners, some idealist and some mercenary, who came to labor alongside them. At the same time, there were very high rates of social mobility as a new managerial and political class was recruited from among workers and peasants. In 1931, Stalin denounced "equality mongering" as a petty-bourgeois deviation, and wage differentials grew within the working class itself. The executives received, not only money incomes several times higher than those of workers, but access to housing and special stores. But then, with the purges that began in 1937, Stalin turned around and attacked the managers and planners as well as the army. That, plus the fact that investment had slowed after 1934, was probably one of the reasons why growth rates declined in that year. Stalin had raised a new bureaucracy above the people; and now he placed himself above that bureaucracy as its absolute lord and master, a position he occupied until his death in 1953.

The justification for all this brutality and one-man rule was a scientistic reading of Marxism that had some warrant in some of Engels's more careless formulations but violated the repeated defense of democracy and self-emancipation of both Marx and Engels. Marxism, in Stalin's version, was a system that explained both nature and society by means of "dialectical materialism" (a phrase never used by either Marx or Engels but popularized by the first Russian Marxist, Georgi Plekhanov). Thus Stalin, as the supreme Marxist, automatically was the infallible interpreter of the objective interest of the workers and the peasants, and if those classes perversely refused to recognize what was good for them, he had the right to impose it upon them. At the same time, the leader was also the supreme physicist, geneticist, linguist — the supreme everything.

This ideological claim was obviously rooted in the fact that the state that Stalin led controlled the entire economy and not just the political structure of the society. It thus went far beyond the limits of a classic dictatorship that simply repressed active opponents of the regime. Now, a workers' strike or an intellectual's disagreement with the central plan was a challenge to the very basis of social authority. And the rationalization of that centralized and supposedly omniscient authority meant, as Hannah Arendt put it, that Stalin had an official, and police-enforced, position on every question, on the playing of chess as well as the nature of the family and the value of music and literature. This was the reality that caused Arendt to describe this society as "totalitarian," that is, as one in which the totality of life was under the control of the dictatorship. Her analysis, like George Orwell's fictionalization of Stalinism, *1984*, accurately described the system at the height — the depths — of its terrorist mobilization, but became less applicable in the years after Stalin's death.

There were, of course, momentous changes in the post-Stalin era, and they are accelerating under Mikhail Gorbachev even at this writing. But the essential, from the point of view of the very concept of socialism, was put in place by Stalin.

Socialism, as defined in Soviet practice, was a bureaucratically controlled and planned nationalized economy that carried out the function of "primitive accumulation" and thus achieved rapid modernization. The state owned the means of production, which made some people think it must be socialist; but the Party and bureaucracy "owned" the state by virtue of a dictatorial monopoly of political power. Such a situation was a moral disaster for socialism, the corruption of the ideal from within, a "false brother" with a superficially plausible claim to authenticity. Thus, even a sophisticated analyst like Isaac Deutscher — who had been a leading Polish Trotskyist — concluded that Stalinism was a barbarous way of moving toward socialism, much as the French Revolution had carried out a progressive historic task in a bloody, dictatorial fashion. But that is to miss the critical difference between a bourgeois revolution, of the kind that took place in France in 1789, and a socialist transformation as imagined not only by Marx but by almost every socialist. Capitalism does not need the conscious participation of the people in order to make its revolution, but that participation is, as Rosa Luxemburg so well understood, the very substance, the heart and soul, of socialism.

After World War II, it was precisely a Deutscher-like confusion on this count that recommended Stalinism, as a model to be imitated or at least borrowed from, to many of the new nations in the Third World. It offered a "Russian" way to make a "French" revolution, a "socialist" rationale for the brutalities of industrialization, which capitalism had pioneered in an earlier era.[3]

IV

THERE WAS A nationalist euphoria in the Third World between the end of World War II and the mid-sixties and it gave rise to many "socialisms" in countries much less developed than the Russia of 1917. When the inevitable disenchantment set in — when, for instance, sub-Saharan Africa lost the capacity to feed itself under the new leftist regimes, and China, once the "pure" revolution, turned to capitalist incentives — the idea of socialism itself was more confused than ever.

Since most of the West had simplistically assumed that the Soviet model was *the* definition of socialism, there were superficial analysts who interpreted these developments as a triumph of capitalism. That the dictatorial, centralized accumulation of capital failed to modernize economies much more backward than Tsarist Russia — not to mention its failure to emancipate people according to the genuine socialist vision — was taken as one more proof that human nature, which was capitalist, would prevail in the end. In the process the Right gleefully accepted Joseph Stalin or Mao as the supreme authority on socialism since that served its polemical aim of proving that "actually existing capitalism" was politically and economically superior to "actually existing socialism."

That the newly independent nations that committed themselves to one or another variety of "socialism" were wildly overoptimistic in the immediate postwar period is clear. That their debacles are to be explained in terms of the flaws in socialist concepts and values and without reference to the intolerable constraints imposed upon them by the very structure of the world capitalist market is ideology, not serious analysis. Indeed, what happened to the Third World during those years — and what is still happening — cannot be understood, as we will see, apart from the *irrelevance* of the classic capitalist model of industrialization for most countries in the world.

That is not a debater's point of the Left designed to deal with the debater's points of the Right. It is essential to the understanding of the contemporary world as well as to the perspective of an internationalist socialism in the twenty-first century.

Let us begin with the vague, euphoric illusions of the time of colonial revolution and national liberation.

In that period, as Gunnar Myrdal showed in his masterful study *Asian Drama*, India, Burma, Ceylon, and Indonesia were all dedicated to something called "socialism." What that meant was very imprecise. In part, it represented the authority of the Russian Revolution, which had caused *moderate* nationalists in both India and China to revise their programs in the 1920s (the attack on Untouchability by the Congress Party, the Three People's Principles of Sun Yat-sen's movement). In part, it was a response to the Soviet experience. Even the non-Communist nationalists recognized the Five Year Plans "as the pioneering attempt of an underdeveloped country to engender economic development by state planning." But there was also a Western influence. In the post–World War II years, government intervention and the welfare state were on the rise in Europe and America, and that had an impact upon Fabian intellectuals like Nehru, the first prime minister of independent India.

More often than not, the high hopes for a government-led and -planned escape from poverty were given the name of "socialism." In India, Myrdal comments, this was "merely a rather vague term for the modernization ideology with an inherent stress on equality as a primary planning objective." And it was associated with an unrealistic sense of the role that the newly independent, but very poor, countries could play in world politics. At the first Third World summit meeting in Bandung in 1955, the emphasis was not simply on completing the process of decolonialization but on the ex-colonies becoming nothing less than a third force as against both the Soviet and American blocs.

Frantz Fanon, the Martinique-born theorist of the Algerian

struggle for independence, was in some ways an extreme spokes-
person for this optimism. Yet his book *The Wretched of the Earth*
had a great influence among Western intellectuals and particularly that stratum that, out of feelings of guilt for the very real
crimes of colonialism and imperialism, became completely un-
critical supporters of colonial revolutionary movements. In an
introduction to Fanon's book, Jean-Paul Sartre wrote, "Europeans, you must open this book and enter into it. After a few
steps in the darkness you will see strangers gathered around a
fire; come close, and listen, for they are talking of the destiny
they will mete out to your trading centers and to the hired soldiers
who defend them."

The notion that the Third World had the power to bring capitalism to its knees was central to Fanon's perspective. If the West
resisted the demands of the new nations, Fanon said,

> the Western industries will quickly be deprived of their
> overseas markets. The machines will pile up their products
> in the warehouses and a merciless struggle will ensue on the
> European market between the trusts and the financial
> groups. The closing of factories, the paying off of workers
> and unemployment will force the European working-class to
> engage in an open struggle against the capitalist regime.

All this, Fanon went on, would be set in motion, not by the
working class of the Third World, which was privileged, but by
the *lumpenproletariat*, "the pimps, the hooligans, the unemployed and the petty criminals. . . . These classless idlers will by
militant and decisive action discover the path that leads to nation-
hood." This was a return to the pre-Marx strategy of the "proletarian messiah," Wilhelm Weitling.

Such fantasies could not survive for long. But it was not until
the sixties that the Third World nations realized that the economic structures of Western hegemony were very much in place
even if most of the colonies had achieved formal independence.
That shift was marked by the meeting of the United Nations
Conference on Trade and Development in 1964 and by the emergence of a whole library of theories about "neocolonialism."
What is significant here is that this turn also meant an end to the

euphoria about the vague "socialisms" of the non-Communist Third World.

The Communist "socialisms" of the Third World that imitated the Soviet model followed a different path, which was not at all vague: the creation of one-party states with the mission of forced and rapid modernization. But they, too, were to encounter the structural limits inherent in the very organization of the world economy. China is obviously the most important case in point.

There is a fascinating history, usually remembered only by specialists, that illuminates the enormous prestige of the Russian Revolution in the colonialized world. In the 1920s, the bourgeois nationalists in China, led by Chiang Kai-shek, later the implacable enemy of Communism and hero of the American Right, became sympathizing members of the Communist International (Comintern). In this strange period, the Bank of China was started under capitalist direction with Soviet funds. Moscow, acting through the Comintern, instructed the Chinese Communists, who had built a base in the urban working class, to make an alliance with Chiang's party, the Koumintang. In 1927–28, Chiang, having used both Moscow and its Chinese followers for his own purposes, turned on them savagely and massacred thousands of Communist cadres (an event depicted in one of the great novels of the twentieth century, André Malraux's *Man's Fate*).

The Communist remnant that survived, led by Mao, was forced out of the cities. At first, it engaged in "social banditry," living an outlaw life in the countryside. Eventually, and particularly after the legendary Long March, it established control over some remote peasant areas. That created the base for one of the most extraordinary developments in modern history, the conquest of the most populous nation on earth by Communist-led peasant armies.

That unprecedented road to power helped define the theory and practice of Chinese Communism after 1949. During the armed struggle, Mao always insisted that the Party represented the working class but, since the Party was totally isolated from the actual proletariat, that had to mean, in Leninist fashion, the ideal working class, "as it should be." But the fact that their mass base was peasant did not turn the Communists into a peasant movement. The Party, the leadership, did not take its cue from the ranks, but debated, decided, and shifted the line from on high. It was of some moment that Mao's policies toward the peasantry changed in tandem with the Soviet international priorities, not with the moods and desires of the people.

In the first years, leading up to 1935, the Chinese Communists attempted to create "Soviets" in the areas under their control and confiscated the property of the better-off peasants. Then, when the Comintern decreed a united front against fascism in 1935, the Maoists not only sought a rapprochement with Chiang but abandoned the policy of confiscation. In 1939, when the Hitler-Stalin pact signaled a revival of a "hard line" in the Comintern, the Maoist attitude toward those better-off peasants became much more severe. Then, in 1941, when the Soviet Union was invaded and found itself in an alliance with the capitalist democracies, the Chinese Communists were once again in favor of coalition and a soft policy toward wealthy peasants.

I obviously compress an enormously complex history in a brief frame. The point is simply to argue that, when the Chinese Communists did take power in 1949, they were independent of *both* the workers and the peasants. The Bolsheviks had to go through vicious internal purges and a near civil war to destroy the independent power of the workers and peasants in the movement that won them their victory. But Mao and his comrades had created a state apparatus based on the Party itself *before* their triumph, and there were no organized forces independent of it. In a remarkably frank speech on April 15, 1958 — during one of his most "radical" periods — the Chinese leader said,

> Apart from their other characteristics, the outstanding thing about China's 600 million people is that they are "poor and blank." This may seem a bad thing, but in reality it is a good thing. Poverty gives rise to the desire for change, the desire for action and the desire for revolution. On a blank sheet of paper free from any marks, the freshest and most beautiful characters can be written, the freshest and most beautiful pictures can be painted.

When the Chinese Communists began to rule, modern industry accounted for around 3.5 percent of the national output compared to 16 percent for Tsarist Russia in 1917, which meant that the real-world limits upon any attempt to create socialism were much, much more severe. Between 1949 and 1955, Mao attempted to deal with these constraints by combining a "Soviet" emphasis on capital-intensive investment in heavy industry and a distinctively Chinese policy of agrarian reform and private peasant plots. Then, in 1955, Beijing suddenly decreed the rapid collectivization of all agriculture, in part because the imperatives of industrialization demanded it. In July 1955, there were 14.2 percent of the peasants on collectives, in May 1966, there were 91.2 percent. This incredible social transformation did not provoke the furious resistance met by Stalin's forced collectivization, but there was enough discontent to lead Mao to permit public criticism of the regime in 1956–57 (this was also partly a response to Khrushchev's revelations about Stalin's crimes).

But in 1958 — when he made that statement about writing on the people as on a blank page — there was the most abrupt shift in line. Hypercollectivization was decreed and the fields were organized on a barracks principle. The result was a disastrous fall in output, the reemergence of hunger and even famine, and Mao himself lost effective control of the Party. In the sixties, he managed to regain power and launched the "proletarian" Cultural Revolution, a movement that began when students broke a strike of workers demanding higher wages (the actual proletariat was not in conformity with the Maoist image of itself). Paradoxically, an antibureaucratic movement of the base was turned on by the Maoist wing of the bureaucracy and after the turmoil and loss of production turned off by the same bureaucracy.

How is one to explain these extraordinary zigs and zags? Are they simply the consequence of Mao's personality, much as the Soviets account for Stalinism without reference to the structures of the society and only in terms of Stalin's "cult"? These personalized theories of world-historical events strike me as less than compelling. In the Chinese case, I would suggest that a Party dictatorship, formed under the egalitarian conditions of armed struggle in the countryside and committed to the Stalinist path to modernity, ran headlong into the limits of Chinese poverty and discovered that an authoritarian will could not overcome them. The peasants were not quite as blank a page as Mao had thought. This proves little or nothing about a socialism based on an advanced economy — or upon a world in which the advanced economies cooperate with the poor nations, out of both self-interest and solidarity, in the common work of eradicating that poverty.

The Chinese Communist failures were repeated in the smaller, for the most part even poorer, countries that took that road (Cuba, Ethiopia, Angola, Mozambique, Vietnam, Guinea-Bissau). And "African" socialism, a Fourier-like vision of skipping the whole phase of capitalist industrialization by building on ancient communal traditions, had to face the most vicious of the colonial inheritances: an area of weak states with boundaries drawn by European imperialists without regard for economics or ethnicity and with a material and technical infrastructure that made failure quite predictable.[4]

V

THERE WERE, WE have seen, structural factors that made it impossible for backward countries, starting with the Soviet Union, to create an authentic socialism and led them to take a path of authoritarian collectivism. Now it is necessary to look at the capitalist nature of the limits that pushed them in this direction.

It is one of the illusions of capitalism that it has found the "natural" economy, the one that corresponds to *homo economicus* as he and she really is. That belief was marvelously exemplified in a 1960 book, *The Stages of Economic Growth: A Non-Communist Manifesto*, by W. W. Rostow. It is of some moment to note that this was a liberal (in the American sense of the word) variant on the basic theme. It was quite influential during the Kennedy administration and helped shape the ethos of the Alliance for Progress, that plan for stimulating a "bourgeois revolution" in Latin America by the judicious leveraging of foreign aid.

In Rostow's analysis, almost all economies go through the same stages of economic growth as Western capitalism, from a period of "take-off," in which the preconditions of change come into existence, to a process of "sustained" growth, which finally achieves the heights of "high mass consumption." "In its broad shape and timing," Rostow wrote, ". . . there is nothing about the

Russian sequence of pre-conditions, take-off and drive to technological maturity that does not fall within the general pattern;
although like all other national stories it has unique features."
The central "fact" about the world of 1960, he concluded, was
"the acceleration of the preconditions or the beginnings of the
take-off in the southern half of the world: South-East Asia, the
Middle East, Africa and Latin America." China and India were
already on the way; Pakistan, Egypt, Iraq, and Indonesia would
"be less than a decade behind."

In a very tough speech on the Third World in 1975, Kissinger
made much the same argument. He attacked the poor countries
for their activism — this was the period of OPEC's first major
price hike and the threat of other raw-material cartels. "Those
who do not want investment from abroad," he threatened the
critics of the multinational corporation, "can be confident they
will not receive it." The core of this stern lecture was the Rostow
thesis, now utilized for conservative purposes. As Kissinger put
it, "Economic development is in the first instance an internal
process. Either societies create the conditions for saving and
investment, for innovation and ingenuity, for enterprise and industry which ultimately lead to self-sustaining economic growth,
or they do not."

In short, the West had found the one sure road to modernity.

This view was an abstraction from history — including Western history. There are few generalizations that can be made about
the capitalist revolution since it happened in very specific ways in
different countries. But it is true that Britain and France went
through a similar process, which was quite different from that of
Germany and Japan. In the earliest variants of the new economy,
there were tremendous upheavals from below as the old society
was challenged — the revolutions of 1640 and 1688 in Britain,
1789 in France — and capitalism evolved spontaneously from that
beginning. In Germany and Japan, as Barrington Moore has
pointed out, there were "revolutions from above" in which the
bureaucracies of the agrarian ruling class made an alliance with
weak commercial classes (the "coalition of iron and rye," as it
has been called in the German case). Capitalist development in
these instances was statist, authoritarian, and was eventually to
take a completely right-wing form of Naziism or military dictatorship.

These differences occurred *within* European capitalism (despite its location, I subsume Japan under that economic category). As Alexander Gerschenkron outlined the progression, in the countries where capitalism started from relatively high levels of development, the factory was the source of capital; in areas of moderate backwardness, funds came from the banks and then the factories; in situations of extreme backwardness, first the state intervened, then the banks, and finally the factories came on line as a source of capital. When one turns from Europe to a colonial world in which the "preconditions" of modernity had been systematically frustrated by the workings of the world market, what did happen — extreme authoritarian, statist strategies of modernization — simply marks a deepening of the trends already discernible on the Continent.

Ironically, Rostow's extreme optimism about the viability of the capitalist model in the Third World, proclaimed as a "Non-Communist Manifesto," commits one of Marx's most spectacular errors. In his writings on colonialism, and particularly on India, Marx, like Rostow, assumed that the "spread effects" of industrialization would operate much as they had in Europe (the one case where Marx got close to the truth was in his analysis of Ireland). The building of railroads had given an enormous impetus to economic development in Europe and America, and this pattern would be repeated in India, where the construction of a rail network would be an important moment in the complete modernization of the society. The problem was, the Indian railroads were not the result of an indigenous industrial evolution, but were imported by the British for *their* purposes.

As Myrdal brilliantly summarized this process:

> Being constructed primarily from the point of view of the British economy, with the aim first of facilitating military security and secondly of getting the raw produce out cheaply and British goods in, as well as providing famine relief, the railways, instead of exerting enormous spread effects as in Western Europe and, later, North America, served to strengthen the complementary colonial relationship and further subordinate the Indian to the British economy.

The result was that "the emergence of an expanding 'free economy' where private initiative would provide the dynamic impulse was rendered almost impossible." In the post–World War II period, the United States, on the liberal Left as well as the Right, ignored these imperialist realities, tried to impose a classic capitalist model on societies that could not sustain it, and explained the appeal of Communism as a plot rather than a consequence of the world that capitalism had created.

Thus, even the most dramatic capitalist success story in the Third World, the rise of the Four Dragons (or Four Tigers) in Asia — Taiwan, South Korea, Hong Kong, and Singapore — was the result of an authoritarian, statist, and most uncapitalist capitalism. Singapore, the wits say, is capitalism led by a Leninist party. These successes were also the outcome of an "export platform" strategy, which subordinated the developing economy to the needs of the imperial centers, a policy that will make life difficult for the "dragons" when the next crisis breaks out on the world capitalist market.

The point is, the first capitalist powers had the opportunity of "evolving" their steel industry out of blacksmith shops, iron production, small-scale steel, and then, after a century of development and job generation, the huge steel factory. But given the discipline of the world market, the Third World country *began* with the most advanced and automated plant, which created an enclave of modernity in a society that remained backward. The displaced peasants of Europe suffered agonies, but the historical process that forced them from the land also created the cities and factories that would employ them, or their children. The displaced peasants of the Third World, more often than not, became a *lumpenproletariat* in the shacks on the margins of the great cities. In Rio, for instance, the great metropolis of one of the potentially richest societies on earth, the *favellas* of the poor can be found within a ten-minute walk of the corporate office towers.

From October 1917 to the present moment, these ugly capitalist imperatives made it impossible for revolutionary movements in the poor countries to overcome backwardness in a socialist way. Fighting odds much greater than those that confronted the first capitalisms, the authoritarianism, inefficiency, and failures of these societies cannot be understood apart from the constraints imposed upon them by many of those who condemn their authoritarianism, inefficiency, and failure. But does this then mean that Stalinism, and the other strategies for forced industrialization, are, just as Lenin said, "barbarous ways of fighting barbarism" and therefore "justified" as socialism by some kind of historical necessity?

Marx helps answer that question. His economic analysis of India (and, by extension, of the colonial world) was, we have seen, fundamentally flawed. His political and moral judgments were not. British imperialism, he argued, was "progressive" in India in the specific sense that it shattered the coherent, complacent poverty of that country and opened up the possibility of the masses winning a decent life for all. That same "progressive" imperialism, Marx continued, was criminal, and he sided with the Indians against the colonialist modernizer. That which *genetically* explains a social phenomenon, Marx understood, does not *ethically* justify it. Similarly, to the extent that the authoritarian accumulation of capital in the Third World "works" — that the Soviet Union has become a modern, if problematic, economy with a much higher standard of living than before Stalin — there was progress and it can be built upon. But it was accomplished by exploitation, violence, starvation, and murder, and the post-Stalin society has institutionalized the authoritarianism of this process, even if in a much ameliorated form. There were, alas, many intellectuals in the First World who simply looked at the statistics, ignored the crimes, and concluded that this progress was "socialist."

The complex truth is that antidemocratic collectivization is historically explicable but not thereby historically justified as "socialist." In part, it was forced to its excesses by "necessities" created by Western capitalism, but it was, at the same time, a functional equivalent of that capitalism, a new mode of exploitation and not of liberation. That one can sympathize with the revolutionaries who had to deal with these intolerable limits is true enough. That one can call their revolutions "socialist" is utterly false.

These distinctions, however, were lost on a good part of world public opinion. As a result, the first phase of the colonial revolution further confused and discredited the idea of socialism.[5]

4

The *Realpolitik* of Utopia

IN THE 1960s, socialist *Realpolitik* gave rise to utopia.

The Keynesian welfare state — a capitalist economy with a socialist (or in America, liberal) government — seemed so successful, so enduring, that both the established Left and its most radical critics believed, in remarkably similar ways, that a new age was at hand. In the 1970s, when that welfare state went into crisis, the disillusionment was all the more bitter because of the exaggerated hopes that had preceded it.

Still, there were real accomplishments in the years of economic growth and social-democratic victories in Europe. The socialists finally escaped from Karl Kautsky's either/or: that capitalism was on one side of a historic abyss and socialism on the other, with an undefined revolutionary leap in between. Now the social democrats came up with transitional programs that made capitalism more humane — even if it remained quite capitalist. It was this most pragmatic of politics that generated a utopian euphoria, which seized the Right wing of the movement as well as the Left.

This description of the hubris of the sixties begins, strange as it may seem, with bankruptcy of the classic socialist analysis in the face of the greatest collapse in capitalist history, the Great Depression. The excessive optimism after World War II was in part a reaction to the paralysis of those despairing years.

In the early thirties, Otto Bauer, one of the most imaginative of the Marxists, described what happened then:

In 1929 as the crisis broke out, the British Labour Party ruled in Britain and the Social Democracy led a coalition in Germany. Socialist parties bore responsibility for the state; *but the economy was ruled by the natural laws of capitalism.* The socialist-led regimes could not ward off the crisis or halt its stormy march toward the credit crisis of 1931. The disillusionment of the masses turned them against socialism. [emphasis added]

The movement — and even as sophisticated an analyst as Bauer — asserted a "revolutionary" rationale for free-enterprise economics at a time when they no longer worked. Capitalism, it was felt, was to be run on capitalist principles, socialism on socialist principles, and the twain would never meet. If the revolution would be provoked by the crisis, then there would be utterly new — but still undefined — ways of running the economy. But short of such an apocalypse, "the natural laws of capitalism" decreed that a depression was the way in which the system corrected its disproportions. There would be programs to moderate the inevitable suffering of the working class — so long as they were not financed by deficits that violated those "natural laws," which Marx himself had described in all their inexorability.

The political results of this stance were disastrous. In the 1930s, fascism triumphed in Germany and Spain (it had already taken power in Italy); there were counterrevolutionary dictatorships in Austria and Bulgaria. A mass rightist movement emerged in France, was stopped by the Popular Front, and then returned in collaboration with the Nazis under the Vichy regime. In Britain, the Tories remained in control throughout the Depression years. There were socialist victories in Scandinavia, but the Swedish Social Democrats were the only ones to come up with an effective response to the crisis.

With the Swedish exception, the thirties seemed to be a time when socialists wandered in a political and ideological wilderness. In one reading of these events, it was ironically an establishmentarian genius, John Maynard Keynes, who saved socialism from itself. After World War II, it is said, the socialists belatedly joined a Keynesian revolution that was, so to speak, handed to them as a free gift.

That was not the case. The shattering events of the thirties did lead to anguished socialist reconsideration during those years, and it prepared the way for the social-democratic Keynesianism of the postwar period. There is considerable evidence to suggest that the socialists, particularly in Sweden, had arrived at a version of Keynesianism well before Keynes published his *General Theory.* In any case, European socialism finally ventured into the *terra incognita* that lay between capitalism and socialism and did so in complex ways that cannot be explained simply by reference to Keynesian theory. That this brought in its train all the ambiguities and contradictions of the mixed economy was both inevitable and a very real progress.

As a consequence, the socialists shaped European society in the thirty years between 1945 and 1975. Their new perspective allowed them not to create socialism but to build welfare states that recognized noncapitalist, and even anticapitalist, principles of human need over and above the imperatives of profit. In the late fifties and early sixties, the success of this "social-democratic compromise" led to basic programmatic revisions in every major socialist party in Europe. A Keynesian capitalism under socialist governments would now generate such growth that, without being forced to redistribute wealth, the surplus would make possible an endless improvement of the quality of social life. It seemed that the socialists had become the normal party of government on the Continent, and their conservative opponents were forced to accept measures they had once denounced on principle.

The new socialist pragmatism led, in theory and practice, to utopias hostile to one another and yet sharing basic assumptions. One of them was the product of the socialist establishment, an idealized status quo that was projected into an indefinite, and trouble-free, future. Another came from implacable critics of that establishment on the New Left who disdained the accomplishments of the social-democratic compromise even as they based their vision upon their permanence. And a third, which was actually formulated in the thirties but had a certain vogue in the sixties, came from John Maynard Keynes, a man who publicly proclaimed his antisocialism.

When the socialist-led welfare states (and the liberal variant in the United States) entered into crisis in the mid-seventies, all of these utopias were dashed. And yet they had introduced significant themes that may become the basis of the realism of twenty-first-century socialism.

I

ONE OF THE PROBLEMS of the orthodox social-democratic Marxists in Germany when the Depression came was that their theories had worked brilliantly for five years.

"Organized capitalism," they had said, was more and more being centralized and planned under the control of monopolies. The social democrats, fighting to democratize that process, could make a temporary alliance with the system, benefit from the growth that resulted, make immediate gains, and even push gradually to change basic structures. One might even say that this was a pragmatic strategy, not totally unlike the post–World War II social-democratic compromise. Between 1924 and 1929, real wages went up, working hours declined, unemployment insurance and other welfare measures were improved. The underlying assumption was that the inherent capitalist tendencies toward crisis had been ameliorated and that a peaceful, democratic transition to a vague and unspecified "socialism" was possible. The benign effects of capitalist socialization were exaggerated in the extreme.

When the greatest breakdown in the history of capitalism took place, Rudolf Hilferding and his comrades had profound political and emotional investments in the status quo that led them to revert to Kautsky's either/or. They had good reason to hope that the automatic workings of the system would restore equilibrium and let them get on with their strategy. After all, Marx himself had argued that capitalist crises eventually functioned to restore the conditions of profitability — not the least by beating down the wage demands of the workers — and to prepare the way for a new expansion.

The German trade unions, however, could not afford such a long view, with its not-so-tacit acceptance of proletarian misery as a historic necessity. Their ranks were decimated by unemployment, and in 1931 they put forward a plan for full employment through deficit-financed public investments. Hilferding and the

Social Democratic Party were outraged with the union proposals, not the least because they, like the conservative economists, feared that deficit financing might lead to inflation! Arguing in defense of the union plan, W. A. Woytinsky, one of its moving spirits, said, "The labor movement needs an economic action program which will show the workers, and also other popular strata, that the social democracy and the unions have come to see a way out of economic misery. Today we have no such program." Woytinsky and the trade unionists were well aware of Keynes's work and tried to get him to come to a meeting of the International Labor Office in 1931 to discuss his perspective, so similar to their own, with the worker representatives. Keynes, who always kept his distance from the class organizations of labor, refused. But even so, the idea of labor "plans" spread from Germany to unions in Britain, Norway, France, Switzerland, and, of course, Sweden. A Belgian socialist leader who had also been active in the German social democracy, Hendrick De Man (often referred to under the French, rather than Flemish, version of his name, as Henri De Man), picked up on the idea of planning, and it spread throughout Europe in the thirties.

This history has been obscured, and one reason has to do with De Man himself. Originally a Marxist, he had become fascinated by the American prosperity of the twenties and argued that scientific management had so deskilled labor that workers were no longer capable of conceptualizing a socialist alternative (this theme was taken up by the French analyst André Gorz in the eighties). De Man, like the Italian Marxist genius Antonio Gramsci and the French socialist André Phillip, was fascinated by "Fordism" in America and saw it not simply as a new technique of production but as a new culture for the masses. Under these conditions, he concluded, the technicians and intellectuals alone had the capacity to be socialist, and socialism itself was now more a question of values than of economic self-interest (Kautsky called it "socialism for the intelligentsia").

De Man's elitist critique of Marx made him a problematic figure and was one reason why socialist history found it difficult to come to terms with him. But much more important was the fact that, when the Nazis occupied Holland, he collaborated with them and was eventually sentenced, *in absentia*, to twenty years in prison after the war. As a result, there are those who suspect that his ideas were authoritarian and do not, therefore, belong in an honorable history of socialist thought.

Yet, there was no necessary connection between De Man's advocacy of socialist full-employment planning within capitalism (considerably focused on monetary policy) and his later collaboration with the Nazis. Even more to the point, the "planning" movement was often consciously counterposed to the old statist — and implicitly authoritarian — models of socialism. The Kautsky and Hilferding vision of socialism, based on a centralized economy, was undercut by the tragedy of the German social democracy, and the new programmatic proposals more often than not emphasized themes of industrial democracy and even sometimes moved in the direction of Guild Socialism.

But the French Socialist leader Leon Blum saw De Man's plan-oriented "neosocialism" as moving in a statist direction, combining economic and political power to a dangerous degree. In appealing to the petty-bourgeois desire for strong leadership in a crisis, which had been a source of fascist recruits, Blum said, the neosocialists were in danger of themselves becoming fascist. That was certainly a possible interpretation of De Man, and it was explicitly made by one of his leading French disciples, Marcel Deat, who moved from Blum's party and eventually became an enthusiastic supporter of the Nazis during the Occupation. But there were other readings of the "planning" strategy that, because they assigned a major role to trade-union participation, were antistatist and even moved in a decentralist, Guild Socialist direction.

Clearly these ideas were also influenced by the Soviet experience, which was anything but antistatist, essentially because the Soviet Five Year Plans were bringing full employment, and at the time most people did not realize the monstrous cost of that achievement.

But on the other side, De Man followed the New Deal quite carefully and used it as a kind of model. And therein lies a very real irony. Roosevelt improvised the New Deal and, as Keynes attested after their only personal meeting, had no theoretical understanding of many of the economic policies he had followed. In 1932, when many of the European socialist theorists were discussing deficit financing, FDR was campaigning against Hoover's excessive spending. During the first six months of his presidency, he actually followed the advice of Lewis Douglas and proposed deep budget cuts in the middle of the Depression. In 1935, when the "Second New Deal" went into effect — that is, when a more Keynesian approach was introduced — it was, in a sense, a turn to *laisser-faire.*

But, as Michael Piore and Charles Sabel have pointed out, it was also an extremely radical move in that the nonideological President did what so many of the European socialists feared to do: *he interfered with the "natural laws" of the market economy.* In France before and during the Popular Front, Leon Blum understood how innovative the New Deal was. Blum, who talked of America under the capitalist reformer Roosevelt much more than of Sweden under a socialist government, noted that Roosevelt was instinctively carrying out policies whose justification could be found in French socialist theory.

In Britain, Keynes's influence was strongest, not the least because the young generation of politician-intellectuals in the Labour Party — Hugh Gaitskell, Evan Durbin, Hugh Dalton, Douglas Jay, among them — were in contact with him or his colleagues. Some of them were suspicious of the inflationary potential of the Keynesian proposals, and all of them thought that Keynes did not go far enough in changing the structures of production, relying primarily on the stimulation of demand. But the New Fabian Research Bureau still prepared the Labour Party for its acceptance of the Keynesian mixed economy in the historic Labour government of 1945. Indeed, Anthony Crosland rightly argued that the Labour Party's "Short Term Programme" of 1937 contained the essentials of the policies carried out by that Attlee government in 1945.

The point is, throughout Europe socialists and trade unionists had come to Keynesian — and more radical than Keynesian — conclusions, independent of, simultaneous with, or even through contact with the master himself. The shock of the Great Depression had forced the socialists of the Continent to decisively abandon their either/or of capitalism/socialism and to begin to explore the difficult terrain between the two systems. John Maynard Keynes was not a *deus ex machina* who saved European socialism from its own sterility, but one influence among many.

Sweden was a dramatic case in point. Its history is very

idiosyncratic, the product of a unique labor and socialist movement. Yet one of the results of that exceptionalism was also a certain universalism, a particular emphasis upon the socialist theme that socialism serves the common good of the entire society. No other European party of the Left gave such a critical stress to the value of human — in addition to class — solidarity. But it turned out that the Swedish Social Democrats had, in their own way, anticipated not only much of Keynes's theory but a central legitimation of the postwar welfare state as well. They made socialist reform the cause of the entire society, not just of one class or political movement.

In a celebrated speech in 1928, the Swedish socialist leader Per Albin Hansson defined the goal of the social democracy as the creation of a "peoples' home" based on "equality, concern, co-operation and helpfulness." It would be hard to imagine a vision more removed from the historic determinism of Kautsky's Erfurt Program. Yet in 1907, Hjalmar Branting, the first leader of the socialist party, had articulated the very "orthodox" attitude that "only when these means of production, in the new, gigantic size they have reached in the era of capitalism, are converted into public property through the large, all encompassing organization which the society constitutes" will the socialist task have been completed.

Why did the Swedes move — very early on — away from the German model? Swedish history and social structure are part of the answer; a number of brilliant individuals who pioneered new ideas is another.

Sweden had been significantly influenced by the Enlightenment, and that in turn affected the emerging business class of the late nineteenth century, which was somewhat cosmopolitan and based on export industry. There were prosperous farmers in the Swedish parliament in the late 1800s and a much larger number of family farms that did not meet the property qualification for political participation. Thus when the society went through a rapid, late process of industrialization, there were allies for the new labor and socialist movement. The Liberals joined in the campaign for universal suffrage and, as the electorate broadened, the small farmers worked for a pension law in 1913 that would cover them as well as the workers. As early as 1911, the socialists responded to the small farmers by dropping from the platform the classic demand for the nationalization of the land and emphasizing cooperatives and small-scale private property instead. At the same time, they rejected the notion that capitalism would inexorably immiserate the working class.

The Swedish working class was organized very early on in the development of capitalism and became a centralized, industrial union movement. At the same time, the employers came together in order to deal with a united labor movement, and the basis was laid for one of the most important characteristics of Swedish society: a national wage bargain between authoritative organizations of both capital and the workers. This is not to suggest that the class struggle was compromised early on. On the contrary. Until 1938, Sweden was the scene of bitter battles between management and labor, and the peace that was concluded that year was on the basis of capital's understanding that the workers had conquered enough economic and political power to make some kind of a deal a necessity.

The main point, however, is clear enough. The Swedish socialists had possibilities of alliances that simply did not exist for their German comrades. They therefore had a fundamentally different attitude toward reforms *within* capitalism. As early as 1908, there had been proposals in parliament for public-works projects that would hire workers at regular wages. In 1918, a Social Democratic–Liberal coalition finally achieved universal suffrage and parliamentary reform, in 1919, the eight-hour day. But in some ways the socialist party's ideology lagged behind its practice. The 1919 Gorteborg Program still stuck to the classic Kautskyan formulations, and in the twenties there were even Social Democrats, under the spell of that unholy alliance between "revolutionary" Marxism and free-enterprise economics, who believed that high wages were a significant cause of widespread unemployment.

The sea change came in the 1920s, and two brilliant economists, Ernst Wigforss and Gunnar Myrdal, were the prime movers.

Ironically, the shift was in part a response to the disappointments of success. The Socialists and the Liberals had achieved universal suffrage and parliamentary responsibility. There was a socialist minority government in 1920, and it appointed a socialization commission, thrusting that hallowed socialist demand into the center of political debate. The result was an electoral setback later on in 1920 as the party lost its historic momentum. As John Stephens described the moment, the Social Democrats "had won 'the battle for democracy' but it had not [as the young Marx had thought it would] 'raised the proletariat to the position of ruling class.' The voice of the people had been heard and it had not supported the socialists." The problem was, Stephens continued — and this was true in every country with the possible exception of Britain — that the workers, and particularly the conscious socialist workers, were nowhere near a majority of the society. They therefore had to appeal to nonproletarian strata to win, and the latter were not in favor of sweeping measures of socialization.

This turn took place at a particularly difficult time. Unemployment was on the rise, and there were not a few socialists who thought that the society had to pay less than the going wage on public-works projects, that capitalism, particularly at a time of crisis, was incompatible with an increase in the real living standard of the people. That might be a profoundly "radical" indictment of the system, but it hardly provided a political foundation for a labor-based movement. At this point, Wigforss and Myrdal became extremely important.

Wigforss was a Marxist critic of vulgar Marxist determinism, Myrdal a thinker who looked to the Enlightenment, rather than the Marxist, tradition. Both built on the work of the Swedish economist Knut Wicksell, who at the turn of the century had developed a devastating critique of Say's Law, the mystical proposition, central to the mainstream tradition, that sellers create buyers and that, if only market forces were allowed to work their magic, an equilibrium of supply and demand would come about on its own. Schumpeter was to credit Wicksell for having anticipated much of Keynes's theory of the importance of aggregate consumption in the economy, and that was, of course, a central theme for both Wigforss and Myrdal. During the twenties, and particularly after another socialist electoral setback in 1928, when the voters rejected radical tax proposals, they worked out an immediate program on the basis of the then astounding proposition that increasing the well-being of the people would make the system productive.

Wigforss and Myrdal were against a "public assistance" approach to unemployment, arguing in favor of deficit-financed investments to put people back to work at full wages. Such an increase in the buying power of the workers, they believed, would not wreck the system. It would save it. They also anticipated the Keynesian concept of the "multiplier," that is, the fact that a dollar of stimulus would create buying power that would put people to work and thus create more buying power so that the total economic effect would be "multiplied." Wigforss was to say that "Keynes' theories strengthened the faith in the correctness of the teachings of common sense and socialism." And Myrdal was to remember that "the *Treatise* [Keynes's book of 1930 on money] and, a little later, his *General Theory* were for us brilliant and significant works whose line was familiar to us and caused nothing like the impression of an intellectual revolution which occurred in other countries."

Moreover, the Swedish socialists saw their ideas within an explicitly socialist framework. In the twenties, when it became clear that there was no political basis for wholesale and rapid socialization, they developed the notion of "functional socialization" to explain what they were doing. Capitalist property, they argued, was not a "thing" to be seized by the state but a bundle of functions — deciding on what technology to produce in what way at what wages at what prices, and so on. And it would be possible to carry out a policy of "functional socialization," of asserting public (but not necessarily state) control over one or another of those functions without attacking private property as such. The gradualist measures were, in short, conceptualized as part of a socialist strategy for structural change — but structural changes that were politically possible.

In 1932, in the midst of the Great Depression, the Social Democrats came to power — but, significantly, with a minority of the vote and only because they had the support of the farmers. Their policies, which were the result of conscious theory rather than the political improvisation of the New Deal, worked. They were, to be sure, helped by a number of external factors, among them the recovery of the German economy under Hitler's military and repressive version of "Keynesianism." But there can be no doubt that the policy shift of the 1920s, formulated by Wigforss and Myrdal (both of whom were to be cabinet ministers in socialist governments), was a significant factor in that success.

By 1938 the Social Democrats had become not simply the governing party of the nation but the source of an ethos for all of

Swedish society. The concept of the "peoples' home," of social-ism as a movement that reached out to farmers, shopkeepers, and white-collar strata as well as to industrial workers, gave a legitimacy to the movement that a purely proletarian ideology never could have attained.

Also by 1938 Swedish capital understood that the workers had, through organization and militancy, achieved an irreversible posi-tion of strength in the society. It was at that point that capital and labor agreed in effect to negotiate their differences in a national wage bargain and to engage in a wary cooperation with one an-other in the work of promoting economic growth. This accord, it must be emphasized again, had very little to do with some innate tendency to compromise on the part of the onetime antagonists and very much to do with their mutual recognition of a new social reality that had been created through conflict. It also established one of the most important characteristics of the Swedish model: that crucial aspects of economic policy were determined not by the state but by a "corporatist" negotiation between organized labor and organized capital.

This left, we will see, considerable room for bitter disputes between antagonistic partners. For now, however, the central point of this survey of socialist ideas in the 1930s is clear enough. There was a ferment in the movement, a break with the old, apocalyptic either/or of the Kautskyan tradition, a new willing-ness to develop socialist programs that could work with and modify capitalism, but that fell far short of a "revolutionary" transformation.

The socialist theory and practice of the thirties, which re-sponded to the tragic defeat of classic social democracy in the face of the Depression, thus prepared the way for the triumph of socialist "Keynesianism" after World War II. At that point, socialists all over Europe became the spokespersons not simply for workers but for the well-being of the entire society that would prosper under the stimulus of social justice.[1]

II

BETWEEN 1945 and (roughly) 1975, advanced capitalism went through an unparalleled period of economic growth and rising living standards for the mass of the people. In Europe, this was, of course, the period of the social-democratic compromise; in the United States it was marked by the hegemony of a Keynesian social liberalism mainly in the Democratic but also somewhat in the Republican party. Indeed, the gains made throughout the West during these years were so striking that they gave rise to no less than three utopias, one of which was actually put into practice.

It is hard to be precise about causation when one is dealing with such a massive historic phenomenon as the Great Prosperity (I take the phrase from Hayek). It is quite likely that a "long wave" of economic growth took place on the basis of innovations that were being prepared during the long wave of economic decline in the 1930s, which suggests that even in the absence of the momentous political changes of these times there would have been a "natural" boom.

But there is also little doubt that the expansion of the welfare state and the commitment of every government in the West to Keynesian full-employment planning were major factors in the unprecedented character of the advance. The "Fordist" strategy of providing a mass-consumption basis for mass production through a range of public programs worked. As a result, a "virtuous circle" was set in motion: increasing investment led to high productivity; higher productivity generated economic growth, which made it possible to have a simultaneous rise in real wages, profits, and social outlays; the expansion of buying power that resulted led to bigger markets, and higher profits; the higher profits made still more investment and productivity possible; and on and on, for more than a quarter of a century.

One consequence was that the money wage turned into the social wage. That is, a growing portion of the citizen's income came not in the form of a paycheck but as entitlements to health care, pensions, paid vacations, public education, and the like (in the United States, which singularly lacked a system of national health, one would also add the "fringe benefits" for medical care negotiated as part of union contracts). It was not an apologist for welfare capitalism but a Marxist critic of that system, Goran Therborn, who computed one of the most dramatic outcomes of this shift. In the advanced capitalist countries, Therborn wrote in a 1984 article, "between one fifth and one third of all household income derives from public revenue and not from property or labour for private or public capital."

That is, income from public employment and from social programs in the West was considerably larger than the money going to the owners of capital (profits, dividends, interest, rent). Therborn's figures were based on 1980 data, and therefore largely excluded the impact of conservative governments in the 1980s, but even the Reagans, Thatchers, Kohls, and Chiracs were only able to attack the margins of social decency, often striking at the most vulnerable. It would have been political suicide to have attempted a head-on assault against the postwar welfare state.

These numbers do not tell us anything about the *distribution* of the publicly generated income, and the data are quite tricky, particularly when we try to make international comparisons. It is true, however, that the middle and upper classes often benefit disproportionately from public expenditure for higher education under the welfare state; that the Social Security pensions in the United States are financed by a regressive tax that favors the rich and discriminates against the middle strata; and so on. We also have much more reliable data on income than on wealth, and there is no doubt that the latter is much more maldistributed than the former. Finally, it must be kept in mind that the expansion of the welfare state was largely financed out of economic growth, not through redistribution. In Sweden, the welfare state with the most conscious egalitarian orientation — and the lowest levels of inequality in Europe — the top 20 percent of the society still received 35 percent of the after-tax income in the mid-seventies (compared to 38.1 percent in the United States and 47.1 percent in France).

Why these national differences? The most significant factor has to do with socialist and trade-union strength. The social-democratic compromise is, after all, a version of capitalism — improved and ameliorated, but a version of capitalism nevertheless. This system can be — and often has been — run by the Right as well as by the Left, which is precisely one of the political problems of the socialists whose ideas were co-opted by their opponents. In *The Transition from Capitalism to Socialism*, John Stephens carefully worked out an international comparison and discovered that the stronger the socialists and the unions, the more redistributive the welfare state. The United States, with no mass socialist movement and a lower percentage of union organization than any European country (with the anomalous exception of France) therefore has the weakest welfare state. Australia, in which a strong labor movement with its own party opted for means-tested public benefits and high, protected wages, is also something of an exception to the rule.

So it is possible to identify a specifically socialist variant of the welfare state, one that is more redistributive and comprehensive than those favored by conservatives. The pioneering work of the Swedish socialists, and the revisions in program and analysis in every European country in the thirties, had made a significant difference. But it led to a euphoric and utopian generalization of the new postwar reality: the socialist perspective was now seen by many of its major leaders as a limitless process of growth-financed social decency in a capitalist economy under socialist political control.[2]

III

THIS SOCIALIST UTOPIA has come to be called the "social-democratic compromise," but it wasn't much of a compromise. There was a brief surge of leftism in the European movement right after World War II even in Sweden, but then the socialists all settled for a situation in which they would regulate and tax capitalism but not challenge it in any fundamental way. The capitalists, in turn, had to concede legitimacy to forms of government intervention that they had denounced as Bolshevism in the not-too-distant past.

What did the socialists surrender? Mainly a rhetoric. That is, there had been no serious social-democratic program for the revolutionary transformation of capitalism since the end of World War I. Even the radical declarations of the Kautskyan period, though they frightened business, were quite vague and rationalized a thoroughly reformist practice. The analyses of the thirties, which came to fruition in the fifties and sixties, all understood that, even for those who in no way had abandoned their commitment to a new society, the immediate and middle-distance future would take place within the framework of capitalism. So when the historic party programs were revised in the fifties to bring them into some kind of consonance with reality, the "Left" critics of the move tended to be traditionalists defending classic phrases rather than an opposition with a political alternative.

The new socialist declarations, like the Godesberg Program of the German social democracy in 1959, were all, in one way or another, committed to the notion of a "social market economy," that is, to a modified capitalism. They tended to put great store in scientifically and technologically generated growth and ignored the environmental costs of that process as well as the attendant bureaucratization, which was to lead to the youth revolts of the sixties. The tragic income gap between North and South was acknowledged as a problem, but it was not a central issue, and feminist concerns were treated in much the same way. The great preoccupations of the years from 1945 to 1960 were "economistic," above all focused on full employment as a response to the Great Depression.

Anthony Crosland's *The Future of Socialism* (1956) is a brilliant statement of this attitude.* It was not simply a book by a socialist intellectual, but also a manifesto of the "revisionist" wing of the British Labour Party, led by Hugh Gaitskell. I take it as a representative statement of the postwar social-democratic mood, which one might define as pragmatic utopianism.

"We stand in Britain," Crosland wrote, "on the threshold of mass abundance." That was one of the key propositions to all of the utopias of this period, not just the social-democratic variant (it was also the basis of Marx's most utopian speculations). Therefore,

if our present rate of economic growth continues, material want and poverty and deprivation of essential goods will gradually cease to be a problem. We shall increasingly need to focus attention, not on universal categories, but on individual persons and families: not on the economic causes of distress, but on the social and psychological causes. . . . We shall rely less on broad, sweeping measures of expenditure than on concentrated measures of aid to limited groups,

---

*Crosland was a friend and I admired his work even when I disagreed with it. My critique has all the unfair advantages of hindsight, but it still regards him as one of the most serious socialist thinkers of the period.

based on patient, empirical social research into the real nature of the need.

That last sentence articulates another central theme of the times: that a value-free, nonpolitical social science would increasingly play a role in practical life.

What about nationalization of industry, which so many — including the left wing of the Labour Party — regarded as the sovereign socialist remedy? In some cases, Crosland said, it could well still be an instrument of policy. But that had to be decided on empirical grounds, case by case, and the classic arguments in favor of public ownership had turned out to be less than convincing. The British industries nationalized by Labour had charged low (nonexploitative) prices that functioned as a subsidy to the largest users, which were capitalist corporations, and deprived the industry itself of the retained profits that should have been a source of its new investments. These public companies were run by bureaucratic authorities under fairly nominal parliamentary control and were often less responsive to social considerations than the private sector.

But Crosland's theory of nationalization was more sweeping than these specific, reality-based criticisms. He attacked the very notion that the form of *ownership* was the decisive determinant of the workers' alienated position in society. In the process, he raised issues that went far beyond the question of nationalization.

Marx, Crosland said, was right in his claim that the control of the means of production by a class that dominated the actual producers was a basic source of the injustices of the society. But was that control necessarily a function of ownership? Or rather, does "it arise inevitably from the underlying technological fact of complex and large-scale factory organization? Surely the latter."

This argument was directed against those in the Labour Party who dogmatically asserted the inherent virtues of public, as opposed to private, ownership, and it was a telling point. By the mid-fifties, socialists certainly understood that a completely nationalized economy in the Soviet Union did not give working people control over the means of production. And under late capitalism itself, as Marx himself had recognized in *Das Kapital*, there was a separation of ownership and control. But in his discussion of industrial democracy — as an alternative to *both* private and public bureaucracies — Crosland himself was something of a Kautskyan.

That is, he assumed that the huge factory was going to be the perpetual rule, that the Fordist organization of work was permanent, and argued — quite rightly I think — that, *under those circumstances*, it was very hard to imagine rank-and-file participation in decision making. Some years later, the Marxist Harry Braverman was to point out that capitalist technology was *capitalist* technology, that is, that it was designed not simply according to engineering priorities but in keeping with social values, and incarnated the inferior position of the workers in the production process. Braverman's conclusion was that socialists should think in terms of an alternate technology rather than envisioning the socialization of an antisocial technology. But Crosland did not consider such a possibility.

The unions, Crosland said, had to be a kind of opposition to the inevitable, technologically based power of management that would exist whatever the mode of ownership. For the simple fact was that someone other than the workers must ultimately make the production decisions. It would be unfair to attack a thinker of the fifties for not having anticipated the technological possibilities of the eighties — the declining importance of scale, the growing significance of cooperative relations at the base, even under capitalism, and the consequent potential for designing a new mode of both work and control. But it was a profound limitation on Crosland's analysis, as he himself later came to realize.*

Crosland did not, however, limit himself to this attack on the cherished dogma of nationalization. He went on to try and rehabilitate private profit for socialists. Profit, he said, was not the diabolic reality that socialists had criticized, for all dynamic societies were forced to use part of the surplus from current production for depreciation and investment. As Helmut Schmidt, the Social Democratic Chancellor of West Germany in the seventies, was to formulate this argument in a famous statement in 1976: "The profits of enterprises today are the investments of tomorrow, and the investments of tomorrow are the jobs of the day after tomorrow."

---

*The last time I saw Crosland before his tragically early death, he told me that he believed that industrial democracy, which he had roundly criticized in *The Future of Socialism*, was basic to the future of socialism.

In Crosland's variant of this thesis, he noted that it was possible for a nationalized board to misuse the GNP surplus every bit as much as a corporate board. Again, the question of *legal ownership* was not at all decisive; the issue was how an enterprise made its decisions and what decisions it made. But, most critically, Crosland asserted that the change in the distribution of income had been so great that profit no longer functioned as it once did. It was possible, he claimed, to have that classic socialist goal, production for use, under a socially regulated form of capitalism.

Thus Crosland wrote:

The statement that production for profit gives a bad distribution of resources (caviar for the rich before milk for the poor) is only a shorthand. What is meant is that production is undertaken for profit: that the distribution of purchasing power determines what is profitable: and that if this is very unequal, then the wants of the rich will be met before the needs of the poor. But if purchasing power is distributed more equally, it becomes more profitable to produce necessities, and less profitable to produce luxuries. . . . Today the redistribution of incomes, and the rise in working-class purchasing power, have banished the worst effects of production for profit by calling forth a quite different pattern of output.

In another context, the same thought was put in compressed form: "Production for use and production for profit may be taken as broadly coinciding now that working-class purchasing power is so high."

The problem with this analysis is that Crosland did not understand the internal contradictions of a situation that, in that period of growth and full employment after World War II, seemed to offer endless possibilities of reform without the need to change any basic structures. That failure led to utopian expectations in the name of a socialist *Realpolitik*. Like Hilferding and the German social democrats of the twenties, Crosland assumed that Keynesian capitalism (which was the new version of "organized capitalism") had put an end to the business cycle. As Lyndon Johnson stated the American variant of that faith in his last economic message to the Congress in 1969, "No longer is the economy a relentless tide of ups and downs." The seventies and eighties proved in dramatic fashion that this was simply not true.

Beyond that, it was not just that Crosland exaggerated the degree to which the welfare state had redistributed income. In 1975, the Royal Commission on the Distribution of Income and Wealth showed that Labour's policies had indeed had an effect in this area in the forties — and that, particularly when account was taken of the ways in which the rich avoided the law, there was still fundamental and structural inequality (Crosland himself recognized, and was appalled by, this fact in the sixties and seventies). But even more basic than this empirical error of prediction was the failure to understand the degree to which the persistence of capitalist economic and social power was a critical political fact as well.

As Crosland put the optimistic proposition, "Naturally the greater influence of the government would signify little if it were simply used to buttress the power, and underwrite the actions, of private business — if the state, in the Marxist phrase, were still the 'executive committee' of the capitalist class. But of course it is no such thing." Indeed it is not, and for that matter Marx never held the simplistic, one-to-one theory of capitalist economic and political power that is so often attributed to him. But that is not to say, as Crosland and an entire generation of social democrats assumed, that capital had lost a preponderant influence on the government. They thought that political and economic power could be segregated or, put another way, that a democratic political order could dominate an undemocratic economic order.

That illusion had a certain superficial plausibility during the glory years of economic growth, largely because corporations were, just as Crosland said, making money out of meeting social-democratic priorities. And yet even in that period there was a tendency, especially in the United States but in Europe also, toward "private affluence and public squalor," in Galbraith's memorable phrase. And when the crisis proclivities of the system reasserted themselves in the mid-seventies and the growth idyll came to an end, even social-democratic governments were forced to follow austere capitalist priorities — including layoffs — because the logic of the "system" demanded it. The French socialist experience of the eighties is more complex than most analysts have realized, but it is certainly true that, despite an absolute parliamentary majority and control of the presidency, the Socialists were, within a year of coming to power, forced to abandon their hopes for a "new mode of life." The constraints of the international money system turned out to be more powerful than the democratic desires of the French electorate.*

In Britain itself, the decay of the central cities of the North, the high unemployment, and the persistent poverty show the power of capital in imposing the costs of an economic transition on the most vulnerable people in the society. The assumption of the fifties and sixties — that mass abundance was at hand — turned out to be a utopia. And capital turned out to be anything but a subordinate partner in the welfare state, which graciously bowed to democratic outcomes. Its power permeated the system even when the socialists were in office.

So the social-democratic "revisionists" who generalized the undeniable successes of the sixties and seventies into an expectation of permanent increases in social decency were wrong. But many of their Left critics made a symmetrical error: they underrated what was accomplished. I am not referring to the true believers who simply repeated the hallowed formulas of old, but of many of the sophisticated neo-Marxists, such as Adam Przeworski and his *Capitalism and Social Democracy* (1985).

Once the social democrats committed themselves to building class-based parties to operate within the framework of parliamentary democracy, Przeworski argues, they were faced with a basic dilemma. Since the workers were not, and did not become, a majority, working-class parties had to choose "between a party homogeneous in its class appeal but sentenced to perpetual electoral defeats or a party that struggles for electoral success at the cost of diluting its class orientation." It was the fact that a majority of advanced society, which was not proletarian, and a minority of the working class itself did not want sweeping Kautskyan — let alone Leninist — "socialization." And this situation did indeed force the social democrats to abandon some of their doctrines. But what else could a movement do when it was committed to *democratic* socialization? Moreover, the workers of Europe freely

---

*I examined the complexities of the French case at chapter length in *The Next Left*. I would simply note here that I believe that the socialists did tolerably well under impossible conditions.

chose the path to the reformist welfare state even though they were given many opportunities — by Communists in their "Left" periods as well as by revolutionary sects — to opt for some abstract vision of "socialism."

Christine Bucci Glucksman and Goran Therborn, writing from a left-wing Marxist vantage point, cogently summarized the reality of the Keynesian welfare state, emphasizing a complexity that eluded both its critics and defenders. They said of the social democrats, "Agents of the stabilization of capitalism and the state, they are also part of the expansion of the working class, of its power, of its increased influence in the last thirty years." One and the same process strengthened *both* capital *and* labor — but left capital in control of the decisive levers of structural power. So when the crisis came, the utopian expectations of the socialist realists came crashing to the ground.[3]

IV

THE SOCIAL DEMOCRATS were not alone in their illusions. Strange as it may seem, some of their radical critics shared their basic — and erroneous — assumptions. The New Left of the sixties was contemptuous of the stodgy social democrats, yet had the very same faith in the boundless possibilities of the economy.

This anti–social democratic utopia was based upon new political movements and social strata. It came to world attention during the events of May 1968 in Paris when a student-led insurgency ignited a national movement and a general strike of the working class and came quite close to overthrowing the then president Charles de Gaulle. This movement was opposed to all bureaucracies, social democratic or conservative, and saw itself as the herald of a near anarchist revolution. It arose with conscious connections to similar developments around the world: to the civil-rights and anti–Vietnam War mobilizations in the United States, the earlier struggle of a part of the French Left against colonialism in Algeria, the German "extraparliamentary opposition," Maoist tendencies throughout Europe including Italy, and the emergence of "Green" environmental concerns in almost every advanced country. In the wake of 1968, this trend also gave impetus to a feminist resurgence, which had much more staying power than the rest of the movement.

The mass base of this New Left was the product of the very social-democratic compromise (and in the United States, liberal triumph) that the movement itself deplored. It appealed to the greatly enlarged student body in institutions of higher education, institutions that had been expanded by pragmatic politicians who believed that knowledge was the key to productivity and productivity the chief constituent of economic growth. It was also a result of the increase in the standard of living and the conviction on the part of masses of people that college was the best way to make it possible for their children to do even better. In this period there was indeed a growth in professional and technical jobs in the new economy, which, in the United States, doubled the percentage of that stratum and made it more numerous than the actual production workers.

There was another factor that is so complex that only one of its aspects can be mentioned here. A cultural revolution was under way in the West in the sixties that challenged moral certitudes and practices with the authority of centuries behind them. Organized, mainstream religion declined in importance, and a variety of Eastern and pseudoreligions proliferated. Drugs, pornography, and casual sex became commonplace, and homosexuals rebelled against a repression that they had once suffered in silence and fear. There were many sources of this phenomenon, but one of them was the official hedonism of the new Keynesian economics. Prior to that Keynesian victory, the dominant economics celebrated saving, the deferral of gratification, the Protestant ethic. Now increased consumption was seen as a driving force for economic well-being for all. Spending money thus became an act of civic virtue.

The new radicals were critical of bourgeois possessiveness — and often the agents of a new possessiveness centered on stereos and motorcycles rather than suburban houses. Their attitudes about morality put them at odds with the working class, which was often social democratic in politics and conservative about cultural issues. Arising in opposition to, and as a result of, the Keynesian social democracy, the New Left looked to the *lumpen-proletariat* within the advanced countries — the minorities, the unemployed, the slum and ghetto dwellers — and to the masses of the Third World as the instruments of revolutionary change.

Herbert Marcuse, a philosopher who had once belonged to the German Social Democratic Party and who was sixty-two years old when the sixties began, was one of the most influential spokespersons of the new youthful utopianism. I take him as a representative figure not simply because he was acknowledged as a guru in Europe as well as in America, but also because his biography shows the interrelationships between the traditional and the New Left. Marcuse belonged to both.

Indeed, his analysis owed more than a little to Rudolf Hilferding and the theory of "organized capitalism," a debt Marcuse acknowledged on more than one occasion. He had known and admired Hilferding, and even though he had long since broken with the Social Democratic Party (at the time of the murder of Rosa Luxemburg and Karl Liebknecht), he contributed during the twenties to Hilferding's review, *Die Gesellschaft*. He also participated in the discussions of the Frankfurt School, which saw the New Deal as a further development of organized capitalism. But in the sixties, and especially in his book *One-Dimensional Man*, Marcuse gave a unique interpretation of Hilferding's theme.

Contemporary capitalism, Marcuse argued at a conference in West Berlin in 1967,

> functions extraordinarily well. . . . We struggle against a society that has succeeded in eliminating poverty and suffering to a degree that the previous stages of capitalism never attained. . . . We have in the United States today freedoms and a living standard, a level of comfort for vast strata of the population that are hardly believable.

But in the process of accomplishing these prodigies, this society had become "one-dimensional." The people are held in thrall by golden chains, by the satisfaction of false, manufactured needs; they are victimized by a technology that manipulates them every moment of the night and day; they have become visionless, conformist, programmed. At the same time, there are the less subtle, more old-fashioned forms of repression turned against the external proletariat in the Third World and the internal *lumpenproletariat* of minorities in the ghettos.

At times, Marcuse talks of such a society as "totalitarian," a label that Leszek Kolakowski rightly rejects as absurdly exaggerated. It may be, as Douglas Kellner has argued, that this is simply a poor choice of words, and that Marcuse never intended the term to be taken literally. But this vision of a controlled anti-utopia — of Hilferding's "organized capitalism" become a means of an oppression all the more terrifying because it is so subtle and benign — was certainly one of the reasons for Marcuse's resonance among the antibureaucratic youth. Their experience with and hostility to the administered and computerized university campus was projected as an image of the entire society.

Ironically, Marcuse argued, the one-dimensional society came into existence at the very moment when a true reign of freedom was possible. There was now an objective abundance — this is clearly a key term of all the sixties' utopias — the clear possibility, for the first time in human history, of abolishing want on a worldwide basis. But it resulted either in the pseudosatisfactions of a programmed consumerism or in a new and vicious form of imperialism and racism. So Marcuse radically reinterpreted Freud in the light of some neglected insights of Marx in an attempt to deal with the new reality.

Freud had made the conservative argument in *Civilization and Its Discontents* that instinctual repression was the necessary condition of economic and social progress. Humans in their "natural" state were creatures of their Ids, prone to violence and lawlessness. But insofar as they sublimated these raging desires, they were able to create economies and cultures, and the more complex the latter became, the greater the degree of repression. Therefore, the progress of civilization was accompanied by increasing discontent as the psychic costs of the achievement became greater and greater. Socialization is achieved through repression.

There was, Marcuse held, considerable truth in the Freudian argument in the premodern, or more precisely preabundance, stage of history. But once society had attained its present productive capacity, only a diminishing part of that repressiveness was truly necessary. The remaining repression of the instinctual life was unnecessary, a means of social domination and not a functional requisite of production. It was "surplus" repression. This notion was clearly related to Marx's distinction between the necessity of direction that arises from the technical conditions of capitalist production — the coordination of a complex process — and that direction necessary to keep the workers subordinate and to maintain hierarchy and class discipline.

In the world of the sixties, Marcuse argued, there was no longer any objective need for this surplus repression, abundance having made it unnecessary. People *could* be liberated, but the same society that made it possible now engaged in ever-more-subtle and all-embracing forms of repression. These utopian possibilities, it should be noted, closely parallel those in Crosland's social-democratic analysis. Society can now control the economy for good or bad — "organized capitalism" has triumphed — and were it to opt for the good, there could be an unprecedented liberation. In making his case, Marcuse quoted at length from a fascinating passage in Marx's *Grundrisse* (the more than a thousand pages of notes in which the themes to be developed in *Das Kapital* were first broached) in which automation is anticipated.

Capitalist socialization, Marx wrote, would eventually put science to work in the production process so that the workers would simply be "the watchers and regulators" of the system, not its drudges. That same development would, by making the individual in charge of automated machinery so unbelievably productive, totally undercut the labor basis of value. What rational connection could there be between pay and output when a single person could "produce" what once had taken a thousand, or ten thousand, workers? Marx did not repeat this argument in *Das Kapital* (although I think it continues to be present implicitly in the discussion of free time). Be that as it may, Marcuse amended Freud in the name of the Marx of the *Grundrisse*.

This led to a poetic and erotic reading of human emancipation. Socialism was no longer going to be a gigantic factory run by the workers. It would be a society in which work was of decreasing importance and play — defined by Schiller as expressing the very essence of humanity, as a kind of painless creativity — would become decisive. Socialism would free the instincts. This view clearly was influenced by the Freudian and Marxist heretic

Wilhelm Reich, as Marcuse acknowledged. It also spoke to the hedonistic side of the new strata, offering a revolutionary interpretation of their not-so-hidden desires.

But since society was controlled and one-dimensional, how would this liberation come about? *Who* would accomplish it? People, Marcuse replied, from opposite ends of the social spectrum: the privileged — the students, the middle-class hippies, the new and highly educated working class of technicians — would rebel against a domination that repressed their souls; and the outcasts, the minorities, the *lumpen*, would join in this attack against simpler and more brutal forms of exploitation. The Third World, Marcuse speculated, was where the new proletariat, which would finally accomplish the Marxist purpose, was being born.

That hope was a delusion. Even if the new privileged strata of organized capitalism became much more radical than they were, and persisted in their idealism, how would they reach out to the hungry masses of Africa, Asia, and Latin America? And why would those masses, living at levels more abysmal than those of the nineteenth-century workers of Europe, fight for a post-materialist society? Even within a country like the United States, most blacks and Hispanics were not seeking total liberation, but integration into the consumer society. And, from a serious Marxist point of view, there were obviously solid reasons why this made sense.

On the other hand, Marcuse, like the social democrats, exaggerated the extent of control achieved by organized capitalism. When the crisis of the Keynesian welfare state came in the mid-seventies, it turned out that the powers that be were not in charge of society to the sinister degree that he and his disciples had imagined. At that moment, or even before, the student revolt of the sixties ended as young people tried to come to terms with a society that now seemed much more demanding, much less tolerant of play and consumption. Marcuse, and those who agreed with him, had mistaken a phase of capitalism for its basic transformation, and in making a radical critique of the system, they had put excessive faith in it.

If Marcuse's analysis — which affected many New Leftists who may not have even read his books and articles — was deeply flawed, the movement that responded to it cannot be dismissed as a simple failure. It sometimes engaged in a simplistic "Third

Worldism," which justified every action of national liberation
movements and thought that because the American intervention
in Vietnam was unconscionable, Ho Chi Minh and his comrades
were *therefore* going to create a socialist utopia. With Marcuse's
encouragement there were even those who denigrated civil liberties in the West as a mere exercise in "repressive tolerance."
Still, this movement opened up windows in the academy,
legitimating the study of Marx and labor history and thereby
broadening horizons for the entire society. The environmentalist
component of the New Left helped create one of the most important mass movements of the modern age, and the campaigns
against French colonialism in Algeria and American policy in
Vietnam were both morally right and politically effective. The
new wave of feminism, which in many instances developed
among women active in New Left movements, has had a lasting
and positive impact upon society.

The practice of the New Left, in short, was often superior to its
theories, which, it must be admitted, bore a certain resemblance
to the ideas of one of the strangest utopian thinkers to base himself on the new Keynesian reality: John Maynard Keynes.

But isn't it absurd to discuss Keynes's ideas in the context of
socialist thought? After all, he had explicitly rejected socialism
on a number of occasions. His colleague and biographer, Roy
Harrod, correctly noted that "his regard for the middle class, for
artists, scientists and brain workers of all kinds made him dislike
the class-conscious elements of socialism." He was, after all, a
product and member of the British establishment and more than
a bit of a snob; his anticapitalist sentiments were aristocratic and
aesthetic. And when his influence became dominant in the
Labour Party after the war, the result was the destruction of the
Marxist Left that had taken shape within the movement during
the thirties. Why then claim that he can be considered a socialist,
and a utopian socialist at that?

There are a number of reasons for doing so, many of which
were outlined in Hyman Minsky's *John Maynard Keynes*. For one
thing, it is quite clear that the socialism Keynes rejected was
either Stalinism or what he called "doctrinaire state socialism"
(what has been called Kautskyism in this book). Thus he wrote in
The General Theory of his opposition to "a system of State Socialism which would embrace most of the economic life of the com-

munity." But then, what serious democratic socialist today would propose such a system?

In a 1926 essay, which explained why he was a Liberal and not a Labourite, Keynes wrote, "I am sure that I am less conservative in my inclinations than the average Labour voter; I fancy that I have played in my mind with the possibilities of greater social changes that come within the present philosophies [of a number of prominent socialists in the twenties whom he names]. . . . The Republic of my imagination lies on the extreme left of celestial space." And in "Economic Possibilities for Our Grandchildren" (1930), he described a humane future in which "the love of money as a possession — as distinguished from the love of money as a means to the enjoyments and realities of life — will be recognized for what it is, a somewhat disgusting morbidity, one of those semi-criminal, semi-pathological propensities which one hands over to the specialists in mental disease."

Keynes concluded: "All kinds of social customs and economic practices affecting the distribution of wealth and of economic rewards and penalties, which we now maintain at all costs however distasteful and unjust they may be in themselves, because they are tremendously useful in promoting the accumulation of capital, we shall then be free at last to discard." Readers of Marx will recognize a significant echo.

These concepts were sufficiently important that Keynes repeated them at the end of *The General Theory*. There he talked of a future in which markets would have a significant role but capital would be socialized, in which the price of capital would fall so low that there would be a "euthanasia of the rentiers." In this setting, the economic issue would finally be solved, and men and women could get on with the serious business of life, which was noneconomic. Keynes was, after all, a man of Bloomsbury, a balletomane, a lover of the arts, and for all of his genius as an economist, he looked upon his own discipline as a necessary evil, or as a prelude. Keynes's attitudes in this, like those of so many of his friends, had been profoundly influenced by the Cambridge philosopher and author of *Principia Ethica*, G. E. Moore. Keynes was to remember that at Cambridge in 1902 Moore opened up "a new heaven on a new earth" for him. The *Principia* taught that personal affection and aesthetic enjoyment were the *summum bonum*.

The point is, the sources of Keynes's utopia were aristocratic, not proletarian — yet it was no less a utopia for that. As he said in 1945 in a toast at the Council of the Royal Economic Society, the economists were "the trustees, not of civilization, but of the possibility of civilization." He looked beyond scarcity to the anti-economics of abundance.

Keynes's hopes, we now know, were as unrealizable as those of the Keynesian social democrats or of the New Left. His Edwardian conviction that all real needs could be satisfied did not anticipate the proliferation of pseudoneeds that would accompany the postwar boom he did so much to facilitate. And the seventies saw an orgy of speculative finance as the rentiers took precedence over the entrepreneurs whom Keynes admired (it should be noted that he had warned against this possibility). Also, Keynes's utopia did not take into account the breakdown of the Keynesian-based social-democratic compromise as economic structures changed drastically in the seventies and eighties.

Still, it is important to understand that Keynes's notion of a "posteconomic" utopia clearly resembles the New Left concern with personal and spiritual, as well as collective, liberation. It is related to Crosland's notion that abundance would solve the material problems and open up a whole new area for socialist concern. Above all, these ideas, from several very different kinds of utopians, are quite relevant to the new socialism that might arise from the present crisis of the movement. They were utopian in their time and place — and perhaps they will be part of the realism of the twenty-first century.

But before considering those futuristic possibilities, it is first necessary to look back to the breakdown of the social-democratic compromise and the resulting crisis, both of these new utopias and of the socialist *realpolitik* that nurtured them as well.[3]

5

The End of Socialism?

"THE SOCIALIST AGE was coming to an end." So Peter Jenkins wrote of the 1970s.

What was happening in Britain was part of a world-wide phenomenon: everywhere in the industrialised democratic world the old manual working class was in decline, trade union membership was falling, old class loyalties were crumbling. . . . In part democratic socialism was the victim of its own success. The welfare societies it had helped to build had opened other and less-collectivist avenues of advance. Affluence had eaten into old class loyalties. Education had provided ladders of escape from the working class. But democratic socialism — or, in the continental usage, social democracy, was inflationary.

If the Keynesian welfare state, or as Jenkins sometimes refers to it, "Croslandite socialism," was indeed the triumph of socialism, then this judgment is clearly right. Its crisis is obvious and all of the socialist women and men will never put the fifties and sixties together again. But if that welfare state was, as I have argued, a phase of capitalism, albeit a phase profoundly influenced by the socialists, then it is at least *possible* that a socialist renewal can take place in the future, much as the original social-democratic compromise itself arose out of the bankruptcy of Karl Kautsky's Marxism.

So I will suggest in this chapter that the breakdown of the social-democratic compromise was an unsurprising, even normal, development of a given "social structure of accumulation" *within* capitalism.* It was not the end of socialism, as Jenkins thinks, or the belated triumph of the eternal laws of economics, as the free-enterprise ideologues claim. Rather, the successful resolution of the problems of the 1930s generated a whole set of new, and as yet unresolved, problems in the 1970s and 1980s. The inflationary trends cited by Jenkins are just one case in point.

Saying this is not to hold that the socialist political crisis that resulted from these events is a mere epiphenomenon of some inevitable process or, worse, that socialists should simply wait around until a new cycle rescues them from their plight. On the contrary. I examine this immediate past in order to find better ways into the uncertain future.

I

WAS THE WELFARE STATE a dangerous error from the very first moment of its existence? So the conservative monetarist theorists think. Not so incidentally, the conclusion inexorably follows that capitalism is the only "natural" economic system and that any interference with its laws is doomed in advance. If that is true then socialism is obviously a fantasy, which is why I take this argument quite seriously.

In that monetarist perspective, the crisis of the Keynesian social democracy results from the fact that the artificially cheap money for social spending and economic stimulus characteristic of the welfare state led inevitably to a misallocation of resources and to inflation. The breakdown of the social-democratic compromise, then, represented the inexorable revenge of the natural laws of the market upon those socialists and American liberals who had flouted them. The prescription was, and is, to cut back on expenditures and to submit to the discipline of the money

*I borrow the term from *Segmented Work, Divided Workers* by David Gordon, Michael Edwards, and Michael Reich. It describes the structures — for instance, the monetary and credit system, pattern of government intervention, and character of the class struggle — that accompany a period of capitalist expansion. The meaning of the term will become clearer in what follows.

supply, which is the "objective" and all-purpose way for regulating any economy.

Now there is no doubt that Lyndon Johnson in 1967 courted inflation by engaging in the deficit financing of the Vietnam War, which he feared the public would not pay taxes to support, or that Richard Nixon's overheating of the economy in 1971–72 as part of his reelection strategy had much the same effect. And the various attempts of governments to use fiscal and monetary stimulus as a way out of the crisis of the mid-seventies — those of the French conservatives as well as of the British socialists — certainly helped to raise prices. More broadly, it is certainly true that, as Keynes himself noted in *The General Theory*, full employment brings inflationary pressures.

Indeed, the connection between the welfare state and inflation was so obvious, and the conservative ideological offensive so effective, that there were those on the Left itself who adopted a variant of the monetarist thesis. In 1976 when James Callaghan, the Labour prime minister of Britain, had to agree, in return for an IMF (International Monetary Fund) loan, to cut social spending, he commented, "We used to think that you could spend your way out of recession, and increase employment by cutting taxes and boosting government spending. I tell you in all candour that this option no longer exists, and that insofar as it ever did exist, it only worked on each occasion since the war by injecting a higher dose of inflation into the economy, followed by a higher level of unemployment as the next step."

Callaghan was wrong when he projected the problems of 1976 back into the entire postwar era. In the fifties and sixties, the benefits of Keynesian management clearly exceeded the costs. But he was right about his own frustrating term of office when the tried-and-true remedies of the immediate past had indeed become a source of stagflation, of a simultaneous inflation and unemployment unthinkable in the earlier period. The question is, was this new development the result of the slow but certain workings of the monetarist laws of the economy, or the consequence of structural changes brought about by the accomplishments of the preceding quarter of a century?

The conservative theories of welfare-state inflation assume in one way or another that there is a "natural rate" of unemployment, defined as that level of joblessness at which inflation will

neither rise nor fall. It is part of the miraculous equilibrium that
the capitalist economy works tirelessly to achieve if only the planners would leave it alone; that point at which all resources, human and material, are deployed with the greatest efficiency
because they are paid their market value. The irresponsible outlays of the welfare state, it is then argued, transgressed this limit
by artificially keeping employment high through fiscal and monetary policies. It therefore prepared the way for inflation. Thus
there are universal market relationships that the Keynesian welfare state violated. And a certain social meanness is the only way
to run a dynamic and successful capitalist economy, painful as it
may be in the short run for those who must suffer for the common
good.

The problem is, the data contradict this thesis on innumerable
points. To begin with, an OECD (Organization for Economic
Cooperation and Development) study of 1985 carefully examined
the performance of the advanced capitalist economies and concluded that there is no relationship between the size of the public
sector and "economic performance as reflected in GDP [Gross
Domestic Product] growth rates, unemployment levels and inflation." Sweden, with one of the most generous welfare states,
outperformed Ronald Reagan's America at a time when he was
cutting social programs. Japan, surely a successful economy, had
the highest rate of social-expenditure growth between 1960 and
1981 of any advanced nation. It is of course true that it began at a
very low base; it is also true that the Japanese corporate policy of
not firing male workers during a recession meant that much less
was spent on unemployment compensation than in Europe.

It is instructive to look at the five countries *least* affected by the
crisis that began in the seventies. Sweden, Norway, Austria,
Japan, and Switzerland have had relatively low rates of unemployment and inflation. Yet the first three nations are examples of
strong social-democratic state intervention and spending; Japan
is a case of a planned capitalism in which government influence
on credit allocation is a major policy tool; and Switzerland is
relatively conservative in economic matters. Yet, as Goran Therborn has shown, what unites these disparate economies is a
common, and very strong, institutional commitment to full employment (even if for left-wing reasons in Scandinavia and Austria and for right-wing reasons in Japan and Switzerland). And

all of them disprove the notion that social spending and cheap money are *the* reason for the current crisis.

Another revealing fact has to do with the timing of social expenditures in the West. The social-expenditure share of GDP in the OECD rose by 10 percent between 1960 and 1975 — but roughly half of that increase took place in 1974 and 1975, that is, immediately following the first oil shock. Until 1973, the share of tax revenue in the OECD economies went up at roughly the same rate as social expenditures. But in 1974 and 1975, in large measure because of the oil shock and recession, GDP went down, tax revenues declined, and the need for social spending went up. This suggests that social spending was to a considerable degree the *result* of the crisis of the mid-seventies rather than its cause.

More broadly, David Cameron has shown that in the entire postwar history of the United States, government spending as a percentage of GNP rose only when recessions occurred. The rest of the time, it was stable or decreasing. In the late seventies, Cameron continued, when Milton and Rose Friedman (the leading monetarist theorists) say there was "rapid growth in government spending," there was actually a decline in those outlays.

It should also be noted that, as Goran Therborn documents, in Japan the successful response to the oil shock was based on a stimulation of domestic consumption, not on exports or austerity. But the most dramatic refutation of the conventional conservative wisdom comes from Reagan's America where, after a vicious monetarist attack on inflation had helped to create the worst recession since the Great Depression, low rates of inflation and an unprecedented government deficit coexisted. In 1983, Milton Friedman, true to his theories, predicted more price inflation that year to be followed by a recession in 1984. He was, as he himself later admitted, "wrong, absolutely wrong." He erred, I would suggest, because "those universal market relations" that were the basis of both his attack on the welfare state and his prophecies simply do not apply.

There was another problem with the right-wing case. "Public spending" lumps together two very different forms of economic activity: direct social investments by the government and transfer payments that expand the markets for the private sector. When it is argued that social outlays "crowd out" the corporations as they bid for funds to finance productive investment, gross, undifferentiated numbers are routinely used. Yet, throughout the advanced capitalist world, and above all in the United States, the transfers, which subsidize the private-sector market, are preponderant. Moreover, there is a perverse element in some of the nontransfer programs, one noted in that OECD analysis. Money for health and education are, after pensions, the largest expenditure categories. But the middle and upper classes get a disproportionate part of those outlays because of their class-based ability to take advantage of them (which is most obvious in higher education but also holds true in the case of medicine).

Thus, the attack on the "egalitarianism" of the welfare state that often accompanies the theories about inflation does not hold. As we have already seen, the social-democratic compromise was simply not that redistributive, even in Sweden. And on balance, the conservative constituencies benefited at least as much as, if not more than, the poor. Would that the postwar welfare state had been as radical as its critics claim it was. But it was not, and therefore the charge that "pampering" the unproductive people at the bottom of the society harmed the productivity and investment opportunities of those at the top is simply not true.

It is not logically contradictory to argue that a wrong policy led to roughly thirty years of unprecedented growth and an enormous increase in the economic well-being of the majority of people in advanced capitalist societies and then, after a lag of one generation, finally revealed its essentially destructive character. Yet it does, on the face of it, invite incredulity. And given the fact that the empirical relationships that this theory posits — between government spending and inflation/unemployment, for instance — do not exist, it is fair to reject the thesis that the present crisis results from the violation of eternal economic laws.

How, then, does a theory of stages explain what has been going on?[1]

II

CAPITALISM IS NOT centrally planned — but then it is not chaotic either. Even in its earliest days there had to be a way to "regulate" its operation. This was done through two very different social structures of accumulation and we are in the process of searching for a third.

Under *laisser-faire* capitalism, roughly prior to the 1880s, that was more or less accomplished by periodic crises. That is, the constant disequilibria of supply and demand were "corrected" after the fact by over- and underproduction, recessions, depressions, panics, and the like. It was, Karl Marx wryly remarked, a proof of the rationality of the system akin to the law of gravity demonstrating its truth by a house collapsing around your ears. But then successful entrepreneurs gave rise to corporations and monopolies; small shops with an artisan work force were replaced by factories with masses of semiskilled workers. Now there were corporations with professional managers presiding over enormous investments of other people's money. Society could countenance the bankruptcy of blacksmith shops and small plants as a necessary and periodic cost of putting the system right; it could not tolerate the regular ruin of the newly established United States Steel Corporation and similar corporate giants.

In terms of this book, there had been a quantum leap in concentration, complexity, and interdependence — in capitalist socialization — as the result of the new factory technology and its corporate organization. Innovative institutions — a new social structure of accumulation — were required to cope with this unprecedented reality. It took a generation of bitter struggle and improvisation to create them.

The socialists, the Fabians as well as Marx and Engels, had seen this trend earlier than anyone else. But, oddly, it was a capitalist genius and crank, Henry Ford, who came to very similar conclusions in the first decades of the twentieth century (the conception of "Fordism," briefly noted in the first chapter and elaborated here, is named in honor of the capitalist who unwittingly did so much to modify capitalism in ways he would have profoundly disliked).

Mass production, Ford understood, could not exist unless there was mass consumption. The enormous increase in output made possible by the new technology that he had perfected — the assembly line — simply could not be absorbed by an economy of low-paid workers. Moreover, a labor force recruited largely from immigrants who had not been disciplined by the Protestant ethic and were forced to work under nerve-wracking conditions turned out to be dangerously unstable. So Ford decided before World War I to pay the incredible wage of five dollars a day and to help buyers finance the purchase of his cars in order to deal with the new challenges of both production and consumption.

More than that, Ford tried to persuade his fellow industrialists that, in their own self-interest, they should increase the pay — and the buying power — of their "hands" just as he had done. He succeeded in winning over converts, usually when there was a crisis — the Rockefellers joined the movement when their hired guns outraged the nation by killing strikers' wives and children in Colorado — and mainly in the ranks of big business. In the 1920s there was also a tendency to use the new discipline of industrial psychology in order to give the workers the feeling, but not the reality, of participating in decision making. The labor historian David Brody called these changes in attitude in the United States "welfare capitalism."

Antonio Gramsci was one of the first to realize how momentous this development was. Fordism, he thought, might mark a "passive revolution," that is, a historic transformation in which the popular energies do not explode from below, as in France in 1789, but are absorbed and tamed by a moderate reformism, as in the Italian *Risorgimento* of the nineteenth century. It was, he said, a response to conditions that were social and psychological as well as economic. Gramsci developed this analysis within the framework of a description of a new stage in the system, of organized capitalism (the "programmed economy," as he called it).

Ford and welfare capitalism made some prominent recruits — Herbert Hoover, who was something of an avant-garde Republican in the early 1920s, was one of them — but he failed to convince the capitalist class as a whole. Big business was mildly and sporadically receptive, but by and large decency toward the workers, even if it helped stop union organization, was seen as an extra cost, putting firms at a competitive disadvantage. Thus when the crash came in 1929, after a decade that had witnessed an extraordinary rationalization of production, a tremendous increase in capacity and productivity ended, just as Ford had feared, with the masses utterly unable to "buy back" the work of their own hands.

The New Deal nationalized Fordism, which infuriated Ford.

Roosevelt somehow improvised a new public framework for capitalism without having any prior plan for or theoretical understanding of what he was doing. The Swedish socialists, we have seen, came to related conclusions but in a systematic and theoretical way. After World War II, the European social democrats followed the Swedish and American models, and the wage was partly socialized in every advanced capitalist country. The interventionist government took responsibility for maintaining full employment, in considerable measure by expanding mass consumption through social programs, but the basic investment decisions and the political power that went with them were still left mainly in the hands of corporate executives.

In this social structure of accumulation, welfare-state benefits and union wages created a market for the output of a tremendously productive factory technology, leading in the sixties to a "virtuous circle" of investment, profit, and rising living standards. In the mid-seventies, contrary to the expectation of the various Keynesian utopias, the system began to break down. The most dramatic confirmation of the obsolescence of the Keynesian strategy came in France in the early eighties. The victorious Socialists in 1981 were committed to a radical version of the Keynesian tactic — they were, they said, "socialists," not "social democrats" — that would stimulate the entire economy by a redistributive spending program targeted to the needs of the most vulnerable workers. Within a year they were forced to put many of their programs on hold; within two years, they practiced an austerity designed to win the confidence of the powers that be in the international money establishment, which had punished them for running up large governmental and balance-of-trade deficits in 1982. That was simply an exercise in classic capitalist discipline and hardly a new problem specific to the most recent stage of the system. What has to be explained is why the French social Keynesianism so spectacularly failed to pay for itself and piled up those deficits in the first place.

Broadly speaking, the Great Prosperity had transformed many of the underlying components of the Fordist structure of accumulation. Instead of the single-purpose machines and standard batches of mass production, there was an enormous increase in the "flexible" technology based on computers, automation, and robots; the blue-collar percentage of the work force declined, and both the professionals and the low-paid service workers became much more significant. The solutions of the fifties and sixties, even in their most socially responsible variant, were simply unable to deal with the problems they themselves had created for the eighties.

In short, the crisis of the welfare state was the consequence of its triumph, not the result of some original sin of an economic policy flawed from the outset. But it is important to become more precise about the new problems generated by its success, even if only in outline. For they are the barrier to the next stage of capitalism — a new and progressive social structure of accumulation — which is to say, to the first steps toward a new socialism.[2]

III

THERE WERE ENORMOUS social costs resulting from the economic success of the quarter century after World War II: environmental degradation, urban congestion and blight, eventually the ruin of the older industrial areas as publicly subsidized corporations followed their private priorities, and so on. Among many other consequences, a "superfluous" population of the marginalized appeared in almost every Western society, and social-welfare costs were dramatically increased not because of the laziness of the new poor but as a result of the actions of corporations. This was the source of Galbraith's "private affluence and public squalor."

In short — and this is the point Crosland failed to grasp — corporate priorities were at work even within a public sector organized by American liberals and European socialists. The new forms of what was still a capitalist socialization made the government responsible for both stimulating private profit and paying the social cost of those profits. This meant that economic success, measured in growing GNP, contributed to the fiscal problems of the state along with failures and crises, such as the oil shock of 1973–74 and the enormous spending that it generated. Thus, a significant portion of the fiscal crisis arose not because policy had been too social but because it had conceded so much to the private sector.

There was a related problem stemming from the fact that the

social-democratic welfare state was based upon growth, not re-distribution.

In the early seventies, many analysts argue, the years of growth led to economic "maturity." As Michael Piore and Charles Sabel noted in *The Second Industrial Divide*,

> The most consequential and long-term postwar development was the saturation of consumer-goods markets in the indus-trial countries. . . . By the late 1960s, domestic consumption of the goods that had led the postwar expansion had begun to reach its limits. . . . Because of this saturation, it became more and more difficult to increase economies of mass pro-duction through the expansion of domestic markets alone.

This led to an internationalization of the system, which we will deal with shortly. For the moment, however, let us focus on the notions of economic "maturity" and "saturation."

Keynes fully expected capital to become less profitable as a boom went on and thought that disappointed capitalists would switch from the overoptimism of rapid growth to an excessive pessimism engendered by merely moderate expansion. One an-swer to this problem, he speculated, would be to raise interest rates in order to discourage excessive investment at a time of seeming capital glut. That, he said wryly, "belongs to the species of remedy which cures the disease by killing the patient." The alternative, Keynes concluded, was the redistribution of income. In saying this, he was true to one of his most basic values, that the "arbitrary and inequitable distribution of wealth and in-comes" was, along with the failure to provide full employment, an outstanding fault of contemporary capitalist society. But even at the moment when Piore and Sabel found markets saturated, there was a new poverty developing within the welfare states and an even larger sector of the population that, if not in abysmal misery, was deprived.

The Keynesian welfare state, as we have seen, was not based on redistribution, but on growth. Even the most redistributive country, Sweden, made only modest progress in reducing the extremes of income and wealth, partly because, with its "cor-poratist" model, it emphasized private sector expansion as a key to social progress. That is why a small country with the most decent welfare state in the world was also the home of some of the most dynamic multinational corporations. At the other extreme, the Keynesian planners in the United States were, for the most part, the adepts of a sanitized, deradicalized version of Keynes, and scrupulously avoided redistribution. The Keynesian welfare state, therefore, got into trouble because it encountered limits to expansion — yet those limits were not inherent in the commitment to social justice but in considerable measure a product of its timidity.

The social-democratic compromise had in its glory days pragmatically accepted the capitalist structure of income and wealth. What matter, the argument went, if the pie is unjustly divided so long as it gets bigger every year and everyone has a larger annual slice? But that pragmatism became a serious limit upon the system once it had exploited the very real economic potential of rather modest social programs.

If Piore and Sabel were wrong in taking this limit as a given rather than as a political choice, they were right about the impulse to international trade that it stimulated. Here we encounter one of the most fundamental structural changes of the postwar period.

The first phase of the "Keynesian revolution" was based primarily on the internal development of the advanced economies. Two major factors were at work. Japan and the major countries of Europe were in ruins because of the war. So world trade was organized under American hegemony and an effective dollar standard from 1945 to 1965. Though the United States profited from its own generosity — the subsidized loans and grants to foreigners returned almost immediately as payments for American goods — its own enormous domestic market was much more important to it. But the Europeans, who historically had been much more dependent on trade, were also focused on their internal economies to a surprising degree. In 1913, French exports accounted for 26 percent of the goods manufactured in that country, in 1959, for 18 percent; in Britain, the figures were 45 percent and 19 percent respectively.

Moreover, contrary to the classic theories of imperialism, the trade that did take place was more *between* the advanced economies than directed toward the Third World. There was now more money to be made by exploiting the new wealth of the North rather than the immemorial poverty of the South. Here, too, the dynamic factor was the internal growth of the richer societies. Between 1948 and 1966, industrial production in the world grew a third more than trade. (These trends will be examined in greater detail when the next chapter takes up the New International Economic Order for the rich created after World War II.)

In the second half of the sixties, these Keynesian successes began to generate new costs. For one thing, the United States succeeded much too well in reindustrializing Europe, and its onetime clients turned into competitors. For another, the boom did indeed "mature" within its self-imposed distributional limits. At that point, just as Piore and Sabel said, the nations looked outward to solve the problems created by their achievements.

At the same time, Japanese automobiles and consumer electronics began to invade the West, but unlike Europe, with its reciprocal trade patterns with the United States, Japan did not open up as a market. As time went on, the Four Tigers of East Asia — Taiwan, Hong Kong, Singapore, and South Korea — followed the Japanese pattern and achieved an export-led growth that eventually was to compete with the advanced economies in major industries such as steel, electronics, and even automobiles. In Latin America, attempts at national self-sufficiency limited the markets for the major economic powers. With the international debt crisis of the eighties, when huge percentages of export earnings had to go to American banks, there came an even more profound limitation on the ability of Latin America to absorb First World goods and services.

The social-democratic compromise had been based on an agreement, worked out in different ways in different countries, between the government, major industries, and unions and/or socialist political parties. But the internationalization of the world economy meant that those industries were no longer national in character. Politically, that weakened labor's power: the workers of the advanced countries were now part of a world labor market based on the ability of capital to move to the ends of the earth in order to get cheap hands. One of the most candid statements about the new position of the worker was made by a vice president of the Goodyear Corporation in the United States, Stanley J. Mihelick. "Until we get real wage levels down much closer to those of the Brazils and Koreas, we cannot pass along productivity gains to wages and still be competitive." That, it should be carefully noted, was an explicit rejection of the essential Fordist wisdom — that productivity gains did translate into higher wages.

If, therefore, the workers were thus subject to a new discipline through the internationalization of the economy, this development freed corporations and capital from national regulation. Multinational corporations could not be controlled in the same way as their national predecessors. Also, the globalization of finance made a mockery of the attempt of central banks and governments to manipulate a money supply that had become extraterritorial. And within the Western nations, the "deregulation" of finance in the seventies and eighties created worldwide opportunities for speculation, which made the Fordist emphasis upon production seem old-fashioned.

During this period, the class structure of advanced capitalism was being radically transformed, and that further undercut some of the political and social assumptions of the Keynesian social democracy.

The shift from goods to service production, the increase in the educated, technical strata, the new technology of computers and robots — all conspired to reduce the percentage of semiskilled and unskilled workers. Even in the manufacturing sector itself, the focus shifted from the mass production of huge batches of standard items — which could now be done in the Third World — to a much more sophisticated, high-tech output of specialty products. This led to what Stephen Cohen and John Zysman call "economies of scope," replacing the "economies of scale" associated with the Fordist factory. The economies of scope are the result of programmable automation that gives a plant the capacity to produce a wide variety of goods rather than, as under the old dispensation, a single good.

To take one example, the American automobile industry has traditionally used two or three basic car configurations as the frameworks for what seem to be different models but are actually variations on a theme. The Japanese, with a much greater emphasis on flexibility, had three times the actual variety in their cars. But in the eighties, when U.S. corporations tried to follow the Japanese lead, the result was a sharp drop in American auto employment. These changes transformed the nature and composition of the labor force and reduced the proportion of those workers who had been most committed to the social-democratic compromise.

At the same time, the new groups of the college educated were, as we have seen, the basis of social movements that were often both radical and opposed to the traditional social-democratic (in America, liberal) working class. Not having gone through the bitter struggles that led to the welfare state, these strata, even though they were the beneficiaries of that state's subsidies to higher education, saw it as just one more bureaucratic institution. Within that framework, environmentalists, feminists, and opponents of the arms race now created the dynamic mass movements, while the labor movement was thrown on the defensive. And suburbanization tended to destroy many of the close-knit blue-collar communities, which had centered on schools, churches, and bars as well as on unions and labor political organizations. In the late seventies and early eighties, these same trends promoted marginalization and the new poverty.

All these economic and social changes were also cultural. In Denmark, for example, there are data showing that young people take more socially insured sick leave than their elders. That fact contradicts the obvious biological reality, that the aging are more likely to be ill than the youth. It also reflects a generational shift in which the benefits of the welfare state become one more fact of life for those who did not have to struggle for them, something to be exploited for convenience. In the United States, Fred Siegel has a fascinating explanation of why the programs of the welfare state remained quite popular even among younger Reagan voters in the eighties:

> Our conventional view of American history places the conflict between the welfare state and self-reliant individualism at the core of post-Depression American politics. But in actuality, *individualism and the welfare state have been marching arm-in-arm over the past three decades. The welfare state is no longer driven by New Deal sentiments of social solidarity. Instead it is the mechanism that, prosperity aside, has freed the individual from the social burdens once borne by family and church and fraternal, work, and community organizations.* [emphasis added]

More broadly, the social-democratic compromise substituted governmental, bureaucratic programs for the community-based response of society to poverty and sickness. In saying that — which is a theme to be found in many conservative critiques — there is no point in romanticizing the past. There is simply no doubt that, for all of the impersonality of the new systems of care, they have led to longer, healthier, and more productive lives. Poor communities, after all, never did have the resources to deal with the crises of life, and their mode of distributing "welfare" often involved demeaning relations of personal subordination. And yet, the new entitlements coincided with, and even reinforced, a certain fragmentation and depersonalization of all of social life, a decline in solidarity, and a rise in possessiveness and what Siegel calls "dependent individualism." A welfare state that sought collective solutions to the problems of working people was put to uses for which it was never intended.

There is another development at work in the crisis of the Keynesian social democracy that is probably the most important single factor in what has happened — and is without a doubt the murkiest factor. I refer to the decline in productivity that occurred in all of the advanced economies in the 1970s.[3]

IV

WHY IS PRODUCTIVITY so crucial?

An American case in point provides the answer. A careful analysis by Martin Baily and Alok Chakrabarti of the Brookings Institution estimated that, had the growth of output per hour after 1965 simply equaled the average rate from 1870 to 1965, production in 1985 would have been 20 percent higher than it actually was. That would have yielded enough additional wealth "to solve many of today's economic problems, most notably the deficit."

Furthermore, had productivity growth continued after 1965 at the pace it held between 1948 and 1965 during the Great Prosperity, output in 1985 would have been a staggering 45 percent higher than it was.

In those golden years of the advanced economies, between 1945 and 1965, rapid productivity increases were at the very heart of the "virtuous circle" of growth. Since the workers averaged an annual 3.5 percent gain in hourly output, there was a mounting surplus that financed more investment (and even more productivity), higher profits, and increased wages, and that made it very attractive to hire new workers to swell the returns from this trend. There was even money "left over" for social decency on the part of the government — which further expanded the market for the cornucopia of the times.

Conversely, when productivity began to decline in the 1970s, classes and strata making demands that in the previous decade were reasonable — and even promoted the common prosperity — provoked tensions, inflation, and new social quarrels. The Keynesian coalition, which had extended from the working class and socialist Left to the sophisticated capitalist Center, came unstuck. This was the problem conservative economists and practical politicians such as James Callaghan overgeneralized into a rejection of the Keynesian model itself.

There is little doubt that the productivity decline played a central role in the exhaustion of the Fordist social structure of accumulation. The problem is, no one clearly understands why. "What happened is, to be blunt, a mystery," wrote Edward Denison, one of the leading American analysts of the phenomenon. But almost everyone agrees that during the mid-seventies and in almost every advanced economy, there was a sharp productivity drop. In France, the increase in labor productivity fell from 5.01 percent in 1950–73 to 3.83 percent in 1973–79 and 3.24 percent in 1979–84; in Japan the corresponding numbers were 7.41 percent, 3.40 percent, and 3.06 percent; in the United States, 2.44 percent, 0.80 percent, and 1.09 percent.

There are enormous difficulties in quantifying this trend. This is, in part, a historical problem, a matter of terms losing their meaning as the structures of accumulation change. The very concept of productivity is associated with and was a "product" of the rise of capitalism. It was a central idea for both Adam Smith and Karl Marx. It allowed one to measure what took place in a huge Fordist factory with a certain precision. What was the volume of output per hour per worker? That was simple enough to calculate in physical units of production.

But when the individual's contribution is completely overshadowed by a science-based technology of automatons and robots — when, in Marx's prophetic words of the *Grundrisse* the worker becomes a "watcher and regulator" of production rather than its agent — how do you estimate productivity? And when there is a shift from goods production to services in the advanced economy, how do you measure the "productivity" of nurses, stock-market analysts, and college professors? In short, the capitalist socialization of the economy not only outruns the control of the Fordist institutions of the Keynesian welfare state, but at the same time the vocabulary of the old dispensation becomes problematic.

Still, there was a real-world decline in productivity, however the term is defined. And part of the reason is the shift from goods production to services, most dramatically in the United States. Service productivity is, as we have seen, extremely difficult to measure. But taking some fairly crude indicators into account, Lester Thurow argues that, in 1983 in the United States, service productivity was 61 percent of manufacturing productivity. At the same time as service occupations were on the increase and lowering the national productivity average, the continuing high productivity in the manufacturing sector was reducing employment.

Martin Baily and Alok Chakrabarti are critical of Thurow — and unpersuasive. For instance, they point out that the percentage of GNP in the goods-producing sector did not decline as dramatically as some people think. But that is to miss the critical point, which is that *employment* in that sector fell for years and then made only a modest recovery during the export boom that began with the falling dollar in 1987. The fact is that most of the new jobs have been in the service sector, and, as Baily and Chakrabarti emphasize in another context, it is precisely in the area of greatest growth where one often finds the new technology employed, not to enhance real-world productivity, but to make "paper entrepreneurship" more efficient.

There is an ironic contrast between European socialism and American liberalism in all of this. Because the labor movement had won positions of strength on the Continent, making it more difficult to fire workers than in the United States, the crisis tendency was to maintain a relatively well paid work force in highly productive jobs — which had the unintended consequence of higher unemployment for those who were left out. In the United States, however, there were 27 million new openings from 1973 to

1987, almost all of them in services, compared to a mere one million new jobs in the European Economic Community. That is one of the reasons why productivity fell to lower levels in the United States than in Europe and Japan.

The rise in service jobs was routinely cited by Ronald Reagan and others as a triumph of the "flexibility" of the American system compared to the rigidities of the European. But that smug comment overlooked some of the basic consequences of the American pattern.

Those new jobs in the United States were primarily service occupations for women and minorities, low paid, nonunionized, and without health, and other "fringe," benefits. *Business Week* reported that between 1980 and 1986 there was a doubling of part-time work at inadequate pay. Such "contingent employment" rose to 17 percent of the total, and 70 percent of the people in this category had no retirement plan, 42 percent were without any medical coverage. The United States government statistics treat a person who works one day a week the same as one fully employed. As a result of these trends, the Congressional Research Service concluded in the mid-eighties, the marked increase in poverty in the United States — the number of the poor rose for five consecutive years after 1979 and has not yet returned to the levels of the mid-seventies — was primarily because of the rise in the number of the working poor. The portion of the welfare poor remained stable.

There was another, macroeconomic, effect of this pattern, one emphasized by Lester Thurow. It was because the American economy took the path of proliferating those inferior service jobs that its productivity declined much more than Europe's. That is to say, this "triumph" was not simply a social retrogression that brought increased poverty; it was also a waste of human resources that put the United States at a competitive disadvantage. American business, faced with the difficulty of finding competent recruits when so many young Americans were dropouts or the graduates of the inadequate schools available to the poor, became alarmed with this problem in the late eighties.

Does this mean that the problem of productivity inevitably involves an impossible trade-off: either higher productivity and more unemployment, or lower productivity and more poverty? The Swedish example suggests that such is not the case. In Sweden, the postwar years saw an enormous influx of women into the economy — female labor-force participation is higher than in any other country — a reduction of hours, and an increase in part-time work. But since the Swedish unions are committed to a "solidaristic" wage policy of reducing the extremes of compensation within the labor force by favoring those at the bottom in negotiations, these new entrants were not consigned to an economic underworld, as they are in the United States. And this was also the result of a commitment to an "active labor market policy," a development that we will examine more closely in chapter 7.

The point is, the productivity trends of the seventies and eighties showed that economic growth, in and of itself, no longer produced new jobs as it once had. Corporations responded to the crisis by firing employees and investing in labor-saving machines, all of which led to extremely high rates of unemployment in Europe and systemic underemployment in the United States. The trend was not inexorable, as the Swedish case shows. But the "virtuous circle" of the Great Prosperity, powered by growing productivity and "natural" labor-force growth, no longer worked. Or rather, productivity did hold up fairly well in the manufacturing sector, but it facilitated replacing men and women with machines.

A second consequence of the productivity crisis stands in stark contrast to the problem just outlined. For in a sense there was, in classic capitalist fashion, "too much" productivity, therefore a glut.

A 1986 article in the *Wall Street Journal* described this irony. "The farming economy, still burdened by tremendous overcapacity, is merely pausing before another long bleed, many economists say. Like the steel, auto and mining industries before it, they suggest, agriculture must adjust to a diminished role in a maturing international marketplace." The "overcapacity" of food production, stimulated by government programs in the Common Market and the United States, coexists, of course, with recurrent famine in Africa. It is now objectively possible to feed every mouth on planet Earth, but the political problems of doing so lead to growing hunger and simultaneous overproduction of food.

The *Journal*'s analysis focuses on the limitations of a "maturing" world economy. But the article was written in 1986, at a time when the austerity imposed by the banks and the International Monetary Fund on Latin America was creating even more hunger in Brazil as subsistence farmland was put to use for export production in the desperate drive to deal with the balance-of-payments problem. Just as the notion of a "mature" market within the advanced countries mistakes the result of specific institutions and policies for a "natural" and "inherent" fact of the welfare state, so the *Wall Street Journal* account of international limits is based not on an inevitability but on the way in which the world capitalist market is now organized.

Inequality within the advanced capitalist nations, we have seen, became one of the limits of the welfare state; to that we now must add that the structural inequality between the nations of the North and South had the same effect. As Baily and Chakrabarti suggest, one reason why innovation seemed to slow in the United States was because demand — mass consumption — was no longer increasing at a brisk pace, and a dollar of research-and-development outlays would no longer have the yield it did in the expanding markets of the fifties and sixties. National and international inequality were, in short, a factor in the drop in productivity.

In this case, and in all the other structural changes I have outlined, the success of the social democracy was a major element in creating the crisis of the system. But then, doesn't this analysis prove that Ronald Reagan and Margaret Thatcher were right? They said that the problems of the seventies were to be located in the mistakes of the socialists and liberals, and they blazed a path to a new period of growth. If so, why talk about a "new socialism" accomplishing what the new conservatism has already achieved?

Reagan, after all, was reelected by a landslide in 1984, and Thatcher won three consecutive elections starting in 1979. Weren't these events popular proof that they had somehow found a new social structure of accumulation? It is important to dispel this notion even if in sketchy fashion, though I am convinced that the events of the nineties will soon provide a most untheoretical refutation of it.

Both Reagan and Thatcher did indeed gain mass support by a

populist attack — not always unjustified — on the arrogant elitism of the planners of the liberal and social-democratic Left when the latter's strategy came unstuck in the mid-seventies. Both spoke in glowing terms of free markets and limits on state intervention in order to promote personal freedom as well as to expand the economy. And both presided over significant growth — but not for the reasons they predicted. For Ronald Reagan and Margaret Thatcher abandoned and even contradicted their basic philosophies in practice even though they continued to celebrate them in theory.

A *Wall Street Journal* analysis by Barbara Timan in 1988 was headlined, "Tory Paradox: In Thatcher's Britain, Free Enterprise Leads to More State Control." Timan wrote of Thatcher: "'We've got to restore the balance,' she said in 1979, 'in favour of the individual against the state.' But nearly a decade later the Nanny State is thriving and Mrs. Thatcher is assuming a degree of power startling in modern democracies." Samuel Brittan, a distinguished British proponent of freedom through the market — and a fierce foe of the Labour Party — called both Reagan and Thatcher "The New Spartans," the practitioners of a militarist and sometimes authoritarian centralism, and took them to task for violating the principles they claimed to serve.

"In the eight years up to 1986–7," Brittan wrote, "UK total public spending on programmes increased by 14 percent after allowing for inflation." By 1986–87, he remarked a little later, "the public spending ratio [to Gross Domestic Product] was still estimated at 44 to 45 percent compared with 43.3 percent in 1978–9, the last Callaghan [Labour] year. . . . The US under Reagan had an even more disillusioning experience with the public spending ratio rising in most years since 1980." As a *Wall Street Journal* editor computed those Reagan percentages, they were over 23 percent of GNP and therefore higher than at the end of the Carter presidency, which Reagan himself had excoriated for its big spending.

This was not a case of hypocrisy on Reagan and Thatcher's part. As a British analyst, Susan MacGregor, described Mrs. Thatcher's policies, "The aim of this social engineering is to change attitudes in British society, shifting it from a social democratic to an 'enterprise' culture. Such engineering, if it is to be carried out effectively in rapid time, requires a strong, centralised, authoritarian state which brooks no opposition and makes no concessions." The first Report of the Reagan Council of Economic Advisors in 1982 was quite frank on this count. "Household choices between consumption and savings and between work and leisure are influenced by after-tax wage rates and after-tax rates of return on capital. *When the government changes either the level or the structure of taxes, it ultimately alters household decisions about consumption, saving and work effort.*" (emphasis added) Washington, in short, was going to see to it that the people became free entrepreneurs, whether they liked it or not.

The point of this exercise was to reduce government consumption in order to increase household saving. But the federal percentage of GNP, we have seen, grew and the American rate of savings sank, that is, the social engineering of the Right proved as fallible as that of the Left. Not so incidentally, this error benefited the rich in both the U.K. and the United States. As Peter Jenkins described the British case, between 1979 and 1986, the real earnings of the bottom 10 percent went up by 3.5 percent a year, and that of the top 10 percent rose by 23 percent. Taxation reinforced that inequality: a family with half the national average wage in 1987 paid a larger proportion of its income in taxes than in 1979, a family with twice the national average, less. As a result, households with five times the average saw their real income grow by 38 percent between 1979 and 1987.

Similarly in the United States. Between 1977 and 1988, average real income went up by $747 and the income of the top one percent by $134,513; in 1979–87 labor income went up by 16.7 percent and property income by 49.9 percent. Indeed, the major single source of the enormous federal deficit under Reagan was the "supply side" tax act of 1981, which raised taxes on the poor even as it provided billions in relief for the very rich.

But wasn't all this justified by the fact that economic growth got under way again? Even that claim is, in the long run, dubious. In the United States, we have seen, the advance was financed by an enormous accumulation of debt — public, corporate, and individual — which, among many other things, changed the position of the nation in the world economy. In Britain, the income from North Sea oil, a windfall that is ending, and from the onetime effect of the sale of government assets to the private sector, allowed Thatcher to simultaneously increase public borrowing *and* cut taxes (in a regressive way).

Am I saying, then, that the recoveries in Britain and the United States were a mirage, that they had nothing to do with a new structure of accumulation? No. For there was one policy shared by Reagan and Thatcher that did have real-world effect: attacking unions and holding down real wages. Samuel Brittan approvingly quotes a journalist on the "darker side" of Thatcherism: "the neglect of inner cities, the rundown in public services and the insistence that the worst off members of society, notably the unemployed, should bear all the burdens of change." And that could, of course, be taken as a fair picture of the Reagan record. On both sides of the Atlantic, then, "prosperity" and depression coexisted for both individuals and entire regions.

The mechanism for holding labor in check was high unemployment in Britain (and on the Continent as a whole) and government-sponsored antiunionism and stagnant or declining real wages mediated by a decline in "good" jobs in the United States. As a result, corporations and the rich, already favored with tax subsidies, were able to make enterprises "lean" and profitable. This was not simply a reactionary — immoral — structure of accumulation; it was unstable as well. The task of finding a progressive basis for economic expansion in the advanced societies, which is inseparable from the drive for social justice, thus remains very much on the agenda and is likely to be enormously complicated when the real costs of the New Spartanism are paid in a recession during the nineties.

More broadly, this brief summary of the Reagan and Thatcher policies points to a central paradox of the times: *that even "laisser-faire" has now become statist, that in practice "free market" policies have been the work of strong, militaristic, socially authoritarian, and debt-financed regimes.* Conservative governments are, in short, unwitting but *dirigiste* agents of an antisocial socialization, not the obedient servants of the law of supply and demand. And the choice for the future is not between an Adam Smith idyll or government intervention, but between top-down and bottom-up socialization. That is why freedom lies to the Left, not to the pseudopopulist Right.

What follows, then, is not a "wish list" but an attempt to outline a socialist future equal to this challenge.[4]

V

THE KIND OF agenda suggested by the analysis of this chapter is clear enough: a program that will help create a new, progressive social structure of accumulation, a next stage of capitalism that is socialistic, if not socialist, because it is based on the expansion of popular participation in decision making as well as of qualitative growth and mass consumption. Here, I will simply sketch these futuristic implications of my analysis of the past in order to establish a framework for the specific proposals in the chapters that follow.

First of all, the immediate demands of the new socialism will be internationalist or else the new socialism will fail.

That is true in the obvious sense that disarmament and an end to the possibility of a nuclear world war are the preconditions of every humane goal. But it also signifies that there can be no "socialism in one country" at a time when the economic and social structures of the world are becoming more international every day. Paul Henri Spaak, the Belgian socialist, once made the biting commentary that the only thing the socialists had ever really nationalized was socialism itself. If that judgment stands in the twenty-first century, then socialism will be, and will deserve to be, finished.

When Willy Brandt became President of the Socialist International in 1976, he understood this imperative and insisted that the movement had to break out of the European ghetto in which it then found itself. Since then there has been a marked increase in the Latin American and Caribbean membership in the International and that fact has had a real impact on the organization's policies. But democratic socialism remains weak or nonexistent in Africa, Asia, and the Middle East. The great scandal of the late twentieth century — which has the terrible promise of persisting into the twenty-first — is still the structured inequality of planet Earth.

If the world continues to become more and more united economically and socially — and there is every indication that it will — the present trends would lead to an intolerable and global class structure. The Keynesian social democracy discovered ways to ameliorate, but not to remove, the inequities *within* advanced capitalist society. The new socialism must make the eradication of systemic planetary inequality one of its most important single priorities. That, as Brandt well realized, is not simply a moral duty. It also creates a new basis for expansion in the North — it is an element in the next social structure of accumulation — through a commitment to ending poverty in the South.

The same point applies to the advanced economies. It is quite possible, we have seen, that the social narrowness of the internal market — even after the gains of the social-democratic compromise — was responsible for declining productivity in the seventies. Hiring the new poor to construct the infrastructure that would end the new poverty is not only a good in and of itself; it is also a means of opening up a new internal market and restoring the dynamism of the entire economy.

That also means that the new socialism should put redistribution on the agenda. The conservatives of the eighties, such as Ronald Reagan and Margaret Thatcher, did not hesitate to use tax policy to redistribute income from the working people and middle class to the rich, all in the name of encouraging investment. This created enormous social costs, borne by the public, huge private profits, and not too many well-paid jobs. In some cases — starting with the United States and Britain — the first step toward redistribution can simply aim to eradicate the inequalities created by prior conservative policies.

There is also a tremendous possibility for growth-oriented redistribution in countering the wastefulness of paper entrepreneurship, with its leveraged buyouts and takeover games. That scandal, pioneered in the United States in the seventies, is becoming Europe-wide in the runup to Common Market integration in 1992. Putting an end to it should be a major priority of the Continental social democracy. The point is, society can clearly reward genuine, real-world innovation (but not unto the generations) without providing enormous subsidies for corporate gambling.

More broadly, there will be a new social structure of accumulation only if the Left understands that growth alone, in the age of automation, will create at least as many problems as it will solve. And that dovetails with the notion of a "qualitative" growth.

A commitment to the expansion of free time — to a reduction of the hours the individual must spend in paid labor in order to achieve a decent standard of living — is obviously a critical component of qualitative growth. But then, social structures of accumulation are not based simply on new modes of consumption; they have to do with production as well. And here the democratic participation of the producers in the decisions affecting their working lives must be a source not merely of less alienated forms of labor but of "soft" productivity gains as well. If one of the reasons for the decline in productivity in the seventies was an increased hostility between labor and management on the shop floor as capital tried to cope with the power workers achieved because of relatively full employment, the democratization of the production process should increase output per hour. This holds true in the clerical and service sectors as well as in the factories, since so much white-collar work has been reorganized on a factory basis in the age of automation.

Politically, it is clear that the socialist movement must take on a new social complexity in response to the radically altered class structure of the developed world. That Kautskyan dream of a revolution made by the workers alone in the name of everyone else long ago proved impossible. But even the new socialism of the thirties, which created a multiclass coalition on the basis of common economic interest, no longer suffices. In the midst of the Great Depression, the Keynesian socialist coalition understandably, and even rightly, defined the tasks of the movement in "economistic" terms.

That situation has now partly changed. For a significant minority in the West, the basic economic problems are at least temporarily solved. The new strata created by the social-democratic compromise grew up with the partial solution to the challenge of the Depression that was the social-democratic compromise and never knew the bitter reality of hunger and want. These privileged men and women were, as we have seen, the political base of a whole series of new political movements that focused on issues not immediately and directly economic. The European socialist parties have been responding to this situation for some time now: the New Left of the sixties essentially joined the Dutch Labor Party; the French Socialists became the improbable heirs of the spirit of the youth rebellion of 1968; the West German Social Democrats have made major programmatic changes in response to the "Greens." And yet there is a sense in which many socialists do not yet realize how central are the demands of those new social movements, above all the feminists and the ecologists.

If the socialist parties simply incorporate those demands into the electoral platforms as a way of reaching out to important constituencies, they will fail. For the themes posed by these movements are essential to the definition of a new socialism. They have to do with the basic principles of the future, not simply with tactics.

John Maynard Keynes, Anthony Crosland, and Herbert Marcuse understood this point from very different ideological positions. They were wrong in their expectations about the imminent end of economic constraints in a socialist utopia, but they were right to see that even the limited gains of the social-democratic compromise had given an importance to issues that were not immediately economic. The new socialism must be concerned with the character of civilization, not just with the allocation of investment. For economic and social development have now made more and more people conscious of primordial injustices that were ignored when simple survival was the central issue. The immediate task has to do with issues of gender, environment, and race that cannot be reduced to class injustice because they are posed *within* every class, the working class most emphatically included.

Education is another case in point.

Mass education has been a demand of the socialist movement from the very first, for it was clearly understood that the capitalist monopoly of culture and learning was one of the most outrageous consequences of class society. But today, with the economic, social, and political centrality of organized knowledge in all economies, the demand for the socialization of knowledge is at least as important as the socialization of industry. When one talks of workers in a plant or an office, or citizens in a community, participating in the economic decisions that shape their lives, they have to have the technical capacity to do so. If corporations or government bureaucrats have an effective monopoly on the technology of decision making, economic and social democracy are not possible.

In their 1987 draft program, the French Socialists speak of a "wager on intelligence" that will make it possible for "citizens to master the evolution of the society in which they live; the cultural stakes are decisive." If there is to be genuine socialization — real control from below rather than mere bureaucratic nationalization — the people must be able to make their own decisions in a technological society. That is, in the contemporary world, not an innate capacity of those who have been kept in an inferior place. It has to be conquered.

This emphasis on gender, race, culture, and environment does not for a moment mean that the economic — or the working class — no longer matters. On the contrary. The mechanisms of gender and racial oppression, of cultural discrimination and environmental degradation, *are* often economic. Poor and working-class women, for instance, are subjected to a double exploitation, as women and as workers. The disproportionate percentage of public money spent on higher education for the children of the middle and upper classes is a consequence of class structure. It is wrong to think that the "quality of life" and personal issues are somehow ethereal and unrelated to the struggle for daily bread or the corporate domination of investment decisions.

More broadly, the working class will continue to exist in advanced capitalism for the indefinite future and emerge in the developing world to the extent that there is growth. More precisely, there are already new working classes in the most dynamic economies. In every Western society, the "dirty" jobs at the bottom of the occupational structure are performed by immigrants or members of racial or national minorities. At the same time, the new technology and organization of work are creating a more skilled stratum of workers and opening up possibilities for socialist conceptions of real participation in decision making on the plant and office floor.

In this context, Stephen Cohen and John Zysman make a critically important point. The advanced societies cannot for long export manufacturing to the periphery and concentrate on building the high-tech factories that will then be run by low-wage labor in the Third World. Hands-on experience with the practical problems of production is, they rightly argue, a precondition of the ability to engineer solutions to them. It is therefore likely that economic necessity — as well as the political movements of the

Left — will force a certain reindustrialization in the coming period. That, too, is a factor in the persistence of the traditional working class.

But then the new socialism cannot focus simply on advanced capitalism and the Third World. At the century's end Communist societies are in the process of basic change. There are, we will see, superficial analyses of this process that interpret every departure from the centralized planning and control of the Stalin era as a step toward "capitalism." That is the result of a simpleminded dichotomy — capitalism or socialism — which misses a crucial possibility of the twenty-first century: an undemocratic and conscious collectivization that is neither capitalist nor socialist. The Communist societies have already taken steps along that road. But it is at least possible that development within the framework of a command economy eventually generates the possibility of democratization of structures that have been collectivized from on high. If that happens, the democratic-socialist dialogue with new forces within Communist society will be a critically important dimension of the future.

Finally, in thus outlining the tasks of a twenty-first-century socialism that arise out of an analysis of the failures and successes of the twentieth-century movement, I do not want to suggest some kind of imminent apocalypse. Far from it. If the first half of this book has demonstrated any one proposition, it is that socialist transformation is the work of a historic epoch, not of a year or even of a decade. "All" that can be accomplished within a generation is to make the maximum structural transformations that will begin to bring the revolutionary socioeconomic changes of these times under the control of the people themselves. In the context of the present analysis, nothing more than — and nothing less than — the creation of a progressive social structure of accumulation is on the agenda of the future.

If that project succeeds, there will still be failures along the way; and even the gains will be ambiguous because the powers that be will often co-opt the best of socialist ideas and put them to antisocialist uses. But if the means of implementing the socialist vision — markets and cooperatives, decentralization and workers' control — are light-years removed from Kautsky's factory society, the vision itself is two centuries old and audaciously new: that the inexorable socialization of the entire planet, which is the future contained in our present, can become the tool, rather than the oppressor, of free women and men.

If we do not at least wager on this possibility, then we would face the intolerable reality glimpsed by Karl Mannheim in 1929: that "after a long tortuous, but heroic development, just at the highest stage of awareness, when history is ceasing to be a blind fate, and is becoming more and more man's own creation, with the relinquishment of utopias, man would lose his will to shape history and therewith his ability to understand it."[5]

6

The Third Creation
of the World

In the second half of the twentieth century, a sophisticated, statified capitalism created an interdependent planetary economy much as an earlier capitalism had transformed the nations of the West. Corporate socialization was now global.

Once again the system blundered into a revolution, unifying the earth as an unanticipated consequence of the transnational pursuit of profit.* But there was an element of consciousness and planning in this process that went far beyond anything in nineteenth-century *laisser-faire* or even in the first phase of "organized" capitalism. Realistic politicians and economists fashioned a New International Economic Order for the rich after World War II. Most of the architects of this system were enthusiastic supporters of "free enterprise," some were social democrats, and none was willing to leave the development of the world economy to the invisible hand of the market.

There are some simplified descriptions of this process that

---

*The standard usage in the United States is to talk of "multinational" corporations, in Europe (and United Nations documents) to speak of "transnationals." I prefer the latter usage and will employ it here. "Multinational" implies that citizens of many nations are engaged in a cooperative enterprise. "Transnational" focuses on the truly critical dimension, that nationally owned enterprises have become independent of their own borders as well as those of other countries. They are corporations that do not merely sell goods abroad — that has been happening since the dawn of capitalism — but produce them abroad as well.

must be carefully avoided, including the left-wing thesis that the postwar boom was *primarily* a result of the exploitation of Asia, Africa, and Latin America. That simply was not true. There was a percentage shift away from Western investment in the poor countries during the Great Prosperity as each economy concentrated first on expanding its own internal market and then on profiting from relations with the other welfare states. So the *relative* economic importance of the underdeveloped nations declined from the point of view of the advanced societies. But the New International Economic Order of the rich was of decisive significance for the Third World itself.

These trends could not be understood within the framework of an enormously influential analysis often used in the Third World: Lenin's theory of imperialism. This is the *locus classicus* of the leftist notion that the affluence of the world's rich depends on the exploitation of its poor. The export of capital to the periphery, Lenin said, was an internal necessity for a system that could not absorb its own surplus because it was incapable of mass consumption. Lenin, in effect, thought that the welfare state was an impossibility, and he therefore could not even begin to anticipate the patterns of the post–World War II era. The obsolescence of his thesis, however, in no way meant that the North had become benevolent in its behavior toward the South. The profits made from the wretched of the earth were now more a cruel convenience than a matter of survival.

When most of the colonies achieved political freedom, they quickly discovered the constraints of an international economy organized according to the priorities of corporate capitalism. Still, there was some progress for some countries, if no basic change in the world structure of domination and inferiority, and this progress even continued in the 1970s when the rich nations had already come to the end of their golden age. However, when the contradictions of success subverted the New International Economic Order, the poor nations suffered even more than the welfare states.

There was a crisis in the South, most dramatically in Latin America and Africa, where living standards declined in the eighties. And there was a related crisis in the North because, even though the Third World had never been the decisive factor in the postwar boom, it was a substantial source of profits. The poor countries could neither manage their debt burden nor continue to serve as a market for the exports of advanced capitalism. They had not been an economic necessity during the glory days, but now their misery threatened the stability of the whole system.

The new socialism will have to provide, not simply practical and immediate solutions to this common crisis of North and South, but solutions that at least move in the direction of changing the way in which economic resources are allocated internationally. That is, socialism itself will have to become international as never before. Promoting the economic development of poor countries will not be enough, though it is a critical precondition of everything else. The socialist point is to do that in such a way as to liberate human beings as well as resources in the South and to increase the equality and solidarity of the world as a whole.

But doesn't that mean that I am talking about a utopia in the ethereal sense of the word? Not in the least. Capitalism created the world — the world as an economic unity — in the nineteenth century under Britain, and then recreated it after World War II under the United States. There is going to be a third creation of the world, because corporate forces are already working at it. Around the globe as within nations, the question is not whether this socialization will proceed apace, but who will guide it, how, and for what purposes. Sophisticated corporate spokespersons are already advocating that international agencies buy up the debt of the poor countries at a discount and thereby relieve the banks of the North from the disastrous consequences of their own investments. This, for strange reasons, is called "free enterprise."

But the socialist concern in this area is not simply that of unmasking the hypocrisy of free marketeers, important as that is. The more fundamental challenge is the fact that, if we cannot move toward a democratic and egalitarian world system, then socialism will turn out to have been nothing more than the best dream the West ever had.

I

THE BRETTON WOODS Conference in 1944 established a New International Economic Order for the rich that functioned fairly well during the Great Prosperity and then contributed to the current crisis.

Bretton Woods marked an attempt to bring the international economy under controls analogous to those that were to become the social-democratic compromise. The end of the war was in sight and the victors — above all, the United States and Great Britain — were concerned that the triumph not end with a return of the Great Depression. There was agreement that the global economic policies of the twenties and thirties had been a disaster, that the insistence on reparations and the repayment of war loans followed by the "beggar thy neighbor" policies in which each country tried to export its unemployment had hurt everyone. There was a consensus that there had to be international cooperation among the great capitalist powers if the economic transition to the peace was to avoid catastrophe.

There were some who were visionary and even anticipated ideas that would become relevant almost half a century later. In 1943, the American National Resources Planning Board issued a statement saying, "We stand on the threshold of an economy of abundance. . . . Only a bold implementation of the will-to-do is required to open the door to that economy. Give the American people a vision of the freedoms that we might enjoy under a real program of American and *world-wide* development of resources, and all of the opposition of blind men and selfish interests could not prevent its adoption." (emphasis added) Indeed, when Harry Dexter White, who was to become the chief American negotiator at Bretton Woods, began to work on these problems in 1942, he saw a World Bank as part of a planetary New Deal.

On the British side, Keynes played a double role. On the one hand, he was the chief negotiator for a nation that he knew was going to be short of cash when the war ended. So his advocacy of new international institutions that would be generous with the debtor nations, and his insistence that the big creditors — which is to say, the United States — revalue their currencies to make life tolerable for the disadvantaged countries was clearly influenced by his national concerns. On the other hand, he had a vision of a postwar order in which an international money ("Bancor") would help facilitate global full employment. Had Keynes's concept of an international monetary fund prevailed — with abundant credit on relatively easy terms — the IMF would have never become the monetarist policemen of the Third World demanding austerity as a price of its support.

The Americans were split on these issues. The New Dealers

inclined toward the open-ended proposals as a means of averting a new depression. The conservative leader, Senator Robert A. Taft, said that the proposed fund "will be like pouring money down a rat hole," that is, he simply internationalized his previous critique of the New Deal and applied it to Bretton Woods (which he opposed). The powerful bankers in New York were suspicious of the "Keynesian" rationale for the new institutions, worried about inflation, and determined to reassert the power of money — *their* power — over planners in the world economy. The Bretton Woods ideas, the American Bankers Association said, "might retard rather than promote enduring recovery."

Henry Morgenthau, the New Deal secretary of the treasury, fought back, warning that the right-wing perspective would allow "five banks in New York" to set world exchange rates and the financial powers of the City of London "to lead us around by the nose, which they have done in the last one hundred years." As it turned out, the American critics and opponents were unable to undercut the Bretton Woods effort entirely, above all because too many people were terrified by the possibility of a new depression. But they did manage to give a distinctly capitalist emphasis to the institutions of international cooperation.

Those institutions — the International Bank for Reconstruction and Development (the World Bank), which was designed to finance the rebuilding of advanced capitalism, the International Monetary Fund, the General Agreement on Trade and Tariffs — were structured on the principle of "one dollar, one vote," which meant that they were under the domination of the largest stockholder, the United States. Later on, that same principle meant that, when Third World countries were admitted to the table, they participated as distinctly inferior members. The new world order, in short, was constructed on the rock of American power and openly dominated by the big capitalist economies.

Still, there was a countervailing principle, part pragmatism, part idealism. In early 1947, American planners saw that the world would soon run out of the money required to buy their country's exports. This, a State-Navy-War Coordinating Committee understood, would mean a further push toward turning a postwar recession into a depression. In June of 1947 the Marshall Plan was announced, dispensing the equivalent of 4.5 percent of the U.S. GNP between 1949 and 1952.

The motives behind this unprecedented act were mixed. They included the idea that priming the Keynesian pump in Europe (and later, Japan) was in the best interest of the United States; a determination to defeat the Communist movements of Europe, particularly in France and Italy, by shoring up the Old World economy; and a commitment to forge economic links that would buttress the political and military unity of the emergent North Atlantic alliance.

At first, the Bretton Woods institutions were the formal expression of American hegemony in the world economy. That economy, in effect, ran on a "dollar standard" between 1945 and 1960, and since the dollar was the new international "gold," the United States was not subject to the monetary and economic discipline imposed on lesser powers. As long as it was the source of goods universally desired in societies that had been ravaged by the war, Washington could print money, for all the world cared. But it didn't have to do that. The new system, Howard Wachtel has shown, was an "economic bonanza" for America: Keynesianism on an international scale worked. Between 1946 and 1959 the purchases financed by American generosity and the new world economic organizations created a balance-of-payments surplus of $58 billion and generated about two million new jobs within the United States.

That this world system was designed for the rich powers was in part the result of the role that bankers and their friends played in constructing it. But there was also a deeper structural factor at work. In 1949, Harry Truman proposed to apply the Marshall Plan strategy in the Third World. His initiative came to be called the "Point Four" program. The problem was, Europe and Japan in postwar ruins were in an infinitely better position for economic development than Africa, Asia, and Latin America. The war-damaged capitalisms had already been through their cultural revolution, and trained, motivated workers and managers were at hand. *All* they lacked was the capital to rebuild, and once that was forthcoming from Washington, recovery was only a matter of time.

But even the most advanced of the Third World countries in Latin America had never been through the social and psychological changes that were a part of the daily lives of Europe and Japan. Truman's Point Four failed not just because it became subsumed under the obsessive anticommunism that dominated American society in the fifties. Even if Congress had voted all the money needed for Truman's original proposal and not turned the whole scheme into a facade for strategic aid to "reliable" anti-Communist dictatorships like Taiwan, the global structures of domination and inferiority would have made a "Marshall Plan" infinitely more difficult to carry out in the South than in the North.

In any case, the most generous intentions of the developed capitalist world never moved beyond intentions. Worse, the successes of the advanced economies soon generated problems that would undercut the New International Economic Order for the rich. And even though the Third World made only limited gains during the boom years, many of the poor countries were to suffer grievously from the crisis of a system that had never been created for them in the first place.

As early as 1961, Washington began to feel economic constraints that had been unknown in the first decade and a half after the war. The balance of payments "haunted all economic discussions" in the Kennedy White House, Arthur Schlesinger has written. The United States, as already noted, succeeded only too well in restoring capitalism in Europe and Japan and thereby created formidable new competitors for itself. The "American century" thus lasted for about fifteen years, and the decline of Washington's relative power in the world weakened Bretton Woods institutions based on the assumption that the dollar was "as good as gold." So when the inflated dollars that Lyndon Johnson used to finance his intervention in Vietnam showed up in Paris, President de Gaulle was outraged with the irresponsibility of his ally. He declared a "Gold War" on America, demanding the precious metal in return for the inflated dollars.

Within ten years of Kennedy's election the new situation was formally recognized in Washington. In 1971 — in considerable measure as part of a plan to assure his own reelection by stimulating the economy — Richard Nixon shut down the American "gold window" (where foreigners were guaranteed an ounce of gold in return for $35) and carried out a competitive devaluation of the dollar. One of the basic ideas of the Bretton Woods system — that stable currencies moving only within a narrow band would facilitate maximum world trade — came crashing to the ground as the monies of the world began to "float" against one another. Over the next decade and a half, the dollar was successively under-valued, overvalued, and then undervalued again, each time with destabilizing consequences, both in the United States and around the world.

There is no point in exaggerating these events. America in the 1980s remains the most powerful single economy on the face of the earth; but it is simply no longer hegemonic in the way it was in 1945–60. A 1984 study by the New York Stock Exchange documents the transition. In 1962, close to the high point of the "American century," there were twelve American industries with at least a 20 percent share in the world market; in 1982, there were only five, the same number as West Germany and Japan. But that still meant that the United States had 35.8 percent of the computer market, 30.9 percent of aerospace, 21.1 percent of agricultural machinery (and these percentages all probably increased when the dollar began to fall and to stimulate manufactured exports a few years later).

How did these developments affect the poor? The post–World War II world market was constructed by and for the advanced powers. As a result, the fate of the Third World, whether in the booming years of the fifties and sixties or after the crisis broke out in the seventies, was determined by events and actors beyond its control or even influence. One way of dealing with this reality was to embrace it. That was the tactic of the Four Tigers (Taiwan, South Korea, Hong Kong, and Singapore), which totally inte-grated their export-led economies with those of Japan and the United States. Their strength was a form of calculated depen-dence.

Other countries, most notably in Latin America, tried a con-trary strategy. They sought, by "import substitution," to create self-contained advanced societies based on their own internal production and markets, and for a while, even in the seventies, it seemed that they were on their way. In 1982, for reasons to be explained, these sovereign powers found themselves so deeply in debt to private banks that, in order to satisfy the "conditions" of the IMF to get the money to pay their bills, they had to contract their internal market by pushing down the living standards of the people.

For a while, the oil exporters of OPEC appeared to be an

exception to these cruel rules. They made enormous profits from the price hikes of 1974 and 1979, and it seemed that the global balance of economic power had permanently shifted. But even in their heyday, their wealth was mainly invested by Western bankers in ways that created the international debt crisis. Once energy-saving responses and recession in the advanced economies — as well as the internal tensions of OPEC itself — led to rapidly falling oil prices, their structurally inferior position became clear again. As for the rest of the Third World, that is, the vast majority of humankind, it was marginal, making no great gains in the good years and suffering terribly in the bad.

The more things change, the more they are the same? Not quite. The emergence of the transnational corporation, the growth of international financial instability, and even terms of trade favoring the rich countries over the poor created serious problems in the North as well as the South. By the eighties, both the sophisticated conservatives and the more astute socialists within the developed societies had understood that these events had made a new international economic order imperative and that the "floating" interregnum that followed Bretton Woods simply would not suffice.

The transnationals flourished in part because they countered the attempt of the newly independent countries to gain control over economic activity within their own borders. If corporations now came not as the sellers of alien goods but as the producers of domestic output, they could exempt themselves from various national (or European Community) tariffs. And even when, in the Third World, restrictions were placed on the repatriation of profits to the transnational's headquarters, this new type of corporation could easily evade the law. By the early eighties, 35 to 40 percent of world trade took place *within* the various transnational corporations; they bought and sold from themselves. So it was simple to transfer profits from a poor country back to the metropolitan center simply by having the center charge very high "prices" for the inputs it "sold" to its own affiliates.

These internationalizing patterns were to have a major impact on the United States. It was not just that the imports were on the rise when the dollar was overvalued between 1979 and 1986; it was that the American companies were contracting out work all around the globe. In 1986, the United States International Trade

Commission reported, 6 percent of the trade deficit, or $5.6 billion, was the result of auto parts brought into the United States by the three major car companies. More broadly, 30 percent of the deficit with the Pacific Rim was due to imports from American corporations operating within the Rim.

These developments were, of course, facilitated by new technologies that made it possible to move goods around the world more efficiently than ever before. One could begin to speak of a "global factory" in which transnationals, often the sworn enemy of national government planning, engaged in nothing less than their own planetary planning. Indeed, the U.S. Trade Commission, a conservative body, noted that the nearest thing to a Communist command economy was to be found in the front offices of worldwide corporations.

At the same time, the terms of trade between the North and the South also worked to shift wealth from the poor to the rich, a development that, strangely enough, was to exacerbate the problems of the North as well as the South. With the exception of two brief periods (the early fifties and early seventies), the prices paid by the Third World for imports from the advanced capitalist economies rose and the prices they received declined. This was offset somewhat in the seventies when the "new middle class" of the South — Mexico, Brazil, Venezuela — grew faster than the Northern economies. But when the debt crisis hit in 1982, the terms of trade took on a catastrophic dimension.

The IMF strategy for dealing with the debt crisis, that is, the advanced capitalist strategy, was to insist that the poor countries get the cash to service their loans by exporting more and consuming less. But with the terms of trade so negative, that became an impossibility. More and more export exertion would simply yield less money. And it also meant that these countries, in Latin America above all, ceased to be markets for the goods from the advanced world.

The international debt crisis, which was a decisive element of this problem, was itself only one aspect of a new international financial instability that had disturbing resemblances to the speculative boom within the United States on the eve of the Great Depression. The OPEC price hikes in the seventies were to play a particularly important role in this development.

At first the quadrupling of energy prices by Third World producers seemed to modify the dominion of the wealthy countries and transnationals. Some years before, in the sixties, the ex-colonies had begun to adopt an economic agenda, often through the meetings and analyses of the United Nations Conference on Trade and Development (UNCTAD), but no one in the halls of capitalist power paid too much attention. But with OPEC's initial success, there was widespread fear that there would be other raw-material cartels — Jamaica under Michael Manley tried to organize the bauxite producers, for instance — and that the North would be denied access to critical resources. For a brief period, *Realpolitikers* like Henry Kissinger publicly explored the possibility of Northern support for some kind of New International Economic Order in return for Southern guarantees on raw materials. But that spasm of pragmatic generosity passed quickly as the Northern banks turned OPEC's triumph into their own advantage — and then into the debt crisis of the eighties.

The OPEC profits were "recycled" by Western banks, and this action was accompanied by paeans of praise to the genius of a system that had turned seeming disaster into a major source of profits. As Harold Lever and Christopher Huhne put it, it seemed that "Santa Claus had appeared in the guise of sound commercial activity, and nobody wanted to shoot him." The quadrupling of oil prices by OPEC in 1973–74 generated superprofits that far exceeded the amount that countries like Saudi Arabia could invest in their own development. At the same time, it created a desperate need for cash to pay for the energy bills of the Third World nations that lacked oil. So the banks — and above all, the "money center" banks of the United States — "recycled" the oil profits and in effect acted as the intermediary for a massive transfer of wealth from the North (the advanced oil-importing economies) to the South (the non-oil poor). At a price.

As a result, there was a major shift in the nature of Third World debt, particularly in Latin America. Private lending took over from official aid and, by 1980, three quarters of the loans were at variable rates, fluctuating with unstable interest rates and scheduled for rapid repayment. As a World Bank analysis put it in 1988, "the vital link between the service cost of a loan and the income stream from the investment it financed had thus been broken." By 1982, the Bank continued, "the process of financing development had become unhealthily dependent on the debtors' ability to obtain new loans to service the old."

In the seventies, however, this last trend was far from obvious. The fact is, the massive transfer of funds from North to South "worked" until 1982. The advanced economies' growth rate declined from 4.4 percent a year in 1967–72 to 2.8 percent between 1973 and 1981; the non-oil Third World registered growth rates of 5.8 percent and 5.1 percent respectively in the two periods. This was true even though there was an enormous unproductive "leakage" as some of those monies were utilized on the increased arms expenditures of the developing world and some were skimmed off by the elites of poor countries and sent back to Northern banks.

By 1982, however, the picture changed radically. There was a huge increase in nominal and real interest rates, largely because the Federal Reserve Bank of the United States was engaged in a savage monetarist assault on inflation without regard for the domestic or global consequences. International terms of trade became even worse for the Third World (the Latin American economies were losing $20 billion a year through this mechanism after 1982); the short-term loans of the seventies came due and had to be refinanced; and there was a deep recession in the advanced world in 1982–83 that caused the export markets of the developing countries to contract. In August of 1982 Mexico's announcement that it could not meet its debt obligations made the world aware of a full-fledged international financial crisis.

These events triggered by the OPEC price hikes were part of a larger trend that was not created, but simply made worse, by the energy pressures.

In the seventies in the North, we have seen, there was a marked slowdown in the growth of the real economy. But at the same time, and for much the same reason, there was a sharp increase in the pace of financial speculation. In the *General Theory*, Keynes had sharply distinguished between "speculation" — forecasting the psychology of the market in order to profit from mood changes — and "enterprise" — forecasting the yield of assets over their entire life. The Americans, he thought, had a penchant for speculative investing in order to make a killing rather than enterprising investment to get a secure stream of income. And he warned of a situation in which speculation would become general and "the capital development of a country becomes the by-product of the activities of a casino."

In 1985, *Business Week* did a cover story on the "casino society" in the United States. Trade in "derivative instruments" — in options and contracts based on market indices — had been proliferating at an alarming rate since the early seventies, it said. As a result, "more and more of what transpires on the trading floors of Wall and La Salle Streets [the site of the financial markets in Chicago, a particularly innovative center in the new finance] has no direct connection to the factory floors of Main Street. . . . The system," *Business Week* concluded, "is tilting from investment to speculation." That prophecy was more than fulfilled in October 1987, when the worldwide "meltdown" of international money markets was set off, in considerable measure, by the erratic behavior of the "derivative instruments."

Finance had, of course, been internationalized along with production, and this American trend took on a global character. Several of the contributors to a volume celebrating the twenty-fifth anniversary of the Organization for Economic Cooperation and Development (OECD) emphasized the problems that resulted. As the Austrian banker Stephen Koren put it, "Floating exchange rates and the accumulation of a huge stock of private and public debt as well as the recycling of petrodollars, seem to have given rise to the separation of capital and money flows from the real economy. . . . With low growth rates and dim profit expectations in manufacture, resources were shifted from the real economy to financial markets."

Raymond Vernon documented what this meant in terms of transactions. The turnover in the world's foreign exchange markets, he wrote, was about $200 billion a day in the eighties — or forty times the value of the average daily merchandise trade. In short, when the world debt crisis surfaced with Mexico's inability to service its obligations to the banks, the whole system was extremely shaky.

At that point the United States government rode to the rescue; so did the International Monetary Fund, which, now that the very stability of *Northern* financial institutions was at stake, relaxed its rigorous "conditions" for loans. As a Joint Economic Committee study of 1986 commented, government policy was totally directed to the salvation of the banks, even if that harmed the manufacturing sector.

By 1985, however, even the Reagan administration had begun to understand that simply insisting on the repayments of the debts was not enough. The United States, and the rest of the advanced world, had lost an enormous Latin American market as the debtors in that area increased their exports and cut imports in order to be able to service their debts. The "Highly Indebted Middle Income Countries" had seen their per capita income fall by a seventh, sub-Saharan Africa by a quarter. This was obviously a catastrophe for the people of those regions, but it was also a loss for the wealthy exporters as well. So U.S. Treasury Secretary Baker called for World Bank, IMF, and private lending to the Third World in order to enhance First World priorities.

The problem was, as U.S. Senator Bill Bradley said at the time, because "the Baker plan calls for new loans instead of interest-rate and debt relief, it creates more debt, not less." The banks themselves shared these doubts, and cut their lending to the fifteen heavily indebted countries targeted by Baker by 8 percent between 1985 and 1987. Many of the banks also made "provisions" for loan defaults, an action that made them even less likely to risk more money in an area in which they were preparing for losses.

If the banks, with the assistance of various rich governments, the World Bank, and the IMF, thus staved off disaster in the North, the results in the South were cruel. In the five years after 1982, the World Bank reported in 1988, no country rescheduling its debts actually reduced the ratio of that debt to GNP. Worse, in that same period there was a total *outflow* of resources from the indebted countries of $85 billion (compared to a $140 billion inflow in the five years prior to 1982). The numbers were even worse for the highly indebted middle-income countries, which suffered an outflow of $100 billion! When the United States loaned Mexico $3.5 billion in 1988, the latter's debt was higher than when it triggered the original international crisis in 1982.

At the end of 1988, the World Bank reported that the poor countries were transferring wealth to the rich economies at a record rate. Estimates for 1988 indicated that the seventeen most heavily indebted nations of the South paid lending institutions

$31.3 billion more than they received from them. At the same time, UNICEF's State of the World's Children report noted that in the forty least developed lands, health spending had been cut by 50 percent during the eighties, a major factor in the death of half a million children who would have survived if the rate of growth in the seventies had been maintained.

On a somewhat more sophisticated level, the CEO of American Express pointed out in 1988 that there had to be actual debt reduction for the Third World because the Reagan administration schemes for new lending simply had not worked. He noted that, between 1981 and 1986, the seventeen most heavily indebted countries, which were major markets for the United States, cut their imports by $72 billion. Therefore, he concluded, international financial institutions, such as the World Bank, had to buy up the debt to save the private sector from itself. And a conservative think tank committed to finding "free market" solutions commented: "It is important for the United States, along with other industrial countries, to find ways to restimulate growth in the developing world. These nations that are still on the threshold of industrialization have the greatest opportunities for rapid growth that can stimulate the U.S. and world economies."

It would be a mistake to cite conservatives who recognize the basic logic of a Northern commitment to the South as a proof of the viability of the socialist strategy proposed by Michael Manley and Willy Brandt. The CEO of American Express, a global and capitalist institution, obviously has a completely different vision of the emergent one world than the new socialists. His insights are designed to transmit the fundamental injustices of the past into the structures of the future, to use state-supported entities, such as the World Bank, to maintain the rule of established and private economic power. And the crisis is far from over, even if the banks have protected themselves to some extent. For the next worldwide recession will involve a degree of financial precariousness unprecedented in economic history.

For all of the complexities, the events of the last two decades have seen the world economy become more capitalist, not less. The initiative has been with transnationals and international banks, and they have made a botch of the globe. Part of the contribution of the new socialism is to simply make that case. More to the point, and much more difficult, it is necessary to propose structural modifications of the rule of capital in order to come up with even short-term solutions to present problems.[1]

II

BEFORE TALKING ABOUT a positive program, however, it is necessary first to emphasize the complexity of the global problem that confronts the new socialism. That makes solutions all the more difficult, yet uncontestably our one world is extremely heterogeneous.

The very concept, Third World, is useful for some purposes and deceptive for others. To be sure, the poorest nations and the most developed of the middle-income economies share a dependence on structures dominated by the wealthy. In that sense both are part of the same universe. At the same time, however, that linkage can obscure the enormous differences *within* the Third World.

The twenty-four Western powers (including Japan) belonging to the OECD contain one sixth of the population of the world (800 million out of 4.8 billion) and control two thirds of the world's gross product. The eight relatively wealthy Communist countries (the Soviet Union plus Eastern Europe) have 400 million inhabitants and a little less than one sixth of the world product. In other words, one fourth of the people of the world possess five sixths of its riches. The Third World is that three quarters of humanity with one sixth of the planet's wealth.

China, with over a billion people, has 2.5 percent of the world product; India, with three quarters of a billion, 1.5 percent. All of Africa has 2.5 percent, and Latin America, 3.5 percent. These structural inequalities are then magnified by the profoundly unequal distribution of income *within* many of the Third World nations. And there are structural differences between, say, China, India, and Bangladesh, where the pressure of population upon resources is a defining fact of life, and Africa, where sheer numbers are not a factor but the absence of stable and articulated nations is, or Latin America, with its oligarchic class structure.

These various differences can be seen operationally when one looks at the disparities among the nations of the Third World. Three countries — Taiwan, the Republic of Korea, and Hong

Kong — account for almost half (45.8 percent) of the manufactured exports of the developing economies. When one adds another eight developing nations — Brazil, Mexico, China, Singapore, India, Malaysia, Yugoslavia, and Argentina — eleven economies account for 81 percent of these exports. Over a hundred nations divide up the remaining 19 percent.

It is obvious that there can be no such thing as a global solution to the problem of international poverty. There can be an international context that facilitates a variety of national and regional responses, but a worldwide master plan is out of the question. Even if the advanced countries became utterly responsible toward the Third World under socialist leadership, they hardly possess a model for the future of the South. Indeed, the Northern nations, their socialists very much included, are even now trying to solve the problems of an ecologically destructive industrialization and a technology that does not generate a sufficient number of quality jobs. Clearly, the poor countries have to find technologies appropriate to their needs.

This does not mean, as André Gorz argues, that if only the wealthy powers would leave the have-not nations alone, all would be well. The Third World's difficulties, Gorz writes,

> are not a result of "backwardness" or inadequate productive forces. Instead they are the result of: 1. The draining of those resources by the industrialized capitalist countries; 2. The political and social obstacles to the utilization of their own productive forces (for which colonialism and latterly the neocolonialism of the multinationals are largely responsible).

The problem with this analysis, as the data show, is that the transnational activities in the Third World are rather narrowly concentrated in a small number of countries. They are not, for example, a decisive force in China, India, Bangladesh, or sub-Saharan Africa. And they were not the major reason for the failure of a country like Tanzania to achieve a decentralized self-sufficiency. If Northern capitalism is hardly the shining image of what the developing countries should become, neither is there a shortcut to utopia in those societies themselves.

In order better to understand these complexities, it is important to survey just a few of the many strategies the Third World has already employed in the struggle for development. About the only thing they share in common is that none of them has succeeded in changing the basic hierarchies of Northern domination. We have already looked at the Stalinist model in some detail. It was, as we have noted, followed by the Chinese in the fifties, by a number of African countries (Angola, Mozambique, Ethiopia), by Cuba and Vietnam, and it had a significant influence even on societies such as India, which opted for democratic industrialization. It is characterized by the use of authoritarian state power to carry through a forced accumulation of capital as part of a process of rapid modernization. It "worked" in the Soviet Union — at tremendous social cost — in the first phase of "extensive" growth but, as Gorbachev has so clearly recognized, it is utterly inadequate for the intensive growth that is the characteristic of advanced economies in the late twentieth century.

Even using the quantitative measures of success applied in the Soviet Union, it is clear that this approach was not adapted to countries that were much poorer, and had much less of a managerial infrastructure, than the Tsarist Russia conquered by the Bolsheviks in 1917. This model, then, is out of favor in the country of its origin, and less and less popular in the Third World. It is also currently going through broad changes in both China and the Soviet Union.

In the eighties, there has been discussion of the significance of the growth achieved by the Four Tigers (or the Four Dragons), South Korea, Taiwan, Singapore, and Hong Kong. Since they account for more than 50 percent of the total manufactured exports of the Third World, that is not surprising. But what is profoundly ideological in the treatment of these four economies is the tendency to treat them as "free market" success stories. The fact is, as the briefest glance at the two leading exporters of the Third World — South Korea and Taiwan — shows, the state plays a central role here, just as it does everywhere else in the Third World.

Until the mid-sixties, South Korea and Taiwan were committed to an "import substitution" rather than an export strategy, attempting, under the tutelage of the government, to create coherent internal capitalist societies. But then Japan, which is crucial for both countries, made its breakthrough and became a critical source of investment funds and contracts, particularly for South Korea. At that point, South Korea and Taiwan had both undergone land reform; and both were, by Asian standards, relatively small societies. There were a number of factors at work that were far from typical of the Third World as a whole, or even of Asia.

When South Korea began its transformations under Park Chung Hee in the mid-sixties, the government poured money into the export sector even as it repressed any attempts to organize the emergent working class. Given the poverty of the people, savings were low and development was financed by external debt. An Economic Planning Board, on the model of the Japanese Ministry of Trade and Industry, played, and still plays, a critical role. This "free market" society has gone through six five-year plans and in 1988 was systematically exploring the subsidized development of seven new high-tech industries. The export manufacture sector is dominated by monolithic, family-controlled, and vertically integrated businesses, the *chaebol* (which resemble the Japanese *ziabatsu* broken up by the American occupiers). Moreover, there is also a Bismarckian dimension to this country: a 1988 UNICEF study points out that it engaged in extensive social spending in order to avoid the increase of poverty that afflicted so many of the poor economies in the eighties.

Similarly, the Taiwanese have been organizing around four-year plans since 1953. The government created the industrial infrastructure with a heavy emphasis on capital-intensive industries (petrochemicals, heavy-machine factories, etc.), and there was also a stress on hazardous-waste operations (plastics, chemicals, petroleum refining, pesticides, leather and tanning). All of this was done under the guidance of the Council for Economic Development, which targeted Twelve New Development Projects in 1978. Moreover, Taiwan, like South Korea, is dependent on both Japan and the United States for markets. Both societies are vulnerable to an economic turndown in the advanced world.

Under the specific circumstances confronting South Korea and Taiwan, an authoritarian, repressive state capitalism led to significant economic gains. That some Western ideologues read this development as a tribute to the power of *laisser-faire* in the Third World testifies to their ideological commitment rather than the cogency of their analysis. There was a related development in

Latin America in the sixties and seventies: militarized free enterprise.

In the four most developed countries of the area — Brazil, Argentina, Uruguay, and Chile — the army did not simply take over the government in classic *golpista* fashion. It came to power with a distinctive economic doctrine, heavily indebted to Milton Friedman and the Chicago school of economics. And it proceeded to implement "free enterprise" policies by means of a police state. It is ironic that capitalism, whose defenders have always boasted of the links between markets and democracy, should have thus become a panacea for fascist, or near-fascist, regimes.

For a socialist, the case of Chile was, of course, the most tragic of the four. There, the Pinochet *junta* overthrew a democratically elected, and socialist, administration under Salvador Allende. In *La Transition Socialiste*, Serge Christophe Kolm developed a fascinating analysis of the internal problems that, even prior to America's unconscionable intervention, were to provide a political and social basis for the military subversion of the regime.

This account puts into sharp focus the way in which the structural problem that bedeviled the socialists in the original capitalist countries — how do you change a system that tends to reproduce itself? — is even more acute in the Third World. It is not simply that socialists must carry out their reforms on a national terrain hostile to them, but that they must prevail against an international complex of power. No longer is the problem simply that of transforming capitalism, which is difficult enough; it is how to transform a *dependent* capitalism. And this is particularly obvious in the case of Chile.

Allende had embarked on a socialist project unique in the Third World: to build democratic socialism on the basis of an expansion of living standards for the entire society rather than upon a sacrifice of consumption to investment. The strategy was an extremely radical Third World variant of Keynesianism. The government would radically increase the buying power of the poorest strata of the society, control prices to be sure that the rise in nominal income would not be annulled by inflation, and thus set off a consumption-led boom. This would, in turn, benefit the private sector as well as the people, for it would vastly expand the internal market and thereby encourage new investment and the creation of employment. At the same time, in a move supported by the Catholic Church and many of the Christian Democrats, the society would take over the foreign-owned copper industry, which was the main source for Chile's hard-currency earnings in the world market.

Some of the problems with this strategy were political. Both the Chilean capitalists and the American copper companies were so hostile to the regime that they were ready to follow policies that in the short run would reduce their profits in order to undermine Allende in the long run. There were other difficulties that were the consequence of the inherited structures of a dependent capitalism. Chilean industry had not been built up on the basis of egalitarian consumption but was designed, rather, to meet the needs of an unjust society. When the masses suddenly were able to buy refrigerators and washing machines, it was impossible to rapidly restructure the entire economy in order to meet that new demand even if the private sector cooperated.

That meant a further inflationary pressure as well as a drain on the balance-of-payments position of the nation: goods were imported to meet the new demand, and the mass buying power in a context of scarcity led to a black-market erosion of the system of price controls. At the same time, by promoting demand through higher wages, Allende, all other things being equal, did limit profits and the funds available for the new investment that he wanted to encourage. Thus, even before Washington put its plans to destabilize the regime into effect, there were internal difficulties having to do with the structural constraints of the existing Third World capitalist system on a socialist government.

But Washington did, of course, intervene. A lesson had been learned at the Bay of Pigs: that direct military attacks on radical regimes in Latin America provoked the populace to mobilize against *yanqui* aggression. President Nixon and Secretary of State Henry Kissinger therefore organized an economic blockade of Chile to create the conditions for internal revolt. The World Bank and the IMF were kept from coming to the aid of the beleaguered society and so were private banks. The American copper companies were encouraged to fight Allende, and everything was done to see to it that the internal economic problems were made all the worse. When money was sent to help finance the opposi-

tion that overthrew and murdered Allende, there was already
tremendous discontent within the society. Indeed, the buying
power of the people was now less than it had been before Allende
became president.

Pinochet came to power on the basis of a coup linked to the
economic subversion of his country by the United States. His
government then consulted Milton Friedman and, after repressing all the organs of popular resistance, imposed "free enterprise" on the society. In this, Pinochet was following in the steps
of the Brazilian, Argentinian, and Uruguayan military. As Albert
Mayio described this military capitalist model in a paper written
for the Joint Economic Committee of the U.S. Congress, the
generals

> believed they could bring about an efficient free market
> economy by major reforms: a large reduction in the public
> sector; a more efficient tax collection system; rigorous fiscal
> and monetary discipline; a sharp reduction in tariffs and
> non-tariff barriers; the elimination of burdensome business
> regulations, and a sharp curtailment in the power of labor
> unions to raise wages above productivity increases.

The net result of this brutal and repressive experiment in "free
enterprise," Mayo concluded, was to weaken the private sector
and lead to an economic performance that compared unfavorably
with the democratic countries in the region. Once these nations
emerged from their authoritarian nightmares, they had to confront the world of the contemporary debt crisis, and it is not at
all clear that economic conditions conducive to democracy will
continue.

When one turns to sub-Saharan Africa the patterns change
radically. Here it is necessary to speak of a developmental *retrogression*. In 1970, Africa largely fed itself; in 1984, a quarter of
the Africans survived because of grain imports. This, as Michael
Manley's *Global Challenge* pointed out, was primarily the result
of three massive trends: the highest rate of population growth a
continent has ever experienced in history; soil erosion and
desertification; and the failure of government policies in agriculture. The debt crisis also had a severe impact, even though most
of the money was owed to official lenders (where it is normally

more negotiable than in the case of private creditors). At the end of 1986, the World Bank estimates, sub-Saharan Africa had a debt of $101 billion, $45 billion of which was concentrated in low-income countries. In the African debtor nations, the eighties have thus far been a time of decline: per capita output has decreased by 16.6 percent, consumption by 12.4 percent, investment by 15.6 percent, and exports by 30.1 percent.

In part these problems were the result of a colonial legacy imposed upon the region. "National" boundaries were set by European powers in the nineteenth century without regard for economic or tribal realities, and colonialism failed to educate the people (in contrast, say, to British imperialism's promotion of an educated bureaucratic stratum in India). Therefore, the problem of administrative competence is, to a degree unknown in the rest of the Third World, a major impediment to economic development. So is the challenge of developing a national consciousness in societies that are still dominated by tribal identities.

At the same time, world economic trends worked against these countries. As Susan George summarized the situation:

> Modern Africa has remained dependent on the same riches — diamonds, copper, gold, food, beverages, fibres and the like — that drew the colonial powers there in the first place. But drastic changes have occurred since the days when African minerals and agricultural raw materials could command high prices on international markets. Technology has run on apace, while African economies have continued to produce for a world that no longer exists. Telephone and communications equipment has entered the fibre-optic era and is junking its copper-wire installations. Miniaturization of practically everything and more efficient processing reduces demands for metals. Plastics are more durable than sisal or hemp. Cotton can be purchased from Peru, Egypt or China. . . . Africa is not well placed to adapt to rapidly changing markets.

The result is that when a country like Tanzania, with considerable assistance from European and particularly Swedish socialists, tried to follow a noncapitalist path to modernity, it was victimized by the lack of internal expertise (which is why the publicly owned corporations tended to become a burden rather than an instrument of change), by the terms of trade for its meager exports, and by the problems of a population even more dispersed than in most African countries. This was true even though the Tanzanian leader Julius Nyerere carried out a vigorous campaign against corruption, a major factor inhibiting development throughout sub-Saharan Africa.

While the failure of African governments to deal with agriculture is a cliché in the literature of underdevelopment, the reality is not quite as simple as the standard description of it. The Africans, it is said — often in the context of an attack on a misguided and sentimental African "socialism" — ignored the rural areas, concentrated on grandiose projects in the cities, and simply did not pay the farmers enough for their produce to call forth the needed volume of food.

But a policy of encouraging cash crops in Africa has often led to production for export rather than for urban consumers. This was true even though critical crops were affected by declining terms of trade and the rising costs of fuel and fertilizers. In any case, only a small fraction of the value of agricultural commodities in Africa actually accrues to the producers. The lion's share goes to the transnationals that control the distribution of the harvest on the world markets.

All of this is not to deny that serious errors were committed by African governments in the postcolonial periods, including the waste of resources by nationalist elites on "socialist" corruption and major planning errors, not only in countries such as Angola, following the Soviet model, but also in a Tanzania committed to a much more participatory form of development. Yet, the objective factors of the colonialist legacy and the terms of trade, which victimized the continent, were much more important. At the same time, it is clear that policies that will address African problems of hunger and desertification will be quite different from those required in Latin America.

One encounters the same heterogeneity when one turns to two examples of attempts at democratic development in the Third World: India and the democratic-socialist experience under Michael Manley and the People's National Party (PNP) in Jamaica in the seventies.

Independent India, under the leadership of Nehru, opted for

what Sukhamoy Chakravarty calls "planned economic development within the framework of a mixed economy." The basic idea
was Fabian and social democratic, the heritage of a nationalist
elite that had been profoundly influenced by the British Left. The
state would take over the commanding heights of the economy
and act as the instrument of national planning; but the private
sector would be allowed to develop on its own. Even at the outset,
as Gunnar Myrdal pointed out, this "socialism" had a considerable rhetorical content, and in recent years, under the prime
ministership of Rajiv Gandhi, the state capitalist component has
been clearly dominant.

Still, it is an enormous accomplishment for a society subjected
to severe economic and population pressures to have persisted on
a road to democratic modernization. To be sure, there have been
deviations from that path — most notably during Indira Gandhi's
"emergency" of the 1970s — but still the level of human rights
and popular political participation in India is higher than in almost any society in the Third World.

The poverty level of the country has also remained very high.
Despite extensive industrialization since independence, India has
remained a rural society. Between 1965 and 1981, for instance,
the peasant percentage of the nation declined only from 74 percent to 71 percent. This was so even though the same period saw
a tremendous rise in agricultural production through the Green
Revolution. In the late sixties, the country was dependent on food
imports for survival; in 1979, it endured the worst drought of the
twentieth century without having to call in outside aid. But this
success set in motion two counterposed trends: in those regions
where it was easiest to introduce Green Revolution seeds and
technology, a new stratum of commercial farmers appeared; but
India's failure to carry out land reform also meant that inheritance laws led to the fragmentation of agricultural holdings and
the proliferation of small-scale poverty units.

At the same time, an inward-looking process of investment in
heavy industry — the Indian share of world exports fell from .79
percent in 1971–72 to .54 percent in 1978–79 — resulted in a
steady increase in GNP without a matching rise in urban employment. This growth was often in the private sector, but with heavy
financial subsidies from the state, and it encountered a typical
Third World problem. In the West during the rise of capitalism,

population growth and urbanization took place simultaneous with the evolution of the new technology. To smooth out a tumultuous history, one can say that industry created openings for displaced peasants. But in the Third World when a country such as India embarks on modernization, it creates an industrial base that is not synchronized with the rest of the society.

This is another way of stating Myrdal's thesis about the absence of "spread effects" in the ex-colonies. Marx imagined that industrialization would have the same transforming power on the capitalist periphery that it exhibited in the center, but this has simply not been true. Third World societies either continue to be primarily rural even though there is a strong and persistent industrial trend, as in India, or else peasants uprooted by the process of commercialization form a huge urban *lumpenproletariat*, as in Brazil.

In any case, India is the example of a democratic and state capitalist industrialization. In Jamaica under Michael Manley there was a brief, and failed, attempt at a democratic-socialist transformation of a dependent economy during the 1970s.

The democratic-socialist model of development applied in Jamaica was based, in Evelyne and John Stephens's fine analysis, on a number of distinctive elements. The process was to be led by the state sector but sought to create a partnership between the government and the private sector as well as to encourage cooperative enterprise. It sought to reduce foreign domination of the economy and dependence on agricultural and other imports; yet it also envisioned joint enterprises under controlled conditions. The most spectacular policy in this regard was Manley's takeover of the bauxite industry and his unsuccessful attempt to organize an OPEC-like international bauxite cartel (there were too many alternative sources of this raw material for the strategy to work).

Perhaps most distinctive of all, the Jamaicans saw the creation of a mass-based political party, with elements of cultural as well as political ideology, as a critical component of their work. The PNP was transformed from a traditional Jamaican political organization, that is, one based on clientalistic appeals, into a very participatory and socialist formation. This meant that the experiment encouraged debate and difference, which, in other contexts, became a problem. Yet it was clearly a precondition for turning an excluded and often manipulated population into one struggling to gain some control of its own destiny.

There were many reasons for failure. As so often happens in the Third World, the movement lacked the trained cadre to run some of the not very profitable enterprises taken over by the government (the hotels, for instance). The working class was relatively small, highly stratified, and had a tradition of intense — clientalistic — internal battles, which made the creation of a serious ideological party all the more difficult. The bauxite takeover was a partial success but fell short of the hopes of the regime. And, to a degree that one cannot assess with any certainty, the United States played a destabilizing role in Jamaica. There is, in any case, no doubt that the Reagan administration showered assistance on Manley's main antagonist and successor, Edward Seaga; the only question is whether, and to what extent, Washington engaged in surreptitious destabilization.

Even if the PNP failed in the difficult task it set itself — and voluntarily relinquished power when it lost a democratic election — it laid out some important principles for democratic-socialist development in the Third World. It understood, however imperfectly, the limits placed on it in a dependent democracy. It sought radical, but incremental, solutions within the framework of the possible. Perhaps the most significant index of its success was that the Seaga regime was forced to respect some of its accomplishments and to phrase its own goals in terms often borrowed, at least rhetorically, from the PNP. At this writing, it appears quite likely that Manley will return to power.

This example, and all the others preceding it, make it painfully clear that the diversity within the Third World as well as the constraints imposed on all of its societies, even the most developed, makes it extremely difficult to formulate an international socialist policy for development.[2]

III

HOW THEN SHOULD the new socialism respond?

Obviously, with a realistic, and even chastened, sense of the limits on the possible. The New International Economic Order of the rich constructed after World War II based itself on a complex, three-hundred-year-old system of global injustice. It will not be quickly dismantled, not even in half a century. Second, these limitations also arise out of the variety, heterogeneity, and weaknesses of the Third World itself. There is clearly no single model of development that is adequate to societies with such different problems and at such radically different stages of economic and social development. Nor is there a single international economic policy that could be adopted with the support of the advanced nations that would somehow open up a path to the abolition of the world poverty. Socialists can, and should, however, make the ending of "absolute poverty," of those depths of misery that sap the very genetic potential of human beings, an immediate goal.

There is no one socialist model *within* the Third World. Socialist movements are going to have to respond to distinctive histories and structures. That is why the positive proposals of this chapter must focus primarily on what can be done to dismantle the international economic barriers to national solutions and to create a global environment in which experiment is facilitated in different countries.

These matters are made all the more complex when one speaks, as socialists must, not of gross statistical growth, but of a democratic and participatory growth in which social liberation is a major factor in promoting economic productivity, for example, where rights for women are seen as a practical, as well as a political and moral, necessity. One must then add the political problem that new departures in the advanced societies are going to require the support of political majorities that will see these measures as working toward their self-interest as well as toward a more just world.

Simply stating these preconditions and limitations makes it obvious that what will be described here are some first steps on a political journey that stretches into the unforeseeable future. But if there is someone who is then tempted to cut this Gordian knot, to propose a decisive and temporary dictatorship that will speed up the process and avoid the temporizing of softhearted social democrats, it must be pointed out that the history sketched in these pages shows how utterly unrealistic this kind of "realism" is.

Still, the prospects are not as bleak as it might at first seem when one begins to identify all the obstacles. One reason is that, starting in 1976, the Socialist International under the leadership of Willy Brandt began to work out the basic concepts of a new internationalism. The report of the SI's Economic Policy Committee chaired by Michael Manley and published as *Global Challenge* goes into considerable detail, even though it is not a blueprint. And what is politically critical is the basic strategic thinking underlying the two reports of the Brandt Commission and the specifics of the Manley Committee.

Fundamentally, the Brandt strategy is based on the assertion that the crisis of the South is deeply connected with the crisis of the North; that the continuing economic gap between the rich and poor nations is not simply an affront to morality and justice but a fetter on the economic development of the entire world. Even the sophisticated conservatives of the North, including Ronald Reagan's treasury secretary (who has, of course, become George Bush's secretary of state), have understood the new interdependence of the globe, that is, that the suffering of the wretched becomes a limit on the markets of the quasi-affluent. While the exploitation of the Third World poor was not — and is not — a life-or-death necessity of the rich economies and therefore *the* reason for their postwar prosperity, it is still significant, particularly in a time of crisis.

Still, one can argue that there is a strange agreement of Left and Right that the growth of the poor countries would be good for the world. But the second element in the socialist approach is not a matter of consensus. It proposes a redistribution of resources from North to South that will create jobs and wealth in the North as well as in the South. The conservative conclusions from the fact of global interdependence are quite different. In essence, they follow the IMF model in which the South is supposed to integrate itself into a world market controlled by the North. Then vastly increased exports will pay off the debts of the past and finance the modernization of the future. In the spring of 1988, Brazil accordingly abandoned its forty-year-old "import substitution" model and explicitly adopted a policy modeled on the success of the Four Tigers of Asia.

In part, this was done because Brazil's attempts to service its enormous debts were starving the country of domestic investment capital. The solution was adopted to invite foreign capital to come into the Brazilian economy, thereby subordinating Brazil to the priorities of a Northern-dominated world market. (The participation of foreign capital under strict controls and as part of a democratic-socialist development model would be a quite different proposition). The policy also means less regulation of national capital and a greater emphasis on internal market forces. We have already seen what this can mean in the case of the militarized capitalism of Latin America, including Brazil between 1964 and 1967.

But the decisive objection to this strategy is not based primarily upon its domestic consequences. For the fact is, the IMF model cannot, in logic or reality, be internationalized, since it proposes a positive-sum result to a zero-sum game. That is, if all of the developing nations are to follow the Four Tiger path and to earn hard-currency trade surpluses by integrating into the world economy, that means that the advanced countries must support trade deficits of the same size. A "competitive" integration of the world economy would thus lead — in the most unlikely situation where it was put into practice — to recession or depression in the North. That is why the cooperative tactic envisioned in the socialist proposals is so important.

The analogy at the base of those proposals is to the Marshall Plan — and it must be used with care if we are not to simplify the challenge before us. On the one hand, there is no doubt that the Marshall Plan more than repaid the United States for its generosity, in that the grants and concessional loans made it possible for Europe and Japan to purchase machines and materials of reconstruction in the United States. The American largesse yielded a clear social profit in enhanced employment and, for that matter, a profit pure and simple for the corporate sector. And it can be cogently argued that a Northern commitment to economic justice in the South could create a new "locomotive" for growth in the North.

On the other hand, the Marshall Plan analogy could give rise to an impermissible optimism. As noted, Europe and Japan after World War II were advanced economies in ruins; they possessed the human skills and knowledge of advanced capitalism, and their critical problem was the destruction of physical plant. Under such circumstances, providing the capital to replace that plant could predictably result in a "miracle." Countries and populations that had already been through the capitalist revolution simply utilized the funds from the United States in order to reconstruct the system.

In the Third World today, it is not just capital that is lacking. Most of these nations have not been through the industrial revolution. Moreover, it is impossible for the nations of the South simply to imitate classic capitalist methods, which do not apply in the unprecedented circumstances we have described; there is no "free market" model as a guide. It is not that politics and the state *are going to* play a role infinitely more significant than at the origins of capitalism; *they are already playing that role even in societies that give lip service to free markets.*

A pervasive state role in the Third World is ambiguous. It is at once a recognition of the validity of the basic socialist insight into the desirability of socialization *and* a possible point of departure for some new forms of authoritarian collectivism. The Stalinist model may well be in deserved disrepute, but more subtle forms of collective domination, like Singapore's "Leninist" capitalism, are still quite viable. And that raises a larger problem. A purely macroeconomic approach to world development would create more propitious conditions for fascists like Pinochet in Chile and "Marxist" dictators like Mengistu in Ethiopia. The benefits, like God's rain, would fall upon the just and unjust. How is one to avoid this indifference to the internal regime in the poor countries without engaging in some new and "progressive" kind of imperialism?

The answer to that question leads to a basic issue: the restructuring of the United Nations and its related economic institutions. For if, under the present Western-dominated structure of international economic institutions, one tried to impose conditions, even conditions prompted by humane sentiments, that would assume that the superior Northerners were going to save the inferior Southerners from themselves. But if socialists envision new forms of participation on the part of the representatives of the poor themselves, then one may speak of a limited, but progressive, conditionality.

Obviously something of a catch-22 is involved here. That is, the representatives of the Third World include the dictators. Still, if there are regional organizations of the South that set policy, then it is possible that democratic tendencies *within the South itself* will play a role in creating truly progressive conditions for participation in this effort.

I have opened up a central issue — that of the creation of new international economic institutions — tangentially, in terms of its relevance to one particular problem. What, then, is the political and planning component of the new socialist economic proposals?*

During the 1970s, the United Nations held a series of ranging discussions on a New International Economic Order. Even though they focused on exceedingly modest proposals that could easily fit into a sophisticated capitalist view of the world — the idea of a fund to stabilize the prices for Third World commodity exports has been institutionalized in the United States for more than a generation in the government agricultural program — the result was inconsequential. When, for a brief time, the Western governments feared that the OPEC cartel might be replicated with regard to a number of import raw materials, there was a prospect of serious negotiations; but as soon as that threat was seen to be imaginary, the interest of the big powers waned.

With the exception of the work of specialized UN agencies — the Food and Agricultural Organization, the World Health Organization, UNICEF, and the like — the UN has mainly produced grandiose resolutions on economic development without any appreciable effect on the way the world is run. Even more to the present point, this failure was built into the very structure of the world organization itself.

The UN was constructed on three very different principles. The General Assembly is based on one nation, one vote and gives the same weight to a small island country as it does to China or the United States. Since this principle is not only undemocratic but utterly unrealistic in terms of the distribution of power and population in the world, it means that the Assembly will perform no more than the useful function of creating an almost universal forum *and* all but guarantees that its decisions will have no force whatsoever.

The economic institutions within the UN "system" — the World Bank, IMF, General Agreement on Tariffs and Trade, and the like — are, on the contrary, based on excessive realism, that is, on the principle of one dollar, one vote. The result is that significant decisions are indeed taken, and that they seriously affect the Third World. But they are made in a setting in which

---

*In what follows, I have been very much influenced by the reflections of Maurice Bertrand, for seventeen years a member of the Inspectorate of the United Nations in Geneva. Bertrand's ideas were set down in a book, *Refaire L'ONU* and in "Some Reflections on Reform of the United Nations."

the major advanced capitalist powers have institutional dominance — and the United States alone has a veto power. Thus the IMF has acted as an international economic gendarme for distinctively Northern conceptions of economic policy in the South. In effect, then, these institutions have promoted the New International Economic Order of the rich created after World War II.

Finally, the Security Council has been based on a somewhat realistic principle of the veto power of the five permanent members, three of them allied in NATO under the effective leadership of the United States, two of them the major, but antagonistic, Communist powers. This has meant that on political issues where there is a consensus, limited concerted action has been possible. But it has not stopped the armed conflicts that have been confined to the Third World since the end of World War II. And the Security Council has not taken up the issues of world economic development that are the crucial focus of this chapter.

Clearly the UN as presently constituted is not an institution capable of taking the lead in even modest measures of global justice based on the common interest of the North and South. Yet with all its imperfections, the UN is a significant starting point for just such an undertaking. It is for that reason that, even though individual socialist governments can make important unilateral initiatives on the basis of the Brandt strategy, the new socialism must make institutional as well as substantive proposals for a reformed world economic order.

This notion is made all the more urgent by the dramatic consequences of irresponsible capitalist socialization in the environment. Without paying any attention to the momentous fact, corporations have created not simply a global factory but a global ecosystem as well. Acid rain, the depletion of the ozone layer, the greenhouse effect, and the shipping of toxic wastes to the poor countries have created a truly international threat to human survival. Nuclear power, as the aftermath of Chernobyl made so clear, has the same impact, and even desertification is the result of a desperate response to a poverty that the North has done nothing to alleviate.

The destruction of the Amazonian rain forest in Brazil because of economic development is a paradigmatic case in point. This action does not simply threaten the ecology of a single nation; by reducing the amount of carbon dioxide that the forest had absorbed, it contributes to the greenhouse effect and a climatic shift that affects the entire world. But how can Northern countries, *which are responsible for at least 80 percent of the economic degradation of the biosphere,* piously recommend to Brazil, already pushed to the wall in the effort to pay its debts to banks of advanced capitalism, that it sacrifice itself on behalf of the world, and particularly, on behalf of the rich of the world? That could be done only if there were an international economic effort linked with a global environmental plan.

These problems cannot be solved within a national framework. Certain technologies and chemicals have to be banned on a world scale; industrial processes have to be designed to be environmentally benign; the Third World cannot be expected to pay the environmental bill for an industrialization it never enjoyed; and so on. But to do these things, as well as to deal with the poverty of the South, requires strong new international institutions.

The crucial task is to create a realistic political forum for serious negotiations on such issues. This means that both power and population have to be taken into account. There are, Maurice Bertrand points out, ten nations with a GNP greater than 2.5 percent of the world product: the United States, the Soviet Union, Japan, West Germany, France, the United Kingdom, Italy, Canada, Brazil, and China. The seven advanced capitalist powers among them are already participants in the Western economic summits. In terms of population, there are seven countries in the world with more than 100 million people: the United States, China, India, the Soviet Union, Indonesia, Brazil, and Japan. Only two of them, India and Indonesia, are not included in the "GNP" list.

Twelve countries therefore represent three quarters of the wealth of the world and more than half of its population. They should be the core of a new Economic Security Council. But how does one represent the other 159 members of the UN, particularly when it is important to have a body small enough to carry out serious negotiations? In posing the question in this way, I am assuming that the General Assembly would remain as a forum in which every nation in the world, no matter what its size, would have a voice. The issue is, how does one construct a forum that is small enough and based on the realities of economic and political power to prove a place for serious negotiations?

Bertrand argues convincingly that regional representation is the best way to ensure the participation of the 159 countries that do not belong to the populous and/or powerful twelve. He suggests — as an example — two representatives from the Latin American region, one from the Caribbean, one from the Arab countries, two for sub-Saharan Africa, one for Eastern Europe, two for Southeast Asia, one for Oceania, and one for the small and medium-sized Western nations. But these regions, it is important to stress, should not be artificial political units created solely for the purpose of representation on the Economic Security Council.

These regional units of a restructured UN could become the sites of development secretariats to coordinate action within a region and between it and other regions. The economic crisis of the seventies undercut South-South trade in which, for instance, 70 percent of Brazil's manufactured exports went to other developing nations. And in 1992, when the European Community will make a major step toward economic integration, there will be the possibility that the socialists of the Community will be able to develop a Europe-wide policy based on the Brandt principles.

More broadly, the new socialists must continue and deepen the beginnings made by the Socialist International under Brandt and take the lead in an internationalist campaign to restructure not simply the world economy but its political structures as well. The New International Economic Order of the rich created after World War II was a conscious and ingenious work of the wealthy. It is time to include the poor in the process.

There are two critical principles in this undertaking. First, there is the understanding that a transfer of wealth and resources from North to South can lead to an increase in wealth and resources in *both* North and South. And second, the achievement of such a transfer requires the creation of new international political institutions for a rapidly integrating world economy that go far beyond anything put in place at Bretton Woods — and yet build on some of the more visionary hopes of 1944. Both of these linked strategies, it has been shown, are based on a combination of genuine moral solidarity and an appeal to an enlightened self-interest.

It is fascinating that something like the concept of solidarity and interest can be found as early as 1907 in the work of Otto Bauer, one of the theoretical leaders of the Austrian social democracy. Living within a multinational Austro-Hungarian empire where the question of nationality was a critical political issue, Bauer wrote, "We do not abstract from the national differences of the workers. Rather, we show that the workers of each nation have it in their own interest that the workers of every other nation satisfy their national cultural needs." The point applies now. What is to be achieved is not the homogenization of the world and the destruction of those local and national loyalties that are the substance of language and culture. Instead, one seeks to break the link between nations and domination, to create a United States of Europe and a Federation of the Planet Earth in which the cultural differences will persist to the enrichment of all.

That points to another fascinating idea raised by Bauer. The theoretical justification for the Northern dominance of world trade has been, since 1815, David Ricardo's theory of comparative advantage. The rich countries, it is argued, are simply submitting to the objective logic of a system in which each nation produces that which it can manufacture most cheaply, with the result that the efficiency of the globe is maximized even though there is no conscious planning. This analysis even proves that a country that suffers from outrageously unfair terms of trade with other nations is still better off despite that fact.

In reality, Bauer pointed out three quarters of a century ago, capitalist enterprise followed the logic of profit in its dealing with the poor countries, not the objective laws of comparative advantage. But, Bauer argued, in a socialist world — or, I would add, even in a world that has taken only the first steps in the direction defined by Brandt and Manley — comparative advantage could actually come into its own for the first time in history. For under cooperative relations of interdependence, it would actually be in the self-interests of what are now the rich countries to allow each country to do what it can do best.

The fullness of that vision is in the unforeseeable distance. It took millennia for humankind to move from the loyalties of family and clan to those of the city and then to the patriotism of the nation-state. The emergence of a global consciousness will not be the work of a decade. It is, rather, the challenge of an entire epoch of history. If the new socialists understand these complexities, they will take visionary first steps in the direction of a new world. No more. And no less.[3]

7

Socialization Revisited

W ELL, THEN, WHAT *is* socialism? After all the qualifications and historic explanations, what is left of an idea that claimed to speak clearly of radical new modes of production and distribution on a world scale?

There are two cultures of the Left in every advanced country now trying to answer that question. As Thomas Meyer describes them, one is based primarily on the traditional working class and its allies and defended the Keynesian model; the other expresses the values of new, and often relatively privileged, social strata. At the polar extremes, Growth for Growth's Sake confronts No Growth. In Germany, this trend takes the form of a surprisingly successful Green party and of the emergence within the social democracy itself of ecological and feminist currents.

By 1984, these developments convinced the German socialists that they had to go through a collective, and public, process of writing a new basic program, an effort still under way. Yet it is already clear from the "Irseer Draft," the first statement of the program produced by a party commission under the leadership of Willy Brandt, that the final text will be light-years removed from the Keynesian economism of the Godesberg Program of 1959.

The "Irseer Draft" talks of the menace to human survival in much of the dominant technology, of shortening the working life and democratizing the workplace itself, of fighting bureaucracy, including the bureaucracies of the social-democratic welfare state, and of putting an end to the Cold War. It is in many ways an attempt to synthesize the two cultures of the Left, demanding "a socially and ecologically responsible industrial society."

So the ideas about socialism discussed in this and the following chapter are not the speculations of an individual, but a personal statement of themes that are becoming more and more important to mass socialist parties as they try to deal with the new economic, political, and social realities. It is precisely because there is such a response that I asserted in the first chapter that the existing socialist movement, with all of its failures, remains the only serious hope for a theory and practice of freedom adequate to the twenty-first century. For it is struggling to define not simply a new social structure of accumulation, important as that is, but the first steps toward a new civilization as well.

That possible synthesis of the work of the "two Lefts" can be put emblematically, for it is expressed in the symbol that has been adopted by socialist parties around the world: a fist holding a rose. That fist is a traditional sign of proletarian power and strength, the rose an inheritance from the youthful revolt of 1968, when it was seen that gentleness and imagination were at least as important as the means of production.

What follows is a brief account of the effort to unite the fist and the rose, of a new socialism.

I

THE NATURE OF work will be radically transformed in the advanced economies within the next fifty years, and some of their most cherished injustices will be subverted in the process. The reason we can confidently predict this future is that it has already begun. As the Office of Technology Assessment of the United States Congress put it in a 1988 study, within a mere two decades "virtually every product, every service, and every job" in America will be transformed.

It would be absurd to think that such a momentous shift in one of the basic constituents of human existence is going to be confined to the workplace. One need only look back a hundred years to the last time something like this happened. The mass-production factory was a crucial part of a transition that redefined the very character of the city, the structure of the economy, the nature of social classes, and the relations of authority in the society as a whole. Its impact was felt in the family, the church, and the ethos of everyday life. Similarly, in 2050, it is not just technology that will be different. The way people live together will be fundamentally altered because of the way they work together.

In these times one and the same "fact" of this kind provides the basis for contradictory futures. We have already seen how the practical necessity of raising the consumption levels of a Third World that is part of an integrated global economy could inform a new, more sophisticated Northern domination over the South *or* be the foundation for a joint liberation of North and South. So, too, with the technological revolution within the advanced societies. It allows for subtle, new kinds of capitalist injustice *or* a new socialism.

It is sobering to remember that, thus far, this transformation has been the work of corporations essentially unconcerned with the societal futures they are creating. The question is, will socialists be as daring as the businessmen, but with a consciousness of what they are doing?

Capitalists, Marx shrewdly commented in *The Communist Manifesto*, constitute the strangest dominant class in human history. All other rulers wanted tomorrow to be like yesterday. But capitalism, the most dynamic mode of production ever, has had to constantly change in order to conserve itself. Thus the bourgeois — the stolid, proper, and pious nineteenth-century bourgeois — was a revolutionary in spite of himself. So it is now, only more so. Corporate bureaucrats have blundered into visionary possibilities.

In the pursuit of productivity and profit, the corporations have been creating an automated, flexible work environment that requires the active participation of at least some of the producers. The ideal worker is no longer the docile machine tender. Suddenly, "cooperation" has become a central managerial value, and the failed welfare capitalism of the American twenties has come back to life. Or rather, that is one of two opposed tendencies now operating in the workplace. Under Fordism, the new technology was forthright: it "deskilled" the producers and was designed to do so. That was not simply an imperative of maximizing productivity; it was also a way of reducing the power of independent-spirited artisans.

Now automation, robotization, computerization, and all the other revolutionary changes both continue and contradict that pattern.* On the one hand, deskilling proceeds apace. The worker on the plant floor with all of his or her knowledge of production becomes the passive overseer of an inexplicable process that is reduced to symbols and digits on a television monitor. The clerk or secretary no longer interacts with boss or supervisor but becomes the prisoner of a routine mandated by the video-display terminal of a computer program.

At the same time, management has been forced to reskill at least some of its employees, learning that "smart machines" work much better if they are run by smart people. In the eighties, for instance, business analysts in the United States agreed that one of the reasons General Motors' massive modernization effort failed was because it ignored the need to invest in the human labor force as well as in robots. GM spent $48 billion on new machinery in the eighties — but the effort was perceived as an attempt to automate the workers out of their jobs. That was a major reason, the *Wall Street Journal* reported in 1989, why the technological strategy did not work "and robots were breaking parts, and computer-software glitches were halting production." Ironically, Ford, which did not have the money to invest on modernization, concentrated on improving communication with the employees and outperformed GM.

But then, even when GM did wake up to its problem and decreed corporate affability from on high, it was clear that the concern was with the production numbers, not the workers. Just as under the welfare capitalism of the twenties, being nice to the "hands" was seen as a way of manipulating them into doing what the company wanted, but not of sharing any kind of decision-making power. The habits of Fordist authoritarianism, in short, have persisted in a technological age that has made them objectively obsolete. That, in addition to its other consequences, perverts an ideal that is central to progressive change.

---

*In what follows I am quite indebted to a fascinating book by Shoshana Zuboff, *In the Age of the Smart Machine.*

In the social-democratic compromise, there were concessions on both sides, but the basic framework remained one of class antagonism and class suspicion. Indeed, the differences between the social commitments of various welfare states is best explained by linking strong working-class political and economic organization with public generosity. Even when capital had finally learned that the rising living standards of the people could be a source of increased profit, it was only as benevolent as it had to be. During the Great Prosperity, there were countless celebrations of how labor and capital had learned to live together and even to like one another. Yet the minute the crisis of the Keynesian economy permitted an attack on the welfare state, Margaret Thatcher and Ronald Reagan carried out a bitter and old-fashioned class struggle against the unions.

Now a manipulated communitarianism in which power relations remain as they were but are voluntarily, even happily, accepted is a distinct possibility as managerial strategy turns toward the feigning of human relations in production. This fraudulent spirit of cooperation should not, however, be understood as mere hypocrisy on the part of the executives. It is a much more profound phenomenon, expressing the collective resistance of an entire class of managers to a threat to their historic authority — a threat that, ironically, results from their own innovations.

The justification for the hierarchical position of managers, Shoshana Zuboff writes, was based on their expertise. They were not, after all, the owner-entrepreneurs of old whose position was legitimated by the "sacred" rights of private property. They were the paid functionaries of capital, and their claim to superiority was based on the decisive contribution their knowledge supposedly made to productivity. Having expropriated the skills of a good part of the work force and, as far as possible, concentrated creativity and initiative in the front office, the executives pointed to their own self-created monopoly of the "scientific" understanding of production as the reason they should command.

With the new technology, however, it is not just that machines become smarter than corporate bureaucrats. It now becomes rational to reskill rather than to deskill, to use the minds as well as the backs of labor. But if the managerial elite is no longer the monopolist of productive knowledge, why should it be accorded the obedience and perquisites claimed in the past? Isn't there a disturbing egalitarianism implicit in the new means of production?*

Zuboff reports a fascinating psychological conflict on the part of the managers in summarizing the data on the transition to automated systems in a number of corporations. The executives, she tells us, always make rhetorical bows in the direction of using the new program to give more initiative to the workers *and* they almost always choose the program that invests in the intelligence of the machines rather than that of human beings. In short, they recognize the liberating potential of what they are doing and then they repress it — and the gains in efficiency it might bring — because it delegitimates their own authority.

At the same time, the technological upheaval affects the society at large and holds out the possibility of a new, and reactionary, social structure of accumulation. By substituting machines for workers, these changes can make many people economically superfluous. There could be a future in which an elite patronizes a sophisticated work force, the middle of the class structure exists somewhat precariously outside the charmed circle of high technology, and a new poverty flourishes in a growing underclass at the bottom of the most productive society in history. That future, clearly, is an obvious tendency in the Western present. The question is whether it becomes a model for the next century.

It is a question because the same trends that pose the danger of a managerial authoritarianism also have a potential for an unprecedented human liberation. This is not only the real-world basis for a new socialism; it also suggests the kind of socialization it must propose.

Marx's anticipation of automation in the *Grundrisse* was premature, yet his analysis applies to the present and future of the late twentieth century. Just as he said, a quantum leap in productivity is making it impossible to base production on a calculus of hours

---

*A quarter of a century ago I noted, in *The Accidental Century*, that Aristotle had anticipated this insight in a strange setting: while defending slavery. If, he wrote in Book I of the *Politics*, "every tool could perform its own work when ordered, or by seeing what to do in advance . . . , if thus shuttles wove and quills played harps of themselves, master-craftsmen would have no need of assistants and masters no need of slaves." Corporate executives are not usually classical scholars, but they have intuited Aristotle's point and it frightens them.

of individual labor. Under these circumstances, the unplanned revolutions of capitalism could burst the seams of the system, and progress would proceed by way of social catastrophes — even of "socialized" catastrophe as carried out by recent conservative governments. And the indicated socialist response remains to control the process of change from below, genuinely to socialize transformations that are the unintended consequences of private innovation. Socialists, who often badly understood their own prophetic insights in images borrowed from the capitalist factory, now have to be as innovative as the changes introduced by capital.

So the nature of the progressive possibilities in the redefinition of the nature of work make it clear that socialization cannot be thought of as a mere shift of ownership title from a private to a public bureaucracy. Productivity gains for a new social structure of accumulation as well as the ethical values of a new civilization require that human beings creatively participate in economic decisions. If hypocrisy is the tribute that vice pays to virtue, then the manipulative communitarianism of the executives is a shamefaced recognition of this socialist truth.

The issues that have just been defined — basic choices between manipulative and authentic communitarianism — will be decided not in an abstract debate over desirable futures, but in a bitter political struggle over how to meet the crises this transition will bring to the advanced economies.

It is outrageous but inevitable that this confrontation over the future of humankind will be focused, to begin with, in the societies of the privileged fifth of the race. For there is no chance that the North-South relationship is going to be completely turned around within the next fifty years. If we are even to begin facing up to global integration, there will have to be giant strides toward such a change. But it is no simple matter to reverse a carefully articulated system of planetary injustice wrought over some four centuries of history.

Most, if not all, of the Third World countries will be fighting to achieve the levels of mass consumption and economic development reached by the West in the period right after World War II. The heritage of injustice makes it highly unlikely that the newest forms of technology will be located in the Third World; they will be found in the advanced economies. That, for pragmatic reasons as well as for moral solidarity, the socialists in those economies must design their response in international terms has already been made clear. But, through no fault of their own, they will do so primarily in those nations in which the technological revolution begins.

Second, the socialist innovation in the advanced countries will take place within a context of periodic structural crises. I say this not so much to insist upon the weaknesses of late capitalism as to point out the very difficult political and economic conditions under which socialists will make their case for new forms of social ownership.

I certainly do not think that any "final crisis" is at hand, that a revolutionary transformation of capitalism is likely in the next fifty years. I think it safe to say that today's advanced capitalist powers will still be mixed economies in the middle of the twenty-first century. If the new socialism becomes a genuine political force, these economies will be far more humane mixed economies, they will be mixed economies in profound transition, but there is no reason to expect that they will be fundamentally transformed. We are talking, then, of crises *of* the system, *within* the system, over the next half century.

Even though one can indeed speak of the coming (and current) "revolution" in the nature of work, that does not mean that all Fordist mass production is going to disappear or that the economies of 2050 will be totally automated and computerized. The vision of an apocalyptic and sudden transition to a people-less production is, as the authors of *Technology, Economic Growth and the Labour Process* have documented, often a figment of fervid leftist imaginations. Artisans survived the age of Fordism, and Fordist modes will continue in the electronic production of the foreseeable future.

Nor does my insistence on the coming crises imply a "vulture" perspective, the notion that a leap in misery will predispose people to accept socialist innovations. First, it is not at all clear that the crises of the next fifty years will be cataclysmic, on the model of 1929. There could be, as Alain Minc described the possibility, a "slow 1929," an uneven series of depressions and recoveries that decimate some regions of the national and international economy even as they stimulate growth in others. Something like that has actually happened in the eighties. Still, there are so many structural problems that a new 1929 cannot be excluded. It is easy, for instance, to imagine a global breakdown of over-production as automation and growth in the Newly Industrializing Countries (NICs) push output far beyond the capacity of the present system to absorb it.

The experience of the Great Depression itself is proof that bad times can make for fascism (Germany) and conservatism (Britain) as well as for new social invention (the United States and Sweden). I stress the crisis-prone nature of the future in order to suggest that events are not miraculously going to extricate social-ism from its present impasse. On the contrary. It means that the socialists are going to have to synthesize their long-run transfor-mations of the way people live and work with short-run responses to serious economic and social disturbances, which is something they never succeeded in really doing in the twentieth century.

Yet these issues will become political even if the socialists are inept. The transformation of the way women and men produce and reproduce their common lives cannot be contained within the old institutional framework. It has been clear since the mid-seventies that the Keynesian social democracy — which was Western society's major response to the social and economic consequences of Henry Ford's technological revolution — no longer works in the old way. The recognition of that sobering fact was followed by a period of romantic conservative illusions about the capacity of "free markets" to order the subversive changes brought about by transnational corporations, automation, and the information economy.

Those illusions cannot survive for long. When they disappear, most likely in the course of a series of structural crises whose intensity cannot be predicted, there will be no choice but radical change. In this context, socialization is the democratic and com-munitarian response to the unprecedented economic revolution now under way. Let me be specific.[1]

II

SOCIALIZATION MEANS the democratization of decision making in the everyday economy, of micro as well as macro choices. It looks primarily but not exclusively to the decentralized, face-to-face participation of the direct producers and their communities in determining the matters that shape their social lives. It is not a formula or a specific legal mode of ownership, but a principle of empowering people at the base, which can animate a whole range of measures, some of which we do not even yet imagine. This project can inspire a series of structural reforms that introduce new modes of social ownership into a mixed economy with Fordist, and even pre-Fordist, survivals.

How does this relate to the once-classic socialist demand for the nationalization of industry? Unfortunately, the way in which this question was posed in the postwar period all but guaranteed a maximum of confusion. The "revisionist" socialists, such as Anthony Crosland and the authors of the Godesberg Program of the German social democracy, did not simply — and rightly — point to the disappointments, and even perversities, of the postwar nationalizations. Their realism was part of a naive belief in the possibility of taming capitalism politically without introducing any structural changes. It seemed as though those who cogently attacked the dogma of nationalization did so in order to abandon the very idea of social ownership itself. They appeared now to be identifying socialism with a Keynesian capitalist welfare state, and the critique of the nationalization dogma was assumed (wrongly) to lead to that conclusion. So the defense of nationalization was taken to be a sign of leftist faith, a view embraced by antisocialists who found that it provided them with a most convenient straw man.

This dichotomy of socialist fidelity and revisionist treason is false. The equation of socialism and the state nationalization of industry, we have seen, was one phase in the movement's understanding of itself and, on this count, a narrow one. Now, under the conditions of technological revolution, it has become the nostalgia of a flawed memory at best, and reactionary at worst. If one is concerned with the truly audacious project of empowering people to take command of their daily lives, that will not be done through the expansion of bureaucratic state power. But to say that is not to give up the vision of social ownership; it is to prepare a fresh way for taking it seriously.

The new socialism must simultaneously make a principled critique of the notion that socialism is the nationalization of industry *and* assert the renewed relevance of social ownership under the unprecedented conditions of the twenty-first century.

Does this mean that socialists must therefore *renounce* nationalization entirely? Not at all.

The point is that nationalization can no longer be seen as the sovereign socialist remedy. It is a question for pragmatic discussion. When one adopts a time frame of fifty or so years, a period in which there will still be mixed economies, there are certain specific circumstances in which nationalization remains relevant. As Alec Nove has shown, there are some economic functions that, by their very nature *as we now understand them*, require large-scale planning and investments. That is, for all of the changes brought about by the information revolution, they cannot be carried out in decentralized units. Power grids as they are presently constituted are a case in point.

Those kinds of enterprises can be candidates for nationalization. But even then, it has to be understood that *the nationalized industry also has to be socialized.* That is true with regard to both their internal organization and their external impact. Most of the public corporations established by socialists after World War II are based on the same authoritarian, managerial structures as enterprises in the private sector. They are subject to democratic overview from the parliament and the executive, but their day-to-day operation is remarkably similar to that of a capitalist undertaking.

As a left-wing member of the French socialist party put it in the early eighties when he was put in charge of a nationalized company, "My job is to get surplus value. . . . To be 'Left' is to have a certain idea of the allocation of national wealth. This has nothing to do with the techniques that must be put in motion to produce that wealth." That will not do as the definition of a socialist attitude (although it may have been an understandable realism in the French conditions of 1982). Even in a large-scale, nationalized firm it is critical that there be as much participation by the producers in daily decisions as possible. For at least half a century, many socialists have talked of democratic structures in such companies, with worker and community seats on the board of directors as well as a managerial presence. It is time to take those ideas seriously.

But that is not as easy as it might sound. Managers, public or private, have staffs, computers, research funds, experts. Workers and communities do not. Thus, one can grant formal rights for participation, but if the participants lack the technical competence to take part in the debate, that is all but meaningless. So, in the society now emerging, one has to look toward the *socialization of information as well as of property*. There have to be funds that allow workers and communities to hire the experts who can translate their intuitive desires into the requisite equations and computer printouts. If there is a certain elitism built into the very nature of the new technology as created by contemporary capitalism, it need not be accepted as a given.

But then, these measures for the socialization of nationalized property extend to all forms of ownership. A fundamental proposition of the new socialism — which is also a basic requirement of the new technology — is the participation of worker representatives in all economic decision-making processes. The Swedish experience with the "wage-earner funds" suggests an ingenious way to do that in the private sector of what will be, for the foreseeable future, a mixed economy.

The original motive for proposing the wage-earner funds was primarily trade union in character. There was an unintended consequence of the solidaristic wage policy that committed Swedish labor in every negotiation to raise most of all the incomes of the least paid. Those corporations with a higher than average proportion of skilled workers made a windfall profit because the pay of their workers did not advance as fast as that of those at the bottom. The basic idea, advanced by the industrial union federation, LO, in 1975, was that some of these profits should be used for "collective capital formation" by being assigned to worker-controlled funds that would invest them in Swedish business. Over time, that meant that the representatives of these funds on the boards of directors of Swedish industry would preside over more and more of the private sector.

This represented a decisive move toward social ownership on the part of a labor movement that, despite decades in political power, had mainly socialized consumption and distribution rather than production; but it did not mean nationalization. The power of the funds would be located in autonomous, decentralized, non-government units. The result would be the creation of a novel form of ownership. It was an ingenious application of the idea of "functional socialization" that first appeared in the Swedish labor movement in the 1920s: in theory, there was no challenge to the continued existence of private corporate property; in practice, critical decision-making functions, which had been legitimated by that private title, would be socialized.

The reaction on the part of Swedish business — a corporate establishment that had flourished under years of social-democratic rule — was sharp, even violent, an anticipation of the defense of authoritarian management that Shoshana Zuboff discovered in the automated industries in the United States. The funds were portrayed as the vanguard of a Stalinist "Gulag Archipelago," and at one point the Swedish capitalists even took to the streets in a demonstration. At the outset of this debate, in 1976, the social democrats were finally turned out of office after forty-four years of continuous power, and some argued that the radical proposal for the funds was one reason for the defeat. So the Social Democratic Party and the unions negotiated, and, in the face of corporate resistance, the innovative ownership aspect of the idea was downplayed and it was now presented more as a scheme for collective capital formation.

When the socialists returned to government in 1983, there was further compromise before the funds became law. No fund, it was decided, could buy more than 8 percent of the stock of any one company, which meant that, even if the five funds created under the statute all put their money in the same enterprise, they would hold only 40 percent of the stock. And the whole experiment would last only until 1990. Rudolf Meidner, the economist who had formulated the original idea, and his associates were deeply disappointed with this turn of events.

Whatever eventually happens in Sweden, it is clear that the idea of decentralized social ownership as a way to socialize a part of the private sector has an enormous potential. The polling evidence of the seventies and early eighties, which did not show widespread working-class enthusiasm for the idea, will be confronted a little later on. What is particularly relevant here is that new forms of social ownership utterly different from the traditional concepts of nationalization are possible.

Now, let us make the happy assumption that, in both the public and private sectors, socialists actually institutionalize the participation of working people in economic decision making. Even then, it must be remembered that socially disastrous decisions can be made by democratic enterprises. That is, socialization has to do with the content as well as the procedures of decision making, and there is no reason to assume that the one necessarily insures the other. The Tennessee Valley Authority (TVA) is one of the few American examples of successful public ownership in the generation of power and flood control. The TVA Board of Directors — appointed by the President with congressional approval — meets in public places, and any citizen can listen to their deliberations. Yet in the postwar period the TVA was as socially irresponsible about the environmental consequences of strip-mining coal as any private company.

How does society discipline nationalized — and all other — industries to respect the environment? By measures that are, at a minimum, national in scope and in some cases parts of international ecological agreements. That is, it is necessary to guard against the "collective egoism" of social property as well as against the rapaciousness and irresponsibility of firms bent on maximizing profit.

Thus far, the possibilities of social ownership have all focused on the difficult cases: industries that, of technical necessity, are likely to remain large-scale over the next half century. This is the sphere where a socialized nationalization, the democratization of some of the functions of private capital, and wage-earner funds are most relevant. But there are, we have seen, much more radical, decentralist, and communitarian possibilities opened up by the new technology.

In Europe in the seventies, there was growth in the number of cooperatives and worker-owned enterprises. In Northern Italy, for instance, small, flexible machine shops controlled by skilled workers have proliferated. In Britain in the seventies, the Labour Party successfully encouraged the co-ops (a trend that was partially reversed by the dogmatic privatism of Margaret Thatcher's governments). And even in the United States, traditionally the most conservative Western economy, the crisis of the seventies and eighties led to worker-owned enterprises (usually, failing companies taken over at considerable sacrifice by their own workers).

It must, alas, be stressed that this trend is as ambiguous as every other tendency in the late twentieth century. Critics of the more romantic accounts of those small Italian machine shops point out that they are sometimes based on the hyperexploitation of family labor. And in the United States, the law facilitating Employee Stock Ownership Plans (ESOPs), which has been used to convert some corporations from private to worker ownership, has often been ingeniously manipulated by non-owning managers to perpetuate their own control and to exclude the theoretical "owners" from any real decision making.

Business Week reported on a classic case of the way in which the old authoritarian relations hold even when the workers "own" a plant within a capitalist context. In 1984, the workers at Wierton Steel in West Virginia created an Employee Stock Ownership Plan and took over a company that would have shut down if they had not acted. The Independent Steel Workers union at Wierton accepted a 20 percent wage cut and a six-year wage freeze as part of the deal. The experiment worked and was often cited as one of the most positive cases of worker ownership in the United States. But by the end of 1988, even though Wierton had been making money, management wanted still more sacrifice: a reduction in profit-sharing payments to the employees from 50 percent to around 33 percent and the right to sell up to 20 percent of the corporate shares to the public in order to dilute the degree of workers' control. All of this was justified in the name of keeping the enterprise "competitive."

There are two critical lessons in this case. First, and this is particularly true in the Employee Stock Ownership Plan structure so often used in worker buyouts in the United States, the rank-and-file's "ownership" can and does remain quite nominal in many situations in which they theoretically "own" a company. Second, it is extremely difficult to build an island of social cooperation in an economy based fundamentally on competition at the expense of the vulnerable. Antisocial priorities are imposed by the market upon the workers even when they do have the vote on the Board of Directors. This is not to disparage all attempts at such worker ownership in a transitional effort to begin to change the nature of the system; it is to emphasize once again how hard it is to change the system when you play by the system's own rules.

Working at home is another important case in point. Until the rise of the capitalist factory, most people worked either in their homes or in the immediate vicinity. The physical isolation of production, the need to "commute" to and from the plant, was part of the overall fragmentation of life carried through by the new system. At the same time, the early unions often had to fight against home work because it was a brutal means of mobilizing cheap child labor. But now, with computers, it is technically possible for there to be a new growth in home-based labor that could undercut union standards and give rise to new kinds of exploitation, *or* provide the foundation for much more flexible and liberating modes of work. Some of the German socialists have already suggested that the movement try to maximize the positive possibilities of this development within a commitment to union standards of work and pay.

We are not, in short, on the eve of some easily achievable technological utopia; here, as everywhere else in the modern world, the ambiguous social consequences of the new inventions will be decided by political, and — dare one say it? — novel forms of class, struggle. At the same time, it may well be possible to go back to some of the ideas of socialist worker self-management that were elaborated in France before the electoral victories of 1981.

There was a rich socialist and trade-union literature in France analyzing how decentralized, autonomous worker enterprises could contribute both to the democratization of social relationships, which is of enormous importance, and to efficiency and productivity. When the socialist government of 1981 ran up against economic realities that forced a retreat, the most innovative of its proposals, like worker self-management, were the first to be dropped or modified. The Auroux laws gave union representatives more time off during working hours, required annual negotiations on wages in plants of a certain size, gave more power to the health and safety committees, and defined new rights of free expression in the factory. These measures represented significant gains for French unions, which had even fewer rights than many of their Western counterparts.

But the Auroux laws, contrary to the original proposals for self-management, did not really empower the workers to make any decisions. They provided only that workers have certain rights to be heard when choices were to be made. The French employers, like their Swedish equivalents, reacted to these rather minimal intrusions upon their authoritarian prerogatives as if a new reign of terror were under way. And the socialists, sorely beset by the attacks of international finance capital, were fairly quick to abandon a part of their program that could not possibly succeed under conditions of austerity. But it would be tragic if those special circumstances were taken to be a definitive judgment on the merits of the idea itself.

There is, however, one rather sobering problem with all of these notions of participatory democracy on the shop and office floors. What if the workers themselves are simply not interested in participating?

In Sweden there was no large popular outpouring on behalf of the more radical version of the wage-earner funds. On the contrary. The polling data showed indifference and even hostility on the part of many working people. Is it, then, right to assume that the direct producers are really anxious to take their "destiny" in hand? Aren't they, rather, concerned with more mundane issues of wages and hours, and even negative about taking on more responsibility at work?

The answer is not only yes, but also that it could not be otherwise. The capitalist attack on artisanal skill, the whole historic process that created a semi- and unskilled labor force, has left a deep impression on society. Labor was widely degraded to the status of a painful means to the pleasurable end of consumption. Under such circumstances, the pessimism about seeking any positive values in work itself expressed by André Gorz in *Farewell to the Workingclass* — a book that looked for social salvation exclusively in the domain of leisure time — was, in some measure, justified. But the circumstances could change, and socialists should not, in any case, turn their backs on such a critical category of human experience as work.

For one thing, the new technology is creating, precisely, new kinds of work. It is, as Gorz failed to understand, *reskilling*. Even more to the point, Zuboff points out that the way in which the hardware and software of the new technology is designed opens up — or closes off — possibilities of much more creative forms of work for masses of people in offices as well as in plants. We should not, then, simply sit back and see if the new forms of work are going to engage people's intelligence. *We should make the engineering of technology a political question, insisting that industry of every kind try to create machines that make jobs creative and interesting.*

Second, there is a sense in which indifference to decision making in the workplace expresses a realism limited to a particular situation, not some deep reluctance to participate that is part of human nature. Specifically, many workers rightly concluded that their active involvement in union activity would not really enable them to affect anything that really mattered in their daily lives. Whenever they did feel that their participation could make a difference, they acted. In the United States, for instance, the rank and file are notorious for not attending union meetings. But when there is a vote on whether or not to accept a management offer, or to go out on strike, there are typically huge turnouts. If, say, the French socialists had been able to legislate something more than advisory functions for those at the base in the early eighties, the response might have been — and could still be — much more positive.

But there is no need to minimize this problem, to dispose of it with the cliché that changed conditions will make for changed attitudes. We are dealing here with the fact that the existing system does not prepare people for socialization, that one is talking of a psychic and cultural change in society and not just of this or that reform of the labor laws. This means that the new socialism has to be as concerned about education and culture as it is about the economy.

There is, however, an even more fundamental problem. All of the innovations in social ownership will work only if there is growth and full employment. To be sure, there are solid empirical reasons to believe that the democratization of economic decision making will result in a tremendous increase in productivity. But we have already seen that those productivity gains themselves might pose a new problem, making it possible to increase output enormously while minimizing human involvement.

Even if one begins to create an institutional framework for the new modes of work, that leaves the problem socialists failed to solve in the 1970s and early '80s: how to control a wrenching economic transition and create a new and progressive social structure of accumulation.[2]

III

ECONOMIC POLICY MUST deal with events that cannot be foreseen and that, particularly in this period, are likely to be surprising, even violations of the "normal" calculus inherited from a different time. One of the few predictions that can be made at the present with some degree of assurance is that much of the future is going to be unpredictable. Further complicating matters, the ability of socialists to introduce long-range, structural changes in a democratic society will be decided by their success in the short run. Effective political coalitions do not win elections on the basis of what they will do for the voters' grandchildren. That is an increasingly important aspect of politics in the age of ecological crisis, but in the main, power is going to go to movements that respond to the problems people have here and now.

It would therefore be preposterous to think that a book looking toward the middle of the next century can be specific about what to do in five years, much less in fifty. What it can do is to set forth some crucial themes and values. The goal can be stated clearly enough: quality economic growth by means of increasing social justice and democratic participation. The assumption of the Keynesian social democracy that, with some adjustments at the edges, corporate-based growth would generate the solution to most of society's problems has to be abandoned. John F. Kennedy made a classic statement of this attitude when he said, "A rising tide lifts all boats." We now know from the experience of the last quarter century that that is not true (and Kennedy himself had begun to suspect that fact). Indeed, one can fairly say that a rapidly rising tide will now sink some boats.

Granted that, even in the short run, the technological revolution requires active government intervention beyond the fiscal and monetary stimulation of growth, how does one achieve a quality and productive full employment? What follows is not *the* answer to that question, but some of the elements that could well be part of the answers.

First there is an international — and regional — "Keynesian" component to the socialist strategy.

National Keynesianism, we have seen, no longer works in a transnational economy. The experience of the French socialists in the early eighties was a dramatic confirmation of that fact as the stimulus decreed in Paris helped to create markets — and jobs — for the West Germans and Japanese at the expense of the French. Even the seeming exception to this rule, the rapid growth generated by Ronald Reagan's military spending and governmental deficits in 1983 and 1984, proves the national limitations on Keynesian policies. That growth was internationally financed, and it took place in the only market that is the economic equivalent of all of Europe.

There lies a clue to the socialist future. The previous chapter showed that an internationalist politics directed toward the Third World could spur growth in the First World as well as in the poor countries. That should be seen by the socialists of the advanced world as a critically important positive factor in their domestic program and not just as an obligation of solidarity. The French socialists, it might be objected, tried to do precisely that in 1981 but rapidly retreated from their commitment to a global New Deal. But that was because France, a medium-sized economy in the midst of a global recession, could not carry out such a policy on its own.

But perhaps an entity as large as a unified Europe could. Europe after the 1992 structural changes in the Economic Community is critical for the revival of *world* socialism. The Continent, with its social-democratic mass movements and traditions, could take the lead in an internationalist economic policy that, among many other things, would create new domestic alternatives for the Europeans. François Mitterrand, in his "Letter to all the French," suggested as much during the 1988 presidential campaign. He stressed the existing successes of the European Space Agency, the production of the Airbus, and the plans for a network of high-speed European trains based on the technology already pioneered in France.

There is also the possibility that events in the Soviet Union and Eastern Europe will broaden that European perspective even more. It is obviously impossible to predict the outcome of the current attempts to overcome the waste and bureaucratic inefficiency of the Stalinist — and Brezhnev — heritage. But if the reformers prevail, there is the potential of extending the European orientation to the Urals. Moreover, as the next chapter will explore, European social democrats might facilitate this development in a post–Cold War world.

The socialist economic policy of the next fifty years must also emphasize productive, job-generating investments and attack the wastefulness of "casino" capitalism.

When Helmut Schmidt was the social democratic chancellor of Germany in the seventies, he made a famous comment that the profits of today are the investments of tomorrow and the jobs of the day after. That was part of the Keynesian euphoria of the times, and it naively assumed that investment would generate rather than destroy jobs and that capital had become a responsible social agent. Even as Schmidt was coining his aphorism, that explosion of financial speculation to which we have given the Keynesian label of the "casino society" was taking place. There was a tremendous surge of "investments" in financial instruments that had only a tenuous connection to the real world of the economy and that generated jobs for stockbrokers but not for displaced steelworkers.

The investment banker Henry Kaufman of Salomon Brothers made a shrewd analysis of this phenomenon in 1986: "Funds sought financial assets, given that there was no need to finance real economic activity" under the sluggish conditions of the seventies and eighties. "Paper entrepreneurship" became, especially in the United States, a substitute for the production of goods and services. Between 1950 and 1960, the ratio of debt to GNP hovered around 1.5; by 1985, it was two times GNP. Even material investments were affected by this trend: they went disproportionately to the hardware and software of a financial industry that expanded rapidly even as the economy itself was in deep trouble. The mergers and buyouts — or the defenses mounted against them — that were part of this same trend were funded largely by borrowed money and often had the consequence of doing real-world injury to productive corporations.

The bull market of the 1980s went through five years of continuous expansion in which the values of stocks had little or no relationship to what was happening in the economy. The result was the "correction" of October 1987, when the New York Stock Exchange saw 20 percent of its presumed worth vanish in the course of a single, traumatic day. More important, this "meltdown" was international, further proof that the American forms of financial speculation had infected the world.

In part, the "casino society" can be seen as an expression of a profound ambiguity in the very language of contemporary capitalism. The same word, *invest*, is used to describe two very different actions: using money to create wealth-producing assets; devoting money to speculation. This confusion is, of course, fundamental to the system. But during the last two decades, it has become a gigantic force in the growth of a particularly parasitic version of it.

Making a clear distinction between these two very different actions, in the practice of governments as well as in economic theory, must be an important aspect of socialist policy in the next period. In the process, a point made by Keynes in the "utopian" last chapter of the *General Theory* has to be expanded. Given his theory that it was the prospect of making profits from satisfying consumer demand, and not the existence of a pool of savings, that stimulated investment, Keynes argued that the economic case for inequality was subverted. The rich, it had been said, had to be paid handsomely for saving and investing their money rather than consuming it. But now that it was clear that investment was spurred by the profits to be made from satisfying consumption, rather than by the abstemiousness of the wealthy, that claim no longer held. Indeed, insofar as it counseled austerity at a time of crisis, it was gasoline on a fire. And if, under conditions of full employment, there were inadequate investment funds, Keynes concluded, that problem could be met by "communal savings."

That Keynesian notion can now be expanded in terms of the events of recent years. The wasteful "casino society," which can do positive harm to the economy, clearly has no right to the enormous rewards that contemporary capitalism confers upon it. Moreover, it is now obvious that retained profits, pension funds, and insurance money — each in its own way a nonindividualistic, "collective" form of saving — are much more important for investment in wealth-producing assets than the decisions of the rich. And all of this gets back to some very important ABCs that were cited earlier.

We know that deductions have to be made from current production in order to finance depreciation and future investment; that will be true in a dynamic socialist society as well as under capitalism. But that does not imply that enormous rewards to banks, brokerage houses, and other financial institutions are justified, particularly when they spend more of their time and energy in wasteful pursuits. Ironically, during the next period, socialists may come to be the champions of a traditional "Protestant ethic" that links rewards to work done in the real world. But they will do so in ways that will maximize egalitarianism and social justice. For it is not only possible but absolutely necessary to link equity with growth and efficiency. Let us be specific.

Tax policy should be used to direct wealth into jobs and production. That can be done in a variety of ways: by giving preferential treatment to capital actually invested in people and work and discriminating against the speculative uses of money; by a levy on passive and parasitic wealth; by inheritance laws that limit the right of passing control over economic decisions from one generation to the next (by distinguishing, as some of the French socialists have proposed, between the transmission of cash and the transfer of voting rights in enterprises); and more generally by "limiting the rewards of success and the punishments of failure" in society. On this last case, we know that the most dynamic capitalist economy of the recent past, Japan, has *less* of a differential between the top and bottom quintiles of income recipients than any Western society.

All of these policies can be justified in terms of maximizing investments, environmental quality, productivity, efficiency, and growth and minimizing the scandalous capitalist wastefulness that became so marked in the seventies and eighties. But at the very same time, such measures move in a direction the social-democratic welfare state, even in its heyday, never followed: toward making the distribution of income and wealth more equal.

In this context, the profound implications of the "collective capital formation," which was a critical element in the original version of the Swedish wage-earner funds, should be pursued. In this case, a policy that contributes to investment and job generation is also a means of economic decentralization, something that management, as we have seen in the case of the new technology as well as in the response of Swedish business to the Meidner proposal, or the funds, opposes, using the rhetoric of individual rights as a screen for the defense of monopoly power.

In this perspective, the workers do not share individualistically in the profits of the enterprise — which usually translates into small amounts of money and zero power. Rather, they share as a collectivity in the social and economic power that those profits have traditionally purchased for the elite. In a time when most trade unionists have been forced to realize that managerial decisions about investment and technology affect their individual fate even more than the determination of wages, such a proposal is not simply an exercise in economic democracy. It is a pragmatic means of defending the immediate interest of working people.

There is also the potential for what an eminently procapitalist American analyst, Peter Drucker, calls "pension fund socialism." In the United States, with its minimal welfare state and its huge outlays for "fringe benefits," corporate pension funds, which are nominally the property of the workers, own a major portion of the American economy (the *Wall Street Journal* estimated their assets in 1988 at $3 trillion). Drucker, totally ignoring the fact that this "ownership" is a legal fiction conferring no real power over how those monies are invested, concluded that the American workers actually were in control of the means of production. Still, that argument, too clever by half, deserves to be taken seriously in ways that would disturb Drucker, who was concerned with rationalizing corporate management.

The Swedish socialists, as is so often the case, provide an interesting example of how this might be done. In the fifties, there was a bitter dispute — in which capital reacted with some of the virulence it was to later exhibit in its response to the Meidner proposal — when the Social Democrats proposed to "fund" the public pension system, that is, to actually invest current payments in order to pay for future benefits on the model of private insurance. The conservatives were aghast because this would create a huge reservoir of monies that would be democratically invested through the government. Needless to say, their predictions of impending tyranny did not come to pass when the measure was actually put into effect. In 1988, Robert Kuttner, one of the most thoughtful men of the American democratic Left, outlined how a similar program for the advanced funding of health care for the aging could help resolve the problem of investment in the United States.

The new socialists, then, should consider how to implement the principle that workers and communities should have an important say in the allocation of all funds set aside, whether privately or publicly, for social benefits. The point should certainly not be one of putting those funds to the riskiest, but most socially decent, uses. People want pensions from pension funds, not moral satisfaction. But with shrewd democratic management, government guarantees, and a certain mandatory pooling of risks, that self-interest can be protected within a framework of social responsibility. (In the United States the pension funds have historically yielded a *substandard* return for the beneficiaries, and it would be relatively easy for democratic management to outperform the private sector.)

These are a few of the ways — illustrative rather than exhaustive — in which the "social socialization" of investment can be more effective, as well as more just, than its corporate collectivization, which is the present fact in a free market disguise. Education and research are two more critical areas for the new socialism, particularly as a response to the transformation of work and the coming necessity of more leisure time.

Education was, in the Western world, one of the very first functions to be socialized. The public schools of the nineteenth century made a massive contribution to productivity and economic growth by continuously upgrading the quality of labor. With the emergence of new modes of work dependent on the application of science to production, this truism becomes even more compelling. If the new computers and robots remain mysterious agencies that are not at all understood by those who tend them, then their enormous potential will be unnecessarily truncated. Clearly, the cognitive skills of the workers are now taking on an importance that was systematically denied to them during the heyday of Fordist mass production.

It is thus significant that, in 1988, *Business Week* devoted a cover story to the problems of recruiting workers in the United States. With the "baby bust" in the marketplace and rising skill requirements even in many entry-level jobs, corporations are spending an enormous amount of time and money finding takers for the least demanding openings. Under these circumstances, the catastrophic decline in educational achievement among the poor — symbolized by the fact that more than 50 percent of the black students in the high schools of New York drop out before they complete the course — is a disaster for both the individual and the economy.

This is so obvious that everyone has understood the point, and not always in ways that will promote the kind of education we need. Shoshana Zuboff has, as we have seen, documented how management, in the course of defending its own authority and prerogatives, often tries to limit the knowledge of the workers to the minimum needed to run the new systems. The other side of that coin is that management — and in this context, whether it is private or public — has its own stunted concept of how the new investments in education should be applied. There is thus a distinct danger that schooling, including higher education, could become totally subordinated to the narrow imperatives of the production system.

It is clearly desirable to have members of the underclass trained in the minimal, functional skills that will enable them to escape the economic underworld. Conversely, in the words of the Office of Technology Assessment, "the combination of technology and large numbers of entry-level people with poor basic education could force (or tempt) employers to produce large numbers of jobs requiring minimal training for people considered interchangeable and disposable." But socialists have to look beyond even this very important point for at least two crucial reasons. One pragmatic reason is that the rounded development of human beings that goes beyond particular skills and enables people to respond to new situations is essential if the new technology is going to be both fully effective *and* liberating. The second has to do with preparing people for a society of leisure time.

The expansion of free time in which people act on their own projects and desires rather than submitting to economic compulsion is a central idea of the new socialism. This demand has utopian possibilities and immediate and very practical applications.

The urban factories of capitalism changed the very rhythms of life. In the predominantly agricultural societies in which most of humanity had lived until the seventeenth and eighteenth centuries, the seasons dictated the pace of effort as well as the liturgies of religion and the celebrations of community. There were times of intense labor — and long periods in which people did not work. One of the first fruits of the capitalist revolution was the fourteen-hour day in England — and the struggle of working people to shorten it. With the separation of work and home and the need to commute, the producers saw most of their lives organized around the working day.

The new technology has already begun to transform this pattern, often negatively. That is, there was a reallocation of working time in the 1970s in the advanced economies in which shocking percentages of the labor force were condemned to the involuntary "free time" of unemployment and economic irrelevance. In Europe, the unions have responded with the demand for maximizing employment by reducing the standard work week. But precisely because this idea is so important, its complexities have to be recognized. If it is treated as a simple panacea it could well be discredited.

To begin with, manufacturing will not, and must not, disappear from the advanced societies in the next half century. Automation is not an end in itself but a way of producing goods more efficiently. If, as Stephen Cohen and John Zysman have suggested, an economy decided to specialize only in the design of robotized factories, shipping the actual work abroad, it would soon fail, for it would have no connection with the practical problems that are the spur to innovation. Even more basic, the contemporary advanced societies have enormous needs for physical investments in environmental protection, public infrastructure, and the facilities to make free time meaningful. When one considers the needs of the Third World and the perspective of a North-South alliance for global justice, this point becomes still more compelling.

Within the most technologically advanced societies, it is precisely the growth of industrial productivity that provides the basis for the radical expansion of free time. If, as Richard Lowenthal believes, the government adopts a policy of reducing working hours but not wages in a period of declining production, the private sector — or for that matter, worker self-managed enterprises — will not hire anyone new, and in fact will try to cut the work force. But if industrial productivity is growing, then there are resources to cut hours and raise wages; those are simply two ways of allocating the gains of productivity. The French socialist government of 1981 was committed to the thirty-five-hour week but encountered these constraints.

There were simply not enough resources in France to finance a rapid 12.5 percent pay increase (which could have been the result of decreeing forty hours' pay for thirty-five hours of work). The socialists therefore proposed work sharing instead: thirty-five hours of work at thirty-five hours of pay, which would have created some openings for the unemployed. Most of the unionists were opposed to taking a pay cut even if it expressed solidarity with the jobless. As a result, there was only a minimal decrease in working time and wages, and the employment effect was correspondingly reduced. Significantly, the goal has not been abandoned — it was reaffirmed by François Mitterrand and the party during the 1988 presidential campaign. But clearly, it can be attained only in a period of economic expansion.

Critical as the demand for free time is, it is wrong to envision an utterly automated society of abundance in the next half century. The "postindustrial society" becomes possible only through a new social structure of accumulation for industrial society. Moreover, a mere reduction in time, even with stable or higher wages, will create new problems — the problems of leisure time.

If society moves toward the four-day week, or the six-hour day, it is taking steps to change the working life or, for that matter, life itself. A social reality in which people spend less than half of their waking hours in the orbit of necessary labor is going to produce a new culture. What kind? Will the free time be organized by private corporations in order to maximize profits? Will it be spent passively, in watching electronic spectacles?

The workplace, as Max Weber understood, conferred an identity on capitalist men and women. In the United States, where this tendency has been carried to its extreme, almost any social encounter begins with the phrase, "What do you do?" for it is the shortest and simplest way to say, "Who are you?" But if what one "does" — paid work — becomes less important, what is the new source of personal and social identity? Ideally, from a socialist point of view, people will now be able to choose rather than submit to their lives. But the capitalist present does not prepare them to do that, for it is based on the old hierarchies and identities. Therefore, education has to do much more than simply prepare individuals for a more effective participation in their working lives. It has to open up possibilities of a creative and expanding nonworking life.

This means that there must be planning that permits people to be spontaneous — physical investments in the facilities, the theaters, athletic fields, do-it-yourself shops, and all the rest — which will open up new possibilities. In this context, education cannot be conceptualized as merely technical or as primarily confined to the early years of life. Clearly, attention has to be paid to the cognitive skills that will allow people to participate creatively in an increasingly democratic economy. But there are also areas of intellectual and cultural importance that have no great economic utility but enable people to lead richer lives. One thinks of music, art, poetry, or, for that matter, hobbies and sports. If society is to open up greater possibilities for the individual, education has a role to play that need not be linked to productivity at all.

The same point applies to research and development. Science as applied to production is, by its nature, social in content even if it is manipulated by private corporations. It is, as Marx understood, a form of "universal labor" that involves the collaboration of the present generations with the accomplishments of the past. And it is not "value-free," a matter of engineering and technique, for value-laden purposes inform research. Indeed, as the last chapter indicated, scientific technology is now international and a potential threat to the survival of the species. Therefore, the proposal for the socialization of the public funds already being used to aid corporate priorities is not simply a matter of democratizing outlays that are social in their very nature. Beyond that, socialist research and development should envision different kinds of technologies from the ones created for the private sector. For part of the scientific mission will be to search out creative and humane technologies.

Implicit in this last point — and in the entire discussion of the way in which social justice and practicality are linked in the socialist project — is an important notion that needs elaboration.

The social consequences of the technological revolution demand not simply new and different kinds of machines but new concepts, and even new statistics, to help us make new kinds of decisions. New statistics? For most people, statistics are not a matter of choice and value but of describing facts. In reality, though, the numbers and concepts now used routinely as the basis for political discussion in the advanced capitalist democracies are based on specific theories, and are only about a half century old. Quantifications like Gross National Product, Gross Domestic Product, National Income, and the like, are aggregates derived largely from Keynes's analysis. Indeed, the American

Employment Act of 1946 created the Council of Economic Advisors, which has turned out to be one of the most successful institutions of mass education in history. It has shaped the vocabulary of economic debate and defined the relevant numbers.

That development represented progress over the mainstream economics that predated Keynes. But those Keynesian concepts and statistics are value-laden. "Gross National Product" is, after all, truly a gross measure and certainly a very capitalist one. It assumes that any activity that yields a profit — be it the production of carcinogenic cigarettes or automobile engines that contribute to acid rain — is to be given a positive weight. If the GNP goes up, no matter what its composition, it is thought that the society is advancing. But that advance could well be a stride toward catastrophe, for example, toward a greenhouse effect that will threaten life itself.

Socialists should therefore propose a new set of statistics based on the QNP and the QIP — the Qualitative National, and International, Product. Constructing such measures will take considerable ingenuity and must be a work of serious research, but the basic idea can be fairly simply put. After computing the Gross National Product, one then subtracts from it all environmental degradation, premature death, wasteful packaging, and uninformative advertising in order to arrive at a figure for a Qualitative Product. And the global costs and benefits of national production have to be calculated as well. If such a series of statistics were available, the relevant facts of political debate would be radically redefined and there would be different kinds of conclusions.

Our minds, our numbers, our daily practices, and our national and international governance have to change if we are to be equal to the revolution that is already under way. If this epochal transformation of human life continues under the control of corporate bureaucracies in the West and undemocratic planners in the Communist world, it will be stunted and likely wasteful. The elites will have to devote real resources to repressing the liberating possibilities of the new inventions. But if the new socialism is prepared to be as socially inventive as the new technologies, if it will pioneer in decentralized and communitarian forms of ownership and even in new kinds of statistics, then it can both move toward a new civilization and create the basis for a new social structure of accumulation.[3]

8

Market and Plan

CHINA, ONE HAS been told since Deng Xiaoping's market-oriented reforms began in the late seventies, is becoming capitalist. So is the Soviet Union under Gorbachev. And similarly with Hungary, Angola, Vietnam, and all the other economies that were once centrally planned and have now introduced markets to achieve efficient production.

If this were simply one more example of a superficial journalistic dichotomy — either a society is planned and socialist or relies on markets and is capitalist — it would not be too bothersome. But it goes beyond that. Serious scholars also employ this facile distinction. And there are still some socialists who feel that tolerating markets may be a political necessity but somehow compromises the basic vision.

The fact is, we cannot evaluate or even describe the workings of markets independent of the social structure in which they operate. The "free choice" of goods, jobs, or investments is one thing in a *laisser-faire* economy of extreme inequality; another in a monopoly or oligopoly system; still another in a democratic welfare state; and quite different in a Communist dictatorship. And, under conditions that must be carefully specified, free choice — without quotation marks — would have a completely new, and potentially positive, significance in any foreseeable transition to a socialist society. In other words, generalizations about the meanings of markets in the abstract are all suspect.

In a sense, the superficial dichotomy of plan and market, an abstraction *par excellence*, is the heir — usually the unwitting heir — of a central tradition in capitalist thought. In that perspective, there is an economic "human nature" that exists throughout history even if it is imperfectly developed in precapitalist societies. The stone tool of paleolithic humanity is thus an embryonic form of capital, the precursor of an automated factory. And a market is a market is a market. Thus the announcement of the emergence of capitalism in China or the Soviet Union is made triumphantly as a proof that the eternal verities have again prevailed.

The point is not just to make a critique of a bad theory. It is to understand the very different relations between planning and markets in various societies, and to free the socialism of tomorrow from the guilt-laden assumption that a market in a social order of increasing equality and popular democratic control is somehow as reprehensible as a market that functions to provide shacks for the poor and mansions for the rich.

Let me put my point most paradoxically: only under socialism and democratic planning will it be possible for markets to serve the common good as Adam Smith thought they did under capitalism.

I am not proposing that the new socialism project a market utopia. In the advanced welfare states, socialists have already removed critical areas of life from the market economy — in every one of them, except that of the United States, basic health care is collectively financed and provided without reference to income — and that process will and should continue. Indeed, the "decommodification" of life is a critical aim of the new socialism. The actual functioning of some of the most important contemporary markets — the capitalist world market that integrates North and South, for instance — is viciously and completely at odds with the virtues still imputed to them. I simply insist that, in the dimly foreseeable and utterly international future of, say, the next fifty years, markets can be an important instrument of free choice rather than of perverse maldistribution if, but only if, they are reorganized within a socialist context. Under those circumstances, the heirs of Karl Marx may well vindicate the hopes of Adam Smith.

I

IT MAY SEEM STRANGE that I begin an analysis of current and future markets by going back to Marx. But, as Keynes said, the pragmatic, no-nonsense proponents of the simplistic plan/market dichotomy often repeat abstractions more than a century old. Marx, I am afraid, is a major source of the current confusion, in part because he provides solid authority for contradictory positions. Even more to the point, a careful reading of *Das Kapital* yields, of all things, a Marxist methodology capable of grasping the positive potential of markets even as that book brilliantly denounces their functioning under *laisser-faire*.

At first glance, there seems to be no ambiguity. It is, one would think, painfully obvious that Marx equated markets with capitalism and socialism with their abolition. The opening chapter of *Das Kapital* defines the "commodity" as the nucleus of the capitalist system. The commodity, of course, is not simply a useful good or service but a useful good or service that is produced to be sold on a market at a profit. Commodities, Marx argued, have existed ever since human beings, in the mists of time, went beyond subsistence production and began to make things to exchange with one another. It is only with the rise of capitalism, however, that commodity production — market production — becomes the dominant activity of an entire society. Is it not inescapably clear, therefore, that the system is *defined* by markets?

Those markets, Marx continues, are pernicious. Where people produced for their own needs — in families, tribes, or self-contained communities — there was misery as a result of the low level of economic development and periodic hunger and famine when the harvest failed or the fishing gave out. But there were not such things as overproduction and underproduction, no economic breakdown that occurred because there was "too much" to be sold at a profit. It was only with the domination of commodity production that poverty resulted from glut. At the same time that this market process regularly plunged masses into a social abyss, it enormously increased the wealth of the successful rich. Markets were, Marx held, engines of social inequality, reproducing elite domination as well as physical products.

So far, the attack on the market is straightforward and principled. But then, when he turns to his central theory of exploitation, Marx becomes more complex. In the calculated over-simplification of his basic analysis — which generations have mistaken for a flawed description of the real world — it was assumed that raw materials, machines, and finance were all exchanged according to their value, and that sellers charged buyers a fair price. Where, then, was the source of profit? In the labor market. The workers sold their labor power like any other commodity. In theory, the resulting wage was the outcome of a bargain between equals, each of which was "free" to deal with the other. In reality, this was a deal between unequals: between a wealthy buyer and a precarious seller trying to keep body and soul together. *The content of the market agreement was, therefore, determined not by markets per se but by the social conditions under which the markets operated.*

So labor markets under capitalism, based on economic rather than political coercion, forced workers to "freely" sell their labor power at a fair value that produced more for the capitalist than it cost. But that opened up the possibility that if one changed the circumstances under which the wage bargain was made, the market outcomes would be different. In an analysis of a historic event of enormous importance for his theory, Marx went on to show that that was precisely what had taken place.

The discussion of the Ten Hours Law, which legally limited the working day in Britain, occupies a central place in Volume I of *Kapital* because it was the basis of a crucial distinction between "absolute" and "relative" surplus value. If one assumes that the worker produces enough to "pay back" his or her wage during only a portion of the working day, then an obvious way to increase profits is to extend that working day. That was the first capitalist strategy. As a result of this savage process, "every limit of morality and nature, of age and gender, of day and night, was destroyed." This was the drive for "absolute" surplus value.

But then, Marx continues, a number of things happened. The physical brutalization of the working class threatened its biological existence and thereby the future of the system itself. The landlords, still furious with the industrial capitalists for having abolished agricultural protectionism in order to cheapen the price of bread and thereby the subsistence wage, were willing to make common cause with the reformers and the workers, and to join in a campaign to put a limit on the working day. The official economists understandably predicted, of course, that such a move would destroy capitalism. In fact, Marx argued, it forced capital to seek more profits by increasing productivity, by working labor intelligently rather than working it to death. And one of the consequences of this political struggle was that capitalism now became oriented toward "relative" surplus value, toward getting more out of each hour of work rather than simply extending the hours. This was one of the many reasons why it was superior — economically and even morally — to the brutal exploitation of the past.

What is relevant here is that Marx regarded the Ten Hours Law — only a minimal humanization of the *laisser-faire* labor market — as nothing less than a "modest Magna Carta," as "the triumph of the political economy of the working class over the political economy of the middle class." A merely reformist change in structure of the labor market could profoundly affect the meaning of the market economy and even give rise to a new epoch in the history of capitalism. I anticipate: these texts provide clear warrant for the notion that, under the radically changed circumstances of a socialist-tending society, markets would have an utterly different meaning than under capitalist *laisser-faire*. Unfortunately, *Das Kapital* also provides solid reasons for arguing the contrary: that socialism must totally dispense with markets. Small wonder that matters get confused.

Ironically, Marx gets into this contradiction in the process of reiterating that markets do not have a fixed, immutable content. In fact, under capitalism they inexorably tend to turn into their opposite; it is the "historic tendency" of competition to culminate in monopoly. At that point, Marx argued, the pursuit of private profit no longer motivates the capitalist to act as the greedy agent of progress by constantly revolutionizing the productivity of the entire society. Now, monopolists "fetter" production precisely because they can dictate to markets and are therefore no longer subjected to the discipline of efficiency. As the system falters, the working class, which needs more productivity in order to raise its own living standard, becomes the economically dynamic class.

This means many things. What is particularly relevant here is that socialism is defined as a monopoly — a democratic, socially conscious monopoly, but a monopoly nevertheless, a system without effective markets. As Radoslov Selucky, who fully understands this contradiction, has put it, in this context "Marx's economic concept of socialism consists of a single social-wide factory based on vertical (hierarchical) relations of superiority and subordination." This is the planned, marketless society with a vengeance. But at the same time, Marx's "political concept of socialism consists of a free association of self-managed work and social communities based on horizontal relations of equality. Whoever accepts in full Marx's first concept has to give up the latter, and vice versa: they are mutually exclusive."

In short, even though Marx in one persona clearly rejected markets altogether, his methodology allows room for the assumption that the markets of a socialist future need not be anything like the markets of the capitalist past. And, more important, his basic political values, his commitment to freedom and human emancipation, are simply at odds with the consequences that follow from his own analysis of socialism as a centrally planned society, as a progressive monopoly. When Karl Kautsky concluded that in the good society the workers would not have the right to change their jobs at will — because there would be no labor markets — he had solid grounding in Marx *and* was contradicting the latter's vision of a truly free and communitarian association of the direct producers.

Piety about an ambiguous tradition should not, then, keep socialists from seeing that markets can and must play a role in the transition to a humane future. All one needs to do is to choose the libertarian Marx over the centralist Marx and then confront reality instead of texts.[1]

II

THE FIRST SOCIALISTS to confront reality, in the sense of actually taking responsibility for the organization of an entire economy, were the Bolsheviks. And their experience, as the Soviet rehabilitation of Nikolai Bukharin in the eighties testifies, is relevant to the present and future.*

---

*I regard communism as an antisocialist system of bureaucratic collectivism and do not see its history as part of the socialist tradition. But even though the Bolsheviks before Stalin, including Lenin, approved measures that laid the basis for the later tyranny, they were in the 1920s sincere and committed Marxists, however wrong, and their experiences do belong to that tradition.

The thesis that any reliance on markets is a sure sign of capitalism, so popular in the eighties with regard to China and the Soviet Union, first surfaced in the 1920s under Lenin's New Economic Policy (NEP). The antisocialist press gleefully reported that the Soviets were making the transition from communism to capitalism because they had turned to market forces, a judgment that turned out to be spectacularly wrong and about as substantial then as it is now.

In the 1920s Bukharin was, we have seen, a champion of "socialism at a snail's pace" that would make use of market incentives. But Trotsky, who was then Bukharin's principal antagonist and the chief defender of "planning" as against "markets," also recognized that the latter had a critical role to play throughout the entire period of transition. Trotsky was ultimately committed to the vision of a planned society that would dispense with markets; but he was equally emphatic that, on the road to that final goal, it was necessary to have a sound currency to measure the market value of investment costs and consumer goods. Stalinist planning — a command economy operated bureaucratically from a single center — was, he rightly thought, a political and economic disaster.

Before turning to Trotsky's advocacy of markets, however, two of Bukharin's particularly illuminating insights in this area are worth noting.

In a 1924 polemic, Bukharin raised the problem of the "tendency toward monopoly" in Soviet society. That, he said, could indeed allow the state to get an extra profit without any effort at all. "But isn't the result of that the danger of parasitism and stagnation? . . . Our economic administrators," he went on, "work for the proletariat, but they are not exempt from human weakness. They can doze off in a beatific quietude instead of being constantly concerned for progress toward communism." In order to keep up the pressure on the bureaucrats, Bukharin said, they must be driven to meet the needs of the people. That means the cheapest prices for the mass of consumers, which can be delivered only if the costs of production are kept to an absolute minimum. Efficiency was thus an imperative of the commitment to a higher living standard for all.

This theme — that the replacement for the capitalist profit motive was the drive to satisfy consumers — was shared by

Preobrazhensky, Trotsky's economic theoretician, who differed with Bukharin only in being much more confident that it would be effective. Stalin, of course, did exactly the opposite of what Bukharin and Trotsky proposed, that is, he cut consumption, turned the state into an absolute monopolist that financed the industrialization of the society precisely through the super profits that could be derived thereby. The result was a system that, by totalitarian pressure, could effectively squeeze resources out of workers and peasants *and* an economy that, as Mikhail Gorbachev realized in the 1980s, had all of the drawbacks Marx — and Bukharin — had ascribed to capitalist monopoly. The Soviet state, rather than the international bourgeoisie, became a "fetter" on production and productivity. In the West there were computers, in the East, the abacus.

In another essay, published in 1925, Bukharin speculated that in his final writings, Lenin had broken with his theory that the road to socialism was along the path of state capitalism, that is, the monopoly stage of capitalism. Lenin's remarks on the importance of cooperatives, Bukharin said, "puts us in the presence of a program that is totally different [from the perspective of state capitalism]." He quotes Lenin: "Now we have the right to say that the *simple development of cooperatives . . .* becomes identified for us *with the development of socialism itself.*" Did Lenin actually go that far? We will never know. But it is at least possible, and even plausible, that before he died, the Bolshevik leader sensed the dangers of centralization in a command economy, what he called "a bureaucratic utopia."

About Trotsky, we need not speculate. In a 1932 essay, "The Soviet Economy in Danger," he wrote:

> The innumerable living participants in the economy, state and private, collective and individual, must serve notice of their needs and of their relative strength not only through the statistical determinations of plan commissions but by the direct pressure of supply and demand. *The plan is checked and, to a considerable degree, realized through the market.* [emphasis added] . . . The blue prints produced by the departments must demonstrate their economic efficacy through commerical calculation.

In his critique of the Stalinist planners in *The Revolution Betrayed*, Trotsky commented that

> the obedient professors managed to create an entire theory according to which the Soviet price, in contrast to the market price, has an exclusively planning or directive character. . . . The professors forgot to explain how you can "guide" a price without knowing real costs, and how you can estimate real costs if all prices express the will of the bureaucracy and not the amount of social labor expended.

Socialist construction was unthinkable, Trotsky said in another passage, "without including in the planned system the direct personal interests of the producer and consumer, their egoism — which in its turn may reveal itself fruitfully only if it has in its service the customary reliable and flexible instrument, money."

There are two aspects to these statements by Trotsky and Bukharin. First, *both* the "Left" and "Right" Bolshevik critics of Stalin agreed that markets were an indispensable element in the transition to socialism (if not, to repeat, in the blessed "final state" of socialism itself). Without them, they argued, the system would become bureaucratic, wasteful, inefficient, and incapable of satisfying those basic human needs that were supposed to be the driving force, and the proof of the moral superiority, of the new economy. Second, Trotsky and Bukharin were right, as at least a portion of the present Soviet leadership has tacitly acknowledged (in Bukharin's case, the admission is even spoken aloud).

Stalin, however, settled the political argument by force and in the process liquidated both Trotsky and Bukharin. He proceeded to a version of total planning in which the omnipotent state swallowed up not just the economy but the whole of society as well.

This does not mean that there were no markets under Stalin. Even in the most extreme days of his rule, people bought consumer goods with money. But the basic decisions with regard to work, production, and consumption were made by a centralized bureaucracy, and almost all the institutions that might mediate between the government and the citizen were turned into "transmission belts" for official policy. In 1938 and 1940, for instance, it was decreed that workers would have a work book identifying their place of employment, that no one could leave a job on pain of criminal punishment for "flitting" from post to post; that the first offense of absenteeism would be punished by "forced labor at the place of employment" (which involved a 25 percent cut in wages), and the second offense by a mandatory jail sentence. This draconian attack on the rights of workers was introduced at the initiative of "trade unions" reduced to organs of state discipline. The most severe rules were not put in place under the siege conditions of World War II, but during the "peacetime" period when Stalin relied on his deal with Adolf Hitler.

The investment and production decisions were fixed according to planned, quantitative targets, which facilitated both waste and shoddy goods. If, a believable joke reported, a Soviet pin factory was assigned a quota of so many tons of pins, it would turn out one monstrously large and unusable pin; and if it were told to produce a certain number of pins, it would achieve the numerical goal with a myriad of pins so thin that they were also useless. The collective farms, as we have seen, were required to deliver their crops to the state at less than their cost of production. Consumer goods were manufactured not in response to demand, but according to a preset planners' decision, which meant that waiting in line to buy items in short supply became a major cause of squandered energy in the Soviet Union.

Yet this system, for all of its intolerable human and social costs, "worked," that is, it allowed the Soviets to create an industrial infrastructure in the space of a decade. Marx, as we have seen, gave capitalism enormous credit for having similarly raised the level of economic development by the savagery of "primitive accumulation" *and* denounced the process as morally vicious. But even if we leave morality aside, this kind of "planning" was laying the groundwork for the economic crisis of the seventies and eighties.

It is possible to make the initial physical investments in modernization in a brutal way. The slave laborers of the gulag could be, and were, driven to dig canals because the productivity of a person with a pick or a shovel is not of great moment. That is what the Soviets now refer to as "extensive" growth, and it corresponds to the period of "absolute surplus value" when capitalism thrived by working people to the edge of death. But the basis of a truly modern system, particularly in the age of automation and the computer, is "intensive" growth, an exponential increase in productivity that rests upon the facility of both human beings and machines. That requires a concern for the quality of work that slaves, or driven workers, will never exhibit. Even though the Soviet economy was significantly modified between Stalin's death in 1953 and Gorbachev's rise to power in the eighties, the institutional bias remained centralist, quantitative, "extensive," which all but guaranteed the declining growth rates of the last decade and a half.

In Stalin's day, however, there was little or no relief from bureaucratic commands backed up by a repressive state. It was this reality that gave rise to the theory of "totalitarianism," the idea that a totally controlled society without any real sources of internal opposition or change had actually come into existence. There was an attempt to mobilize the economy by a state that absorbed all of society into its dictatorial political system. In theorizing about this phenomenon, Hannah Arendt wrote in her influential *Origins of Totalitarianism* that "total domination succeeds to the extent that it succeeds in interrupting all channels of communication, those from person to person inside the four walls of privacy no less than the public ones which are safeguarded in democracies by freedom of speech and opinion." The aim, she said, was to make "every person incommunicado."

There were political consequences. If there were no possibility of internal change within the Stalinist empire, that made a hawkish Cold War policy of "liberation" all the more logical, since there was no hope that, as the original American "containment" theory of 1947–48 held, time and history would eventually soften Soviet policy. Arendt's book appeared in 1951 when Stalin was still alive; a second edition, with an epilogue to deal with the anti-Stalinist rebellions in both Poland and Hungary in 1956, came out in 1958. Even then, Arendt was convinced that the Khrushchev reforms in the Soviet Union had already run their course, that the system was returning to type.

On a more superficial — even frivolous — level, Friedrich Hayek, normally a serious thinker, declared in *The Road to Serfdom* that the British Labour government of 1945 was a precursor of a totalitarian system. This was an attempt to make the case that Stalinism was an inherent tendency of any socialism, even a democratic socialism, a proposition that has been refuted by every event that has occurred since it was first stated.

Stalinism terrified its external enemies as well as its own people. Yet it turned out that opposition and criticism had not been abolished as Arendt thought. Hardly was the tyrant dead than some of the most repressive features of the regime were modified. In 1956, Khrushchev gave his famous speech in which he began to acknowledge the bloody historical record. Contrary to Arendt's 1958 speculation that the event was a momentary aberration, the anti-Stalin campaign was most marked between the Twenty-second Party Congress of 1961 and Khrushchev's downfall in 1964. These were years in which the Soviet leader tried to energize the Party and the people behind a vision of a rapid transition to "communism," that is, to a consumer utopia in which the Communist bloc would enjoy higher living standards than the capitalist West. This was, Seweryn Bialer has argued, the last attempt to take the official ideological goals of Soviet society seriously, and Khrushchev "will pass into the annals of Soviet history as the last true believer in the ideals of the original Bolsheviks to hold a leadership position. His successors care about their own and their country's power, not about communism."

Still, when the gerontocratic, bureaucratic Brezhnev era followed the charismatic Khrushchev period, the Soviet government committed itself to raising the living standard of the workers and the collective farmers more than that of the new middle class. For one thing, this was a period of labor shortage, and that gave the factory hands, who were no longer tied to the job as under Stalin, some informal leverage. Also, there was considerable social mobility as the economy expanded in the postwar period and more and more bureaucrats and engineers had to be recruited from the children of those at the bottom.

In the process, however, a fateful bargain was sealed between the regime and the workers, one that is expressed in a venerable Soviet joke. The workers got security and a certain level of consumer comfort, but they were not expected to show initiative — a suspect quality in a "planned" society — and, in any case, the "extensive" growth structures inherited from Stalin were not built with creativity and productivity in mind. So, the saying went, the government pretended to pay the workers and the workers pretended to work. There was a national minimum, a welfare state for those at the bottom, but it was shoddy and the beneficiaries became conservative time servers. By 1983, Tatyana Zaslavskaya, a sociologist and economist who was connected with the reformist, Gorbachev wing of the Party, was writing about a catastrophic degeneration of the work ethic in Soviet society.

As early as 1970, Brezhnev admitted "that we have entered a stage of development that no longer allows us to work in the old way but calls for new methods and new solutions." Throughout the decade, there were discussions of very limited market reforms in calculating the real costs and benefits of investment and some interest in the changes taking place in Communist bloc countries such as Hungary. In 1978, the Soviet leader talked of "uninstalled equipment worth several billion rubles unused in warehouses." In July of 1979 an "avalanche" of reform and change was decreed — but nothing new happened.

The most dramatic break with Stalinist orthodoxy took place in China, not the Soviet Union, under the leadership of Deng Xiaoping.

Mao had turned on the Soviets as early as the late fifties. The "Great Leap" was a repudiation of the model of centralized command planning, of giant factories, and a celebration of the utopian potential of the people. But if the content of both the Great Leap and the Cultural Revolution was critical of Stalin's path and the Cultural Revolution in particular, the mode of leadership was still quite Stalinist. That is, Mao believed that he could "write" on the Chinese people whom he compared to a blank page. From on high he engineered a revolution from below, a reality that became quite apparent in mid-1968 when Mao turned off the enthusiasm of the Red Guards that he himself had originally decreed and relied on the army to enforce his will. Decisions were, in short, still made on a political basis by small cliques — or by one man — and behind closed doors.

Mao died in 1976, and there was an interregnum under Hua Guofeng that lasted until Deng took control in 1979. At that point the government decreed that individual peasant families, under the "household responsibility system," could — after paying their taxes, selling a quota of their output to the state, and meeting fees to the collective that still owned the land — dispose of their surplus in any way they wanted. Industrial enterprises were made more autonomous, and they, too, could decide how they used their surplus. Some radicals wanted to go further. They proposed to make the market, rather than the plan, the basis of the economy, to have "regulation" rather than control — and to significantly increase political pluralism. And some of them looked to the Four Tigers of East Asia as models of blending "private entrepreneurship with public ownership, market forces with government regulation, and organizational pluralism with political order" (the quotation is from Harry Harding's *China's Second Revolution*).

In the wake of the 1979 changes there were problems, and the moderates counterattacked the radicals. But in 1983 there was another period of reform, with enterprises given much more latitude to take initiatives on their own, a strengthening of the "household responsibility system," and a new emphasis on foreign trade. In the retail sector, markets became more and more important, the Sheraton and Holiday Inn chains began to manage hotels, capital markets were created, and some enterprises actually sold stock. At the end of 1984, the conservative columnist William Safire wrote in the *New York Times* that the biggest event of the year had been "the embrace of capitalism" by the Chinese Communist Party.

This assumed that markets per se, without any regard for their context and content, are always capitalist, an oversimplification not very helpful for explaining what is going on in China. In the midst of the reforms, for instance, Deng at all times insisted on "four cardinal principles": Marxism-Leninism, Mao Zedong thought, Party leadership, and continuation of the existing state structure. In 1986, two years after Safire's discovery of capitalism in China, 68.7 percent of the industrial output came from the state sector, 29.2 percent from collectives, and 0.3 percent from private enterprises. In retail, the respective figures were 39.4 percent, 36.4 percent, and 23.9 percent, which did indeed mark a significant shift. But exactly how a statified economy, run by a single party that uses markets to forward its own planned policies, qualifies as "capitalist" is a mystery.

As John King Fairbank put it, "Anyone who concludes that Chinese agriculture, having seen the light and wanting to be more like us, has gone 'capitalist' is making a grievous error. The contract system [Fairbank's translation of the "household responsibility system"] must be seen as the latest phase of statecraft, how to organize the farmers in order to improve their welfare and strengthen the state." A little later Fairbank writes:

> The Deng reforms are not bringing Western-style capitalism to China, except for the state capitalism of corporations that make deals with foreigners, but rather they are bringing an expanded form of what might be called "bureaucratic socialism". . . . In other words, a modernization that elsewhere has generally produced a new middle class, in China seems likely to produce a local and mid-level leadership that remains essentially bureaucratic.

There is no point in trying to suggest, as many who blithely assert that capitalism is about to work its magic in China have done, that Deng's shift will be accomplished in a painless way. In the areas of China specializing in export production, there are already abundant reports of child labor and other forms of exploitation that are reminiscent of the most ugly days of early capitalism. The Fordism that will come to such countries will be, in the phrase of three acute French analysts, "bloody" (*sanguinaire*).

At this writing, it is impossible to say how the economic reforms put into practice in the Soviet Union at the beginning of 1988 will change that society. Gorbachev has obviously decided to take seriously the need for "intensive growth," productivity, qualitative rather than quantitative measures of output, and the use of market criteria in investment policy. In a major report to the Party Central Committee in February 1986, the Soviet leader told his colleagues that "we must radically change the substance, organization and methods of the work of the financial and credit bodies. Their chief aim is not to exercise petty control over the work of enterprises but to *provide economic incentives and to consolidate money circulation and cost accounting, which is the best possible controller.*" (emphasis added)

That means a fundamental reorganization of the State Planning Committee, one of the most powerful bureaucracies in the society. It would also put the state in conflict with the least efficient enterprises. And it opens up the possibility, in a society that has prided itself on guaranteeing a job to every citizen (even if inefficiently), that unemployment, or at least firings, would become a necessary concomitant of market policies.

Dealing with that problem — putting market mechanisms at the service of social priorities rather than in command of the economy — is an area in which democratic socialists have contributions to make. But before turning to those specifics, it is important to locate the possibility of a democratic-socialist dialogue with Communist reformers in a much larger context.

It may well be that the changes now taking place within the Communist world define the beginnings of a new era in the relationship between democratic socialism and communism. The definitive split between those two ideologies occurred in the 1930s when Stalin appropriated a socialist rationale to create a new, antisocialist system. The resulting hostility was not based on misunderstanding. It was the consequence of a real-world conflict between fundamentally different conceptions — and the actual practice — of how to organize not simply society, but the world. And it was, of course, made all the more acute by the fact that most of the effective democratic-socialist parties in the world were European and supported the Atlantic Alliance in the Cold War.

That geographic dimension of the ideological quarrel was one of its most disturbing aspects, as Willy Brandt openly admitted when he became President of the Socialist International in 1976. Democratic socialism was "Western," largely confined to a European ghetto; communism was "Eastern" and a road of forced modernization for backward economies; and there was a nonaligned Third World in which, in most cases, "socialism" had strong authoritarian tendencies.

The economic and structural sources of that ideological geography have not been abolished simply because Communist reformers have changed their attitudes toward markets. China remains, for all of its real progress, a very poor country, subject to the vicious antisocialist constraints Marx outlined well over a century ago. The Soviet Union is obviously at a higher economic stage, but the institutional weight of its Stalinist history puts an enormous limit upon change. And it is, of course, true that in both the Soviet Union and China reform has come from concerned bureaucrats, none of whom propose mass democratic participation.

At the same time, the old-line Soviet conservatives, committed to defending the essential structure of the state, are right: it is extremely difficult to segregate economic and political change, to embark on a course of liberalization in the one sphere without opening up the other. It is not an accident that *glasnost*, with all of its evident limitations, and *perestroika* were introduced together. It is impossible to demand initiative and creativity from a labor force that, the moment it leaves the job, is not allowed to think aloud and to discuss freely. Does this mean that democratization will follow quickly and inevitably upon markets? Obviously not.

Yet, *possibilities* exist, not the least because no one knows where reform will lead. And that offers openings for democratic socialism that have not existed for more than half a century.

The internationalist commitment to linking disarmament and economic development in the Third World outlined in chapter 6 could create engines of growth in the First World, both capitalist and Communist. Without entertaining any illusions that the outbreak of peace would lead to the rapid democratization of Communist societies, it is nonetheless true that a negotiated end to the Cold War would create the conditions in which democratic tendencies in the East would have the greatest possible play. There is no way the socialists can intervene directly in Communist societies. But those democratic tendencies could be accentuated if the democratic socialists realized that they have some solutions to offer, through dialogue, to the reformers in the Communist countries.

One example: the adoption of market criteria of efficiency by Communist reformers could, we have just seen, mean that workers will lose their jobs in inefficient plants. But doesn't that show that the Communists are, willy-nilly, driven to accept the classic capitalist discipline, with its special cruelty toward those at the bottom? Not necessarily. For one of the most imaginative socialist attempts to deal with that problem — and one of the most creative illustrations of the use of markets within a planning framework — might become germane to the Communist reformers. I refer to the Swedish active labor market policies.[2]

III

AS FAR BACK AS the 1920s, the industrial unions of Sweden, the Swedish Labor Federation (LO), had declared their concern with the low-paid workers of the land and the forests. But it was not until 1936, with the metalworkers taking an important role, that the notion of a "solidaristic wage policy" came to the fore, and only in 1951 was it decisively formulated. According to that concept, the unions would use their bargaining power to reduce the wage differentials within the working class by maximizing the gains for the lowest paid in negotiations with the employers.

There were a number of reasons for adopting this attitude, one of which had to do with a refusal to accept the verdict of the existing labor markets. Under "normal" capitalist circumstances, the employees of the most backward sectors would receive lower wages than those who worked for advanced, highly competitive companies. But the labor movement, LO concluded, should favor the universalistic principle that there should be the same pay for the same expenditure of effort throughout the entire economy. That meant that the unions should have a conscious policy of reshaping the outcomes of the labor market. While this tactic was adopted on "trade union," not feminist, grounds, it was one of the reasons why women in Sweden were to reach near parity with men. They benefited from a policy directed not to their gender but to the inferior position to which the "normal" workings of markets would have assigned them.

That policy was definitively adopted in 1951. Then, however, the economic environment was completely different from that of the thirties. Instead of mass unemployment and depression, there were full employment and the danger of inflation. How could the solidaristic wage policy, and all the other social goals of the unions, be made compatible with price stability? The answer was formulated by two union economists, Gosta Rehn and Rudolf Meidner, and it was taken up by LO.

Ten years before economist A. W. Phillips published his famous article on the relationship between joblessness and wages, the Swedish unions had already identified what came to be known as the "Phillips Curve."* That was the theoretical basis in almost all of the Keynesian countries of the 1960s for the notion that there was an inevitable "trade-off" between full employment and price stability, something Keynes himself had believed and Phillips had documented as a historic fact during a century of British experience. But the Swedish unions and socialists were not willing to accept periods of unemployment, even at relatively low levels, in order to deal with inflation and to make other social priorities possible.

As Meidner and his associate Anna Hedborg put the LO attitude in a retrospective of the early 1980s: "It is not necessary to accept the trade-off of the classic Phillips curve and to make a choice which must ignore at least *one* extremely valuable social goal, either full employment or economic stability."

Prior to the adoption of the active labor-market policy, particularly in 1949–50, the Swedish unions had effectively experimented, as had their Western equivalents, with an "incomes policy" as a way of dealing with the problem. That is, the unions voluntarily accepted a two-year moratorium on wage increases and took upon themselves much of the responsibility for dealing with inflation. Relying on the "general" mechanisms of economic policy, it turned out, was a most fallible instrument for fighting wage increases. For despite the moratorium, there was an upward "wage drift," which was the result of local conditions, of pieceworkers making more money, of entire new categories of labor coming into the market, and of other factors that escaped the macroeconomic net.

Wage restraint posed the incongruous issue of unions policing workers' demands rather than fighting for them. It also affected both the solidaristic wage policy and the efficiency of a national economy that was very much oriented toward competition on the world market. Ironically, the refusal to countenance low wages meant that marginal enterprises, which could survive in other economies, were subjected to the most extreme pressure, since

---

*In "The Relation between unemployment and the rate of change of money wages in the United Kingdom, 1861–1947," Phillips argued that low unemployment led to higher wages (and inflation) and joblessness to a downward pressure on wages.

they had the highest number of the underpaid and were therefore targets of the solidaristic wage policy. They could solve this problem either by becoming more productive — which would raise the efficiency level of the entire economy — or by going out of business. The Swedish socialists did not retreat in the presence of that last possibility (and the relevance to the Soviet problems of restructuring is, I assume, obvious). They proceeded to change the consequences of that market outcome by selective measures that saw to it that the workers would not suffer as a result of shutdowns or rationalization.

Local labor exchanges were created under the direction of a national Labor Market Board, and a whole range of programmatic options was made available for dealing with the specific conditions of an enterprise or industry in a given area. There was job retraining, public-works employment, a sophisticated system of identifying new openings, aid to employers in creating new jobs, subsidies to cover the moving costs of those who had to go to a new region, and, in many ways last and least, unemployment compensation. In 1979, for instance, the Swedes devoted only 10 percent of the labor-market funds to jobless benefits, compared to 31 percent for retraining, 13 percent for support to cooperating employers, and 45 percent for other measures to help the individual find new work. The goal was not to tolerate even subsidized joblessness, but to find useful work for every single citizen.

There is no reason to depict these policies as utopia in action. There were grave difficulties in the seventies and eighties because of a slowdown in Western growth, and a good part of the success of the socialists after their return to power in 1983 was the result of an old-fashioned competitive devaluation of the currency. But there were also new measures of public employment to deal with the specific problems of youth joblessness. However, I don't want to go into the actual workings of the system in any detail. Instead, I want to generalize from this rich experience to an overall socialist attitude toward the relationship between plan and markets.

How, one might ask, can policies designed to defend workers against the impact of capitalist markets be used as a model for the socialist future? Isn't this objection reinforced by the fact that those policies were adopted as pragmatic trade-union responses to a specific economic problem? In fact, a conception of the relationship between markets and plan is implicit in this Swedish history, which could be quite relevant to the new socialism of the twenty-first century.

That positive aspect of Swedish policy was well stated by Jacques Attali in 1978, a time when he, and the entire French socialist movement, was quite critical of "mere" social-democratic solutions. "Plan and market are two inseparable sites of the encounter between the production of demand and supply," Attali wrote. "The plan participates in the creation of a market liberated from the logic of capital; the market transmits the collective demand elaborated under the plan to the enterprises." Translated into Swedish: the plan decommodifies the labor market and treats workers as human beings, but it does so in response to signals from that labor market.

In putting these considerations in their larger context, I will expand on my insistence that utopia will not be at hand during the next fifty years. In the last chapter, that judgment placed limitations on some of the more exuberant proposals for moving immediately to an economy of free time. Here, it operates as an argument in favor of the continuing relevance of efficiency in the foreseeable future.

Marx thought that ultimately there would be so much abundance that "economizing" would no longer be necessary — that, as Alec Nove put it, resources would be available at a zero price. As this utopia, anticipating automation, was formulated in the *Grundrisse*, science as applied to economic ends would so exponentially increase productivity that there would no longer be the possibility, much less the necessity, of measuring and compensating contributions to output in terms of hours of labor expended. At that point, "*the surplus labor* of the masses has ceased to be the precondition for the development of universal wealth and the *non-labor* of the few is no longer the precondition of the development of the universal power of the human brain."

Nove is right to reject this automated utopia as a guide to the formulating of socialist policy in the contemporary world. Whatever unimaginable potential there may be in technology, total abundance will not happen in the next fifty or a hundred years, particularly if one takes the Third World into account. Yet I think that Nove misses the importance of real-world approximations of that utopia. Hunger could be abolished in the next period even if scarcity cannot, because the world already has the capacity to feed itself. Even if speculations about an age of free time and plenty must be located in the future, it is important that socialists begin to engage in them here and now. Shouldn't we begin, for instance, to define the hours required of a working life and then think of how many ways in which human beings could arrange them?

Still, for the world as a whole, economizing is clearly on the agenda. The question, then, is how does one economize in socialist fashion?

In a democratic-socialist society constrained by scarcity and committed to the global abolition of poverty, the surplus product would be socially and democratically allocated. So long as the producers and/or the ecosphere are not violated in the process, such a society will, on grounds of solidarity and social justice, be as concerned with efficiency as is capitalism. That "efficiency" will be defined in a different way than under capitalism — to express social goals and not just private interest — is obvious. But there is still a moral as well as an economic necessity to minimize the human and material inputs in production — in the public sector as well as the private — in order to have a maximum surplus product for the work of justice.

Let me be specific on how this implies the use of both planning and market principles. It was and is one of the great accomplishments of social democracy to have removed the minimum necessities of health care from market allocation. But in both Britain and Holland that accomplishment was under severe attack in the eighties, in part because the socialization of health care does indeed increase demand as "ordinary" people insist on the same kind of care that was once available only to the elite.

But it is also true that the nonmarket sector can develop inefficiencies of its own. And that opens it up to the attack of "privatizing" conservatives. In Thatcher's Britain, for instance, 10 percent of health care was provided through private health-insurance policies, and in the discussion of National Health in the 1980s there were more than a few who wanted to extend the scope of for-profit care. Indeed, Mrs. Thatcher tried to quintuple its role, and in many cases the assault on public health is being led by corporations from the socially backward United States. This, in turn, threatens one of the single greatest socialist triumphs over the "logic of capital."

When the National Health system was created by the 1945 Labour government, it was established as a *universal* entitlement. In part, this was an appropriately negative response to the means-testing of social programs in the Depression; in part, it was the assertion of a basic socialist principle that medical care should be a right of the citizen, not only of the poor citizen. With privatization, however, there is a tendency toward the "Americanization" of the entire system, that is, toward the creation of two separate systems of medicine, a publicly financed one for those at the bottom and in the middle of the income distribution, and a privately financed one — providing superior care — for those at the top.

The private-enterprise attack on socialist universality is, it should be noted, an inherent tendency of a society that is no longer entirely capitalist and certainly not yet socialist. Under such circumstances, private profit makers will try to "cream" off the affluent functions in a given sector and graciously allow the state to socialize the remaining losses. That trend cannot be successfully combatted simply by appealing to egalitarian value systems (although in Britain in the eighties, it is clear that there is enormous political support for national health). The public sector has to respond to the private market attack — to markets — by controlling costs without sacrificing quality or the principle of universalism. In the mid-eighties, the Swedish socialists also addressed this issue. They have introduced reforms that seek to achieve private, market levels of efficiency in the public sector without compromising the basic commitment to services based on need.

Sometimes critically important ethical problems — which deserve to be dealt with in a calculus more humane than that of profit and loss — are involved. Medical technology now makes it possible to prolong a life of sorts for the very old if major, and rather expensive, investments are made in sophisticated technology. Is that a morally and socially sound use of resources? In *Setting Limits*, the bioethicist Daniel Callaghan argues that, in the name of other health and social priorities, one cannot make such an open-ended commitment to maintain life without regard to cost. In Britain, he notes with approval, National Health has emphasized "improving quality of life through primary-care medicine and well-subsidized home care and institutional programs for the elderly rather than through life-extending acute-care medicine." In the United States, with its two-tier health structure, there has been a tendency to invest in the high-tech care of those who can pay for it.

The American experience, however, includes a little-known history of success with implications that go far beyond medicine. The Neighborhood Health Center program was begun in 1965 under the aegis of the Office of Economic Opportunity, the main federal agency of the War on Poverty. Its premise was that the traditional organizational modes for the delivery of health-care services were not appropriate to the poor, that it was imperative to locate community centers in the immediate neighborhood of those in need. The centers were not only able to facilitate dramatic health gains in those neighborhoods; they turned out to be more cost-effective than the traditional, hospital-dominated system financed by third-party insurers. But, as Paul Starr has suggested, they were not followed up in the Nixon and Ford administrations because they contradicted conservative ideology. They experienced a brief revival during the Carter presidency and were then subjected to renewed attack during the Reagan years.

This example has implications that go far beyond this specific case. In 1988, a remarkable American study, *Within Our Reach* by Lisbeth Schorr, documented how, throughout the entire range of social programs, efforts that were decentralized, informal, and face-to-face — in dealing with problems like teenage pregnancy and school dropouts and training poor women to work with young girls as advisers on what help was available — were much more efficient than the standard bureaucratic procedures. In West Germany, an "alternative movement" that began in the sixties pioneered in the cooperative delivery of social services.

So it is that the German socialists' draft of a new long-range program argues for decentralization and cooperative modes, with the actual involvement of those being helped wherever possible within the framework of the welfare state. As the influential German socialist leader Oskar Lafontaine put it, social services "must be organized with the least bureaucratic expenditure. One must consider how social security can be expressed in organizational forms of immediate human solidarity and individual self-determination." And nonstatist social services are sometimes more effective than those provided by "professional" bureaucracies.

Questions of efficiency — sometimes posed as profound choices relating to life and death — are important even in the nonmarket sector, even when they are answered in cooperative and decentralist ways. That point relates to the broader concept of the commitment of the new socialism to *decentralized* forms of social ownership. It is not merely in the delivery of social services that such an approach opens up new spaces for personal freedom and creativity. It also provides for the possibility of bottom-up control of the economy on a human scale.

Either, Alec Nove argues, there is a centralized and authoritarian plan for the allocation of resources or there must be markets. There is, he asserted in a debate with a sophisticated "orthodox" Marxist, Ernest Mandel, no third possibility. Nove, I think, overstates this counterposition, and Mandel projects a vision of a democratic planning that is at least possible. The problem is, Mandel's model requires heroic consumers who would be willing to attend endless meetings in order to ensure that they get exactly what they want. I am not sure that is feasible; I am quite sure that it is not desirable. For one of the most effective arguments against socialism, as Oscar Wilde realized long ago, is that it would create a society with interminable meetings.

More broadly, Nove is right if one is serious about decentralized social ownership. What is the point of having a variety of forms of participatory control at the base — in nationalized industries, cooperatives, small private enterprises — if all of the critical decisions are to be made centrally? That would obviate one of the greatest gains that could come from the new structure of ownership — namely the encouragement of independence and invention on the part of workers. For one of the sources of socialist productivity should be that liberation of creativity that, under capitalism, is smothered by the antagonistic relations on the shop floor. One need not be lyrical and futuristic about this possibility, since Japanese capitalism understood it long ago and has long tried to manipulate an appearance of cooperative relations and even to provide a lifetime guarantee of employment, which allows the employee to suggest innovations that might even eliminate his or her job.

The French notion of "worker self-managed socialism" (*socialisme autogestionaire*) was subverted by the events that caused the socialists to make a radical change of course while in power. But that concept has a relevance to the socialism of the future. It is of some moment that all of the proponents of this approach understood that, if there is to be genuine grass-roots autonomy, then there must be a market space — modified by planning priorities, of course — in which the democratic enterprises are free to exercise their communal imagination and interact without supervision from above.

If, however, all decisions are made by central planners, even if they are working under the instructions of the people, one would lose that new source of productivity. For the latter requires that the enterprise — private or public, large or small — has the possibility of coming up with new ideas and products. That leads to what must seem to be a very heretical thought for a socialist: that there must be sources of individual and collective gain in this process.

Of course socialism will be marked by the expansion of non-material incentives, by the degree to which people will strive for excellence on social grounds or simply because it is its own reward. But so long as there is scarcity and discretionary income, so long as there must be a *social* concern with economizing inputs and therefore linking performance and success, there will be a need for material incentives. And that situation will most certainly obtain for the foreseeable future. Obviously socialism will at the same time seek to radically narrow the inequality characteristic of capitalist society — which is not, as the system's defenders claim, a functional necessity but a matter of ethos and legitimated greed. No one will ever be punished for failure by unemployment or the denial of necessities; no one will be rewarded for success by being given a privileged position unto the generations.

The insightful — and heterodox — Yugoslavian Marxist Svetozar Stojanovic has made a most important point in this regard. On the one hand, he wrote, worker self-management can lead to a "decentralized oligarchy," to an egoism, a collective capitalism, of the democratic enterprise. In that case, the logic of capital takes on a communal form within the framework of the market. On the other hand, "self-management is not only threatened by statism, but also by a utopian image of human nature, which leads to the naive expectation that self-managed groups produce rationally, without being challenged by competition. In a system without competition, solidarity turns into its opposite, into parasitism." The market is not a sufficient condition for the socialist functioning of self-management, but it is a necessary condition.

Doesn't Stojanovic suggest a much larger point: that markets, even under optimum socialist conditions, inherently encourage self-seeking and even greed? That they are antithetical to a society based on solidarity and cooperation?

Yes and no. There is no doubt that, with the rise of the mass standard of living in the advanced Western capitalist countries, millions have been liberated from the primordial struggle for necessities and have freely chosen paths of culture, learning, and service. So we might optimistically hope that rising levels of material satisfaction, even if far short of abundance, will change human motivation and make people impervious to the corruptions that have historically accompanied competition. At the same time, however, we know that the youth of the West in the sixties, sometimes proclaimed as a "postmaterialist" generation, were often as acquisitive as their elders, different only in what they coveted, disdaining suburban comforts and exalting consumer electronics. Even more dispiriting, not a few of these rebels became well-adjusted members of societies with chronic poverty and unemployment.

Socialists should not wait passively to see how these ambiguities work themselves out. The labor market can be consciously shaped to provide more opportunities for socially meaningful work not requiring heroic sacrifice. The prejudice for the private over the public is, after all, an artifact of a system that carefully favors the former over the latter. In other words, the psychological reaction to a socialist use of markets is not a given, but a policy issue. At the same time, to repeat an earlier warning, there is no socialist market utopia. Making self-interest — including collective self-interest — the instrument of community purpose will be a contradictory, and even dangerous, idea for the foreseeable future. It is also necessary.

Integrate Stojanovic's point with the Swedish labor-market experience. One of the aims of the Swedish unions was to counteract the market outcome according to which workers in advanced companies get higher wages than those in less successful industries. But at the same time, the Swedes did not abolish the labor-market mechanism itself; they restructured it to meet their priorities instead. In the case posed by Stojanovic, a similar solution would be appropriate: planned policies to see to it that the productivity of worker-managed enterprises would be, in some measure, shared by the entire society — without abolishing the local incentives for that productivity.

There must be room in the new socialism for initiative from the base, and one of the ways of encouraging that is through markets that will reward the most innovative producers. A cooperative should be motivated, say, to produce medical technologies that would make the nonprofit health sector more effective and free resources for other purposes; a hospital should be able to use its expertise to choose between medical technologies, picking the one best suited to its needs. This is particularly important, as Nove insists, in the area of capital goods where the "consumers" consist of other enterprises that must make a self-interested assessment of what they buy.

Jacques Attali suggests that there must then be room for *failure* in a socialist society. An incompetent cooperative or an ineffective management in a socialized industry wastes human skills and materials that could be put to a better social use, and, as the Swedish socialists have understood within the context of capitalism, there must be socially acceptable ways of putting an end to such activities. The resulting "discipline" of markets must not be vicious, as it is in the present, where entire communities were sacrificed in Britain under Margaret Thatcher in order to make industry "lean" and competitive. But, particularly if one is serious about the commitment to abolish world poverty, there must be *a* discipline. Here the issue is not whether there are to be markets, but what kind of markets with what kind of consequences.

That generalization applies to the area in which there is the most obvious case for socialist markets: consumer choice.

In the capitalist theory of "consumer sovereignty," it is the individual in the marketplace who dictates the patterns of production. In reality, monopoly capital produces whatever will yield the largest profit, and uses all the wiles of psychology and science to make sure that the consumer chooses what is good for the corporate bottom line, while at the same time many essential and even desperate human needs — say, for affordable housing in the decaying central cities — are not met. Above all, under the consumer "democracy" of contemporary capitalism, the votes are determined by income and wealth, and the market is thus a mechanism for transmitting the desires of the privileged.

As Anthony Crosland suggested in *The Future of Socialism*, however, if there were a much more egalitarian society, then *and only then* would the essential virtue of markets really come into play. They would function as a decentralized and instantaneous device for registering the needs of people as determined by the people themselves. That they cannot do under contemporary capitalism; and one of the basic socialist critiques of the prevailing system is therefore that it systematically rigs and frustrates that same free choice that it claims to be its greatest virtue. The new socialists can and should argue that their policies would lead to the liberation of markets from the conscious manipulation to which they are subjected under capitalism.

That is why it would be wrong to counter the advertising industry by an authoritarian — or even democratically, but centrally, planned — determination of what will be available to the people. Of course, the programming of desire is pernicious, above all when it exalts profitable pseudoneeds above less profitable real needs. But the alternative should be socialized consumer information, education, a commitment to the proposition that the people, if they are not systematically misinformed, are quite capable of making intelligent decisions for themselves. Prior to the banning of cigarette commercials on television, there was a period in the United States when the antismoking lobby was given free television time for public-service announcements, computed as a percentage of the time of the paid advertisements. Those television spots were some of the most effective instruments of public-health education.

An article by Diane Elson that was critical of both Mandel and Nove focused on one of the essentials. Markets, the extravagant claims of their defenders to the contrary notwithstanding, often function to obscure information rather than providing it. Therefore, it is necessary to talk about "socializing" the market, that is, of the government using computer and television technology to provide consumers with objective knowledge for their choices, something that enterprises, public and private, might not want to do.

In at least three areas, then — the efficiency of the nonmarket sector, the relations between decentralized democratic enterprises, consumer choice — markets have an important role to play in the new socialism.

Markets are obviously not acceptable to socialists if they are seen as automatic and infallible mechanisms for making decisions behind the backs of those who are affected by them. That is indeed a profoundly capitalist notion, and the new socialism should reject it out of hand. But within the context of a plan, markets could, *for the first time*, be an instrument for truly maximizing the freedom of choice of individuals and communities.

I would not, however, use the phrase "market socialism" to designate this process, since it implies that what *defines* socialism is the market relation, which is a contradiction in terms. What is critical is the *use* of markets to implement democratically planned goals in the most effective way. That, it must be said, involves a danger: that the means will turn into ends. There is no guarantee that this will not happen short of a people genuinely committed to solidaristic values and mobilized against the threat inherent even in the planned employment of the market mechanism. But the alternative — authoritarian central planning — is not a hypothetical and avoidable difficulty; it spells the end of socialism, as the Communist experience has so abundantly proved.

The aim, then, is a socialism that makes markets a tool of its nonmarket purposes. And it is not totally utopian for the new socialists to argue that, in liberating markets from the capitalist context that frustrates their virtues, the visible hand can use the invisible hand for its own purposes.[3]

9

Visionary Gradualism

C AN THERE BE a visionary gradualism?

Why, it might be asked, pose such a bizarre question in the first place? Because the analysis of this book suggests that the new socialism can face up to the challenges of the next half century only if it finds a way to yoke together these contraries.

On the one hand, it is clear that there is no such thing as a socialist apocalypse, a sudden leap, to use the classic Marxist formulation, from the "kingdom of necessity to the kingdom of freedom." Modern society is so complex that, even in the unlikely event of a political revolution in the West, fundamental change — of human consciousness as well as of technology and institutions — takes a great deal of time. We are talking, then, about a transitional epoch, not a day, a year, or even a decade.

On the other hand, if one is concerned with the survival and deepening of freedom, justice, and solidarity, there is no alternative to socialist change. During the last fifty years or so, there has been a profound transformation of the conditions of human life under the aegis of unwitting corporate and conservative revolutionaries as well as social-democratic and (American) liberal reformers. This emergent world is built upon a technology with tendencies toward authoritarian elitism *and* human emancipation. "All" that socialists have to do in order to forward that emancipatory potential is to make this process transparent and subject to democratic control. And this must be done while simultaneously winning political support from a majority of the people for the short-run governments that are the only possible agency of long-run democratic change.

Is that conceivable? I am not sure. But since it is a precondition for the survival of freedom, justice, and solidarity — none of which are guaranteed by some benign providence — it has to be carefully examined. It is not only necessary but perhaps even possible that the socialist movement be both visionary and gradualist.

I hear the ghost of Karl Marx responding to my argument with righteous anger. He would denounce it as a utopian scheme worthy of a German professor, a revival of that academic radicalism of the 1840s that he pilloried as "True Socialism." Where, he would ask, is the social class in the advanced economies that will undertake this task of transformation? Where is the historic movement actually progressing toward this goal?

We come here to an essential component of the present socialist crisis. What real-world force(s) will be the agent of socialist change? For if none exists, then brilliant new programs are at best electoral rhetoric and at worst testaments of delusion.

I

THE CLASSIC MARXIST analysis argued that the internal development of capitalism generated the conditions for its overthrow, including the creation of a working class whose self-interest drove it to the universal emancipation of society. In *The Communist Manifesto* capitalism was pictured as inexorably simplifying itself into a gigantic proletariat and a tiny bourgeoisie, destroying almost all the intermediate strata in the process. "The proletarian movement," Marx and Engels wrote, "is the independent movement of the immense majority in the interest of the immense majority." There was thus no need to worry about the question of democracy since economic development was creating a homogeneous and conscious majority, that is, an inherently democratic force.

The mature Marx realized that he had been wrong, that intermediate strata were proliferating, not disappearing. The problem was (see chapter 1) that Marx committed his error in *The Communist Manifesto*, an enormously popular and widely read pamphlet, and corrected it in the course of an obscure academic analysis, *The Theories of Surplus Value*, which was not published until more than twenty years after his death. Even more to the point, though he recognized the facts that contradicted his youthful prediction, he never incorporated them into a revised theory of the working class as the agent of socialist revolution.

Actually, the history of "classical Marxism" and the rise of the modern socialist movement in the years between 1880 and 1914 can be interpreted as an attempt to deal with the fact that Marx's "realistic" predictions about the working class were not coming true.

Kautsky knew, from the development of "organized capitalism" as well as from the revisionist attack on Marxist orthodoxy led by Edward Bernstein, that the massive and homogeneous working class of the *Manifesto* really did not exist. Nor was it just that the proletariat was not becoming a majority. There were divisions in the working class between those who were trade unionists and those who were socialists, those who joined Christian or other unions and those who followed the social democrats, and between the bureaucracy and the rank and file. If the workers were an internally divided minority within the society rather than a coherent majority, how could they play the role that Marxism assigned them? Because history would eventually rendezvous with the socialist possibility once the new middle strata were proletarianized, Kautsky replied. The classic scenario would still be played out, even if in ways its authors had never imagined.

Rosa Luxemburg saw the same problems as Kautsky, but with a greater emphasis on the bureaucratization of the socialist movement. Her response was a refusal to wait until history corrected the deviation of reality from Marxist theory. Rather, she looked toward the spontaneous interaction of the trade unionists and socialists at the base that, under conditions of crisis, would restore the unity and élan of the movement and allow it, after a long detour, to accomplish its preordained mission. The general strikes of the Russian Revolution of 1905, Luxemburg said, were not simply the result of the specific conditions of tsarist absolutism. They exemplified the universal consequences of international capitalist development, and backward Russia had only pioneered the tactics of mass mobilization from below that would be taken up in the advanced capitalist countries.

Edward Bernstein went far beyond Kautsky and Luxemburg in

revising socialist doctrine. He was quite willing to repudiate large chunks of Marxism that he felt were the products of Hegelian metaphysics, even while insisting on the value of Marx's economic analyses. The victory of socialism, he argued, would not come from the working of "immanent economic necessity," and it would have a distinctively ethical component. Moreover, Bernstein wanted to reach out to the new middle class that he saw as an irreversible feature of the system. "The social democracy," he wrote, "will not dissolve this society in order to proletarianize all of its members. Rather, it works ceaselessly to raise the worker out of the social position of a proletarian and to make him or her into a citizen."

So the historic force making for socialism in Bernstein's analysis was multiclass and based on ethics as much as economics. Since there was not going to be any dialectical leap into the future, on the Hegelian model, the movement would proceed through reform rather than revolution. But for all his moderation and empiricism, Bernstein was, like Kautsky and Luxemburg, a prisoner of a kind of evolutionary optimism. He assumed that the business cycle was becoming less of a problem and that a gradual transition to socialism — with a considerable and quite unrealistic emphasis on the importance of cooperatives — would be relatively easy to achieve.

Antonio Gramsci was more tough-minded and revisionist than Bernstein, even though he remained a dedicated Communist until his death in 1937. He anticipated many of the ideas in this chapter and therefore will loom quite large in it.

But before turning to Gramsci's analysis — which has become extraordinarily popular among socialist and Marxist intellectuals in recent years — let me suggest a reason for not taking it seriously. One of the critical elements in Gramsci's perspective is a radical revision of the traditional Marxist timetable. In 1848 Marx thought that the revolution would triumph in a matter of two or three years; in the 1850s he postponed the date by half a century. August Bebel, we have seen, told the delegates at the Erfurt Congress of 1891 that most of them would live to see socialism, and Rosa Luxemburg agreed. But Gramsci did not belong to that period of "classical" Marxist illusions. He lived through the social-democratic betrayal of the antiwar commitment in 1914 and the end of the euphoric phase of the Russian Revolution —

and, what is more, wrote from within an Italian fascist jail. He said that socialism was not imminent at all, that it would come only at the unforeseeable end of an entire historic epoch. He was a herald of a socialism based on the experience of defeat, of what Perry Anderson has called "Western" Marxism.

Is the popularity of this pessimistic view due to the fact that, by deferring it to an indefinite future, it makes it impossible to falsify the socialist possibility? That certainly could be the case, and the reader should keep this possibility in mind while reading my borrowings from Gramsci. Yet, Gramsci did grasp the significance of "Fordism" very early on and saw the necessity of a coalition politics, which did not become clear to many socialists until well after World War II. That is, whether he was right or wrong on the prospects of a distant socialist future, he was more successful than most analysts, whether socialist or not, in identifying political trends that did not come to fruition until long after he died. He should, then, be taken seriously, even if some might want to add a pinch of salt.

Hegemony was a key concept for Gramsci. A class did not rule a society, he argued, simply on the basis of its critical economic functions, much less solely by repression and force. It secured voluntary acceptance of its position — hegemony — by shaping the cultural, ideological, psychological, and spiritual life, by permeating the society with its values. This was not a conspiratorial or instrumental theory in which, say, the capitalists cleverly "used" ideology to dupe the masses. During the rise of capitalism, the bourgeoisie did not simply pretend to represent the interests of the vast majority of the society in order to mask its own narrow purposes. It did in fact represent that majority interest. Capitalist values internalized by the noncapitalist classes were an organic element of a historical transition, not the Machiavellian device of a wily ruling class. So Gramsci argued that Henry Ford's automobile-assembly line was not simply a technology but also a basis for creating a new human psychology.

How did this analysis impinge upon the notion that certain historical forces would bring about socialism? No longer, as in Kautsky, was it the independent action of the workers alone that would emancipate them and the other dominated classes. Now it was necessary to create a "historic bloc" in which the working class was the decisive factor, but in which other classes and strata were part of an alliance and exercised real influence upon it. Politics, even compromise, thus became much more important, since socialists had to unite heterogeneous forces around a common project. And the historic bloc had to counterpose itself to the old order culturally and ideologically as well as economically and socially. It had to seek nothing less than a "moral and intellectual reform" of the society. Like the Protestant Reformation, it was the carrier of a new morality and a new worldview, of a change in the way people think and feel. This meant that the transition to socialism would be much more protracted and profound than most socialists, including Marx, had thought.

Gramsci developed these ideas in Mussolini's jails, and his *Prison Notebooks* were not published until after World War II. Only gradually did they become an influence on contemporary socialist thought. Ironically, the insights of this independent but very Marxist genius led to conclusions quite similar to those of the arch-revisionist of Marx, Edward Bernstein. It became impossible to think, even with Kautsky's or Luxemburg's qualifications, that a homogeneous working class would inevitably lead in the socialist transformation. So a Gramscian strategy, with its emphasis on alliances between classes and strata and its appeal to moral values, clearly pointed in the only direction that contemporary socialism could take.

But can one radically change the traditional socialist theory of how the movement is constituted without calling into question the traditional definition of socialism? It was not an accident that the postwar revisions of socialist theory, such as the Godesberg Program of the German social democracy or Anthony Crosland's *Future of Socialism*, tended to ignore the vision of a fundamentally different society and to settle for a humane, social-democratized capitalism. Both the Germans and Crosland were right to recognize the fact that, unless socialism reached out far beyond the working class, it was condemned to permanent minority status if it remained committed, as it must, to democracy. Was the price of that insight a politics of increments that surrendered any sense of visionary alternatives?

Another question: Did the very vision of socialism itself require the old faith in the working class as a collective Messiah? Leftist critics of the social-democratic revisionists were utterly myopic when they denied the new facts of political life and simply appealed to the old Marxist faith in the working class. But they were on much stronger ground when they charged that their opponents had abandoned not only one tactic for the achievement of social- ism but the very notion of a new society as well. Only, some of the true believers did not notice that, even if their accusation was true, the basic question remained: Had realism now dictated the jettisoning of the socialist goal itself together with the proletarian strategy for reaching it?

The answer can be determined only by political and social struggles in the future. If, however, it does turn out that socialism is obsolete, that does not mean that internationalization, automa- tion, and biotechnology will have a benign effect upon humanity — only that they will transform our lives while we play no role in the process, that is, that they will most likely forward neither freedom nor justice. That possible outcome is utterly unaccept- able.

Alain Minc coined his phrase "the slow 1929" to describe the possibility of an economic crisis as profound as the Great Depres- sion but taking place in fits and starts, festering rather than ex- ploding. I think we are living through a "slow apocalypse," a transition to a new civilization that could occur before we are even aware of it. If that revolution, which is in progress, makes us, we will lose ourselves; if we make it, there is at least hope for freedom and justice and solidarity.[1]

II

FIRST, LET US define the social fragmentation that did so much to subvert the classic strategy for achieving socialism, after which we can turn to the difficult task of showing how socialism might be able to unify the various elements behind the vision of a new society.

We begin with the class structure of advanced capitalist soci- ety, which changed much more than even the mature Marx ever imagined in his most self-critical moments.

Social classes, most people forget, were "invented" by capi- talism. Understanding that fact is a key to their constantly chang- ing nature and the reason why changes in this crucial category have done so much to undercut socialist hopes in recent years. Hierarchies and inequalities existed almost from the beginning of human time, but they were established politically, not through the workings of a dynamic economy. Peasants under European feudalism were born and died peasants and, with the exception of a handful who rose in the church bureaucracy, it was absurd to think that they could change their status. It was the fateful separation of the economic from the political, one of capitalism's greatest triumphs, that created fluid social classes based on a temporary conjuncture of wealth and power rather than "estates" or "orders" determined by heredity. A penniless prince remains a noble; a bankrupt bourgeois is declassed. Under capitalism, there is a history of shifting internal structures that are infinitely more dramatic than those of any prior system.

In most of the major capitalist societies of the nineteenth century — the United States is an outstanding exception — the largest single social class was not capitalist at all: the peasantry. It was usually (but not always, for instance in Spain) a bastion of conservatism, of the traditional ways. There were workers, many of them women and children, and, until the emergence of the Fordist factory at the end of the century, many of them skilled and exercising some kind of control over the daily routine of the job. There was the bourgeoisie itself, which, to complicate matters, rarely led in the creation of bourgeois society (in England, capitalism was largely the work of landowning aristocrats; in France, of middle-class Jacobins; in Germany, of Junker plantation owners). And there was a petty bourgeoisie that was made up of small businessmen and shopkeepers as well as lawyers and doctors.

At the end of the century all of these classes and strata remained, but with significant new additions. The rise of the corporation and the gigantic factory created the semiskilled proletariat, a new class of nonowning managers, and a stratum of "employees," including the women who became secretaries and used that radical new invention, the typewriter. There was also a significant shift within the capitalist class as the entrepreneur gave way to the board chairman, and investment bankers, who assembled the financing for the huge undertakings of the new corporations, took on greater importance. *Laisser-faire* was being replaced by organized capitalism.

After World War II, the class structure of capitalism became even more complex. The Keynesian welfare state expanded government employment at both the national and local levels, and a public-sector work force appeared whose wages were paid through taxes that, through no fault of the public employees, often discriminated against private-sector workers, thus creating a new source of divisiveness within the labor movement. The peasants all but ceased to exist in Europe, while the farmers of both the Continent and North America remained a potent political force. An intermediate stratum of college-educated technicians emerged — without the decision-making power of the upper managers but with considerably more income and status than the clerical employees.

At the same time, society redefined the meaning of age.

"Adolescence" was an innovation of the capitalist middle class. Prior to its creation, young people, except for the aristocrats among them, had gone to work as soon as they were physically able. Now the growing productivity of the economy allowed the better-off to exempt their children from that rule, and the growing sophistication of the economy made it rational to extend their education and defer their entry into the labor market. After World War II, both semiaffluence and the growing prestige of learning as an important "input" in the generation of wealth saw more and more young people participate in that trend. A youth culture came into being, and social-class divisions were intersected by new kinds of generational differences.

At the same time, the service sector expanded, in part because rising incomes permitted people to spend more money on restaurants and entertainment. That was perhaps most visible in countries such as France and Italy where the Americanization of mass culture put an end to the two-hour midday family meal. And in Europe and America it meant the emergence of a stratum of workers in small, difficult-to-organize units, often made up of youth and/or minorities. This is just one example of another enormously important trend during the past forty or fifty years: the intersection of race, gender, and age with social class. New divisions emerged within what was a new kind of working class.

Because of its slave heritage, America was more of a multiracial society than Europe. But from the end of the Civil War to the first decade of the twentieth century, violent political repression and economic mechanisms saw to it that Lincoln's Emancipation Proclamation remained a hollow promise. In that first period of juridical freedom for blacks, there was a continuation of almost total social and economic subjugation. At the worst, the ex-slaves, or their children, became "sharecroppers," which was nothing but a capitalist form of peonage. In the period prior to World War I, blacks did begin to move to the North, but the Depression reversed that trend and it was not until the postwar era that there was a vast migration out of the agricultural South into the cities, thereby changing the racial geography of the United States.

There were real gains for those blacks who arrived in time for that last great expansion of Fordist mass production — and for their children who took advantage of the growth of expanding public colleges and universities. But for blacks as a group — and Hispanics and the other minorities who arrived in the United States without skills or entrepreneurial traditions — the end of the postwar boom was a disaster. Many of the rungs of the occupational ladder up which other groups had climbed were eliminated. The new jobs created in the 1970s and 1980s were disproportionately in the lower-paid service sector, minority unemployment was twice as high as that of whites, and economic forces thus institutionalized racial inferiority even though Martin Luther King, Jr., triumphed over legal racism.

In Europe the great influx of immigrants and "guest workers" was a phenomenon of the postwar boom. From around the Mediterranean periphery — Greece, Turkey, Yugoslavia, the Maghreb, Spain, and Portugal — unskilled workers, and even ex-peasants, moved into the lower reaches of the labor market. And in America, there was a mass migration of Latinos and Caribbeans, many of them "undocumented" men and women who had evaded the border patrols and were easy to exploit because of their lack of legal status. In both North America and Europe, men from the dominant racial and ethnic groups no longer performed the low-paid, dirty jobs that were relegated to minorities, further reinforcing stereotypes of incompetence and laziness that many people were only too anxious to believe. In France in the early eighties, the Communist Party responded to racist currents in the working class by demagogically attacking the North Africans. When the Communist hold on workers began to erode, a significant number of them moved to support the neofascist movement of Le Pen.

At the same time that racial and ethnic divisions became more important, there was a significant influx of women into the labor market. The Swedish "solidaristic wage policy," with its class-based emphasis on raising the wages of the least-paid workers, operated, we have seen, to raise the income of the entry-level jobs filled by women. In other countries, particularly in the United States, women were concentrated in the bottom third of the occupational structure, in clerical and retail jobs, and received only about two thirds of the male wage.

Thus, throughout the advanced capitalist world, there was a "new" working class with the number of semiskilled blue-collar workers in relative decline and a disproportionately minority and female labor force occupying the low-paying jobs in the expanding service and white-collar sectors. With the end of the postwar boom in the seventies and the ensuing high rates of unemployment, there was a new poverty as well, exacerbated by the cuts in the welfare state made by the renascent governments of the Right. In many countries, youth and children were particularly victimized by this process, and a new distinction arose within the working class: between a proletariat, with unionized and relatively secure jobs, and a "precariat" of casual workers, participants in the "underground" economy, which was a sort of late twentieth century *lumpenproletariat*.

Marx had not nominated the workers to be the decisive agency of socialism simply because they suffered exploitation. He saw the specific conditions of their existence — concentration in huge cities and in factories, participation in an intricate and increasingly scientific division of labor, a disposition to form unions — as reasons why they would be a much more dynamic force than dispersed peasants living in cultural backwaters. But the problem of the new working class I have just described is that, more often than not, it is broken up in small units, spread out throughout the society, and engaged in simplistic, and sometimes isolated, tasks. The new working class often seems much less impelled to trade-union and political action than the old.

Finally, the welfare state itself created another division. A good portion of its outlays was devoted to the care of the aging — not only in the form of pensions, but in the high percentage of public medical expenditures that went to older people — and these monies were essentially financed by the younger generation in the work force (Sweden, with its "funded" public retirement system, was an exception). Matters were made worse by the fact that, most notably in France and the United States, the cost of these expenditures was disproportionately borne by the traditional working class. Still, there was a collective self-interest on the part of the aging to maintain their own living standard, and that was a source of political tensions between them and their "children," the younger generation.

If, as Marx himself finally realized in the 1860s, class differentiation rather than class concentration was the basic tendency of capitalism, that trend became much more visible precisely at the moment of modest blue-collar triumph under the social-democratic welfare state. The timing was not an accident.

Obviously, race, gender, and age were not the inventions of the 1960s. But it was precisely the quickening pace of political as well as technological change that sometimes transformed those immemorial biological categories into dynamic social forces. For instance, European peasants and American blacks had spent decades shuttling between rural and urban society as part of a reserve army of the unemployed and underemployed that supplied the labor power for periodic booms. But in the postwar period, many of them were driven out of the fields as a result of the huge gains in agricultural productivity and forced into a permanent "attachment" to the labor force. In the civil-rights struggles of the American sixties and in the Italian strikes in which Southern immigrants played such a role in the seventies, those changes became the basis of a surprising militancy in people who had once been marginal.

The youth and student explosion of the 1960s was similarly related to deep-lying trends. The expansion of higher education was in part a public response to the needs of the postwar economy for more trained technicians and researchers. Society, for its own good reasons, assembled a generation of the young in mass institutions of learning that had never existed before. Sometimes the revolt that followed was an angry protest against the crowding and bureaucracy of the new universities; more generally, however, the students had acquired the leisure and knowledge to discuss injustice and to challenge not only the educational system but the structure of society as well.

The students and young graduates thus became the shock

troops of the antinuclear movement — the Campaign for Nuclear Disarmament in Britain in the late fifties was a harbinger of the sixties — of opposition to the American intervention in Vietnam and of NATO's deployment of Euromissiles. The most dramatic example was the explosion in Paris in May of 1968, when a student-initiated protest spread to the working class and came close to deposing President de Gaulle.

That energy also flowed into one of the most significant movements of the age: that of the environmentalists. Here, too, timing was not a matter of accident. Ecological damage accumulates, and in some cases, as with the depletion of the ozone layer and the greenhouse effect, there is a long period of deadly incubation. So the public only gradually became conscious of the real costs of the boom. Eventually, however, the polluted rivers and skies could no longer be ignored. Many of those who responded were college-educated activists who had earlier been involved in other movements. It seemed logical to some, for instance, to proceed from protesting nuclear weapons to demanding an end to nuclear energy per se.

The environmental movement — with the Greens in West Germany the most successful political example — appealed to a genuine sense of kinship with the universe analogous to the awe of primitive religions, to a respect for the basic constituents of existence, of earth, air, and water, which goes back to the earliest phases of humanity. It was sometimes organized by people who had been social democrats or ultra-left Marxists, and it mixed dangerous utopias, such as the idea of zero growth, with extremely serious and compelling defenses of the ecosystem. When the movement sometimes simply challenged new investments without proposing alternative sources of work, it found itself unnecessarily on a collision course with the traditional working class.

The women's movement was also organized mainly by college-educated feminists, but it went much deeper than that. The middle-class activists had entered the universities in the fifties and sixties and participated in the new militancy. But they discovered that even in "revolutionary" organizations they were assigned traditional female tasks: to provide food, sex, and typing. At the same time, the welfare state was "commodifying" aspects of life that had once been the preserve of unpaid women's labor in the family: day care, frozen foods, and household appliances changed the basic necessities of life. Moreover, the new standards of consumption often required two incomes, while new attitudes toward personal relations — premarital sex and single parenting, for instance — undermined the traditional family.

Because they were pushed into inferior positions with lower rates of pay than men, a consciousness of gender difference and solidarity developed among many working women. Italy, to the consternation of the Vatican, voted in a referendum to approve both divorce and the right to abortion. This development, and disputes over scarce jobs in a period of high unemployment, often led to conflict with traditional blue-collar men and even with some of the unions.

But all this is not to imply that those blue-collar workers were simply passive and that the social movements were all the product of an educated elite. On the contrary. In the late sixties, there were waves of working-class militancy in the United States and throughout Europe. History remembers May 1968 in France as a student revolt, but the general strike that followed actually led to greater changes — very large increases in both the minimum and average wages — than those achieved by the student revolutionaries.

Still, profound transformations had taken place. The working class had clearly been the most dynamic social movement in the Western world from, say, 1848 to the end of World War II. To be sure, there were feminists, antislavery abolitionists, and pacifists early on in the nineteenth century who played a significant role in the origins of socialism. But those insurgencies were dependent on hundreds and thousands of individual commitments that waxed and waned. The labor movement, as both a political and an economic force, was rooted in a struggle for daily bread that confronted the worker whether he or she had made a moral choice or not. So the unions had a solidity, an organizational continuity, that none of the other movements could achieve.

But once race, ethnicity, gender, and age became militantly self-conscious as a result of changes in the structure of society, they acquired a power they had never before possessed. Ironically, however, these new sources of social energy often weakened the Left by dividing it between competing constituencies of the old and the new. There was a "dealignment" of class politics noted in almost all of the Western electorates, with significant blue-collar defections to Reagan, Thatcher, and Kohl. At the same time, there were middle-class splits from the socialist movement, notably the social democrats in Britain and the Greens in West Germany.

These fragmenting trends are far from finished. Computerization and automation will probably simultaneously reskill and deskill traditional factory workers, with social and political consequences that can only be guessed. One of the most fundamental challenges to a new socialism, therefore, is to find a way to politically unify social forces that in recent years have spent a fair amount of time frustrating and fighting one another. How is this to be done?[2]

III

A REJECTION OF THE classic Marxist focus on the working class as *the* decisive class, acting either independently or even in coalition, does not mean that one should adopt the superficial view that social class in general, and labor in particular, has now become irrelevant. During the next half century in the advanced economies, there is going to be a significant blue-collar stratum and an even larger sphere of workers organized into unions. These people were, are, and will be of critical importance to the new socialism.

Let us for a moment assume the worst case: the unions do not respond to the challenge of the new occupational structure and become institutions of a declining portion of the work force. Even so, there will still be millions in manufacturing. In fact, in the United States in the mid-1980s there are more such workers than there were in 1970, and the Bureau of Labor Statistics projects that this classic labor force will be a million and a half men and women larger in 1995 than a quarter of a century earlier. What confuses many people is that the *relative decline* of the Fordist occupations often coexists with an absolute increase in numbers.

There is also a factor impossible to capture by numbers and statistics. That is the social weight of the blue-collar working class, still concentrated in relatively large enterprises and unionized. In politics, its collective character gives it an importance — and often financial resources — that cannot be measured simply by counting heads. Ten thousand workers who belong to a union with a political-action program are of greater influence than ten thousand professionals who may well, as individuals, dispose of considerably more income.

Moreover, assuming the worst, if the automation trend continues under authoritarian direction, there may be new openings for the unions. For under those conditions, deskilling and an old-fashioned, utterly obsolete emphasis on managerial rule could well provoke rebellion in the ranks. In a well-known study of continuous-process industries in the United States, the sociologist Robert Blauner discovered that it was just such issues that angered workers laboring under otherwise excellent conditions. In this context, it is well to remember that the "experts" at the annual meeting of the American Economic Association predicted in 1932 that unions in the United States had no future. This prophecy was made on the eve of the most dynamic organizing surge American labor has ever known.

Indeed, the growth of public-sector unionism throughout the West in the postwar period — the unionization, so to speak, of the welfare state itself — is proof that the service sector is not a permanent refuge from organization. A recent analysis of the class composition of social-democratic parties in Western Europe and Britain by David Hine shows that white-collar workers — clerical, technical, and managerial, and quite often unionized — have been playing a growing role in the socialist movement for some time now. Such people obviously have a distinct self-interest in, as well as an ideological concern for, the welfare state.

In the late 1960s and early 1970s, some theorists on the Left looked to the emergence of a "new working class" of the educated and skilled employees of the most advanced industries. Serge Mallet, for instance, argued that this stratum played a particularly dynamic role in the events of May 1968 in France. Some of those analyses were an attempt to "save" the classic Marxist schema by conceptualizing new phenomena under reassuringly old labels ("working class"). But even if a good number of the college-educated militants of the sixties had turned to private consumption and self-gratification a decade later, Mallet had identified an important trend. There is indeed a conflict between, on the one hand, the professional and personal autonomy of many scientists, technicians, and middle-level managerial cadres, and, on the other, the structures of authority under which they work.

That last trend could well be accentuated by automation. Though it is true that the United States is exceptional in the high percentage of managerial employees compared to those actually engaged in production, it is still of some moment that about a million middle managers, roughly one third of the total, lost their jobs in the decade that ended in 1988. One reason is that computers can perform any task, including many managerial functions, that can be reduced to a programmable routine. It is also conceivable that the deskilled version of clerical work — reducing clerks and secretaries to puppets of a video-display terminal — could bring an assembly-line quality into the office and lead to a growth of unionism.

Even under the worst-case scenario, the unions will remain a significant economic and political force in the years to come. Another possibility is that new social strata become open to the appeal of unionism as a result of the very trends that diminish the percentages of the classic working class.

At the same time, the new socialism has to demonstrate convincingly to those concerned with the environment, the Third World, sexism, and racism that *the quantities of economic life are central to the quality of all life.*

The environment is an obvious and cogent example. Whenever industry feels itself under competitive pressures, one of the ways to reduce costs and increase profits is to impose on society the costs of degrading the ecosystem. The private "savings" from the despoiling of the environment are already a major source of problems that threaten human existence itself. It is not enough, as free-market enthusiasts propose, to force the corporations to pay for their own mess. For in many cases, unconscionable harm can be done by that mess whether its costs are internalized by capital or not.

At the same time, there is an almost inevitable conflict between the Greens (I use the term generically, not in reference to any specific political party) and those workers who see environmentalism as a threat to their jobs. As a result, two major groups with an interest in challenging corporate power could well become antagonistic.

Clearly, if this happens, both the environmentalists and the trade unionists will lose and capital will win. The same could be true in the movement to gain equality for women and minorities in the workplace. If one assumes future chronic high unemployment and a secular decline in the number of well-paying jobs, there is simply no way that antiracist and antisexist demands can be put into effect.

The economic, then, is hardly irrelevant. As it is refracted in social class in general, and in the working class in particular, it will remain a major factor for the next half century. And it is a critical concern for constituencies dealing with issues such as race, gender, age, and global justice. But this is not to say that the new socialism is simply the old doctrine in a somewhat more sophisticated, multiclass form. If it is *primarily* economistic, it will fail utterly.

It is not just a matter of tactics, of appealing to social strata and movements that, for a variety of historical and structural reasons, are concerned with values and culture. On a much more profound, strategic level, it is impossible to sustain a new conception of society on the basis of narrow, incremental demands.

Beyond strategy, the very conception of socialism requires an emphasis on values, on the noneconomic as well as on the economic. If socialization is no longer thought of as the automatic consequence of the economic development of capitalist society, as a transition from capitalist monopoly to socialist monopoly; if, on the contrary, socialization is understood as the conscious control of their destiny by the people; then it is clearly a goal that extends to all of society, not just to the economy. It involves a shift in culture, in psychology, in the very self-conception of individuals who have previously accepted a subordinate condition.

Actually, there were adumbrations of this point in the classic Marxist writings. In an 1894 letter, Engels clearly implied that under socialism the economic would become *less* important. After all, economic determinism operated precisely in societies that did not, and could not, have a clear analysis of the social process. But when there was socialist planning, consciousness would become much more important than it had even been before. In "The Changing Function of Historical Materialism," one of the essays in *History and Class Consciousness*, Georg Lukacs argued that since Marxism in power would mean the domination of the

"superstructure" over the base, the Marxist methodology itself
would change. More recently, Jurgen Habermas has persuasively
argued for a politics based on a rational, communicative search
for social consensus as a complement to more class-determined
struggles.

But it was Gramsci, of course, who, among the Marxists,
understood this transition most profoundly. What had been contemptuously called mere "superstructure" by the vulgar Marxists
would take on a tremendous importance.

I turn, then, to the morality and culture of the new socialism.[3]

IV

I HAVE NO WISH to turn socialist parties into proponents of
an official *Weltanschauung*. One of the gains of the social-
democratic revisions of the 1950s — and this is true from an
authentic Marxist point of view — was to give up the notion that
the social-democratic party was necessarily committed to Marxism. Such a philosophic and theoretical commitment narrowed
the movement by excluding many, especially people of deeply
religious convictions, who agreed with its program but not with
Marxism.

Here, I want to talk about the values of solidarity, freedom, and
social justice, which are shared by Marxists, non-Marxist human-
ists, and followers of every major religion in the world, and can be
reached by many intellectual and ethical routes. The validity of
those different paths is not unimportant and deserves to be vigor-
ously debated, but it is not a matter to be settled by a political
party.

Nor am I proposing that socialism be a substitute religion.
Socialism is not an explanation of all of the fundamental problems
of life, of the meaning of death, the existence of evil, and so on.
Socialists may well address those questions, and Marxism, as an
atheistic humanism, makes a stoic response to them. But socialism itself deals with putting an end to the *unnecessary* evil of the
world that is caused by economic and social structures. No more,
no less. A good society may well give rise to even more intense
religious reactions than the needless suffering of unjust social
systems. In any case, there is no socialist answer to Ivan

Karamazov's question of why an innocent child should die — and such deaths will occur in the best of societies humanity will ever achieve.

Finally, I am not proposing ethereal and lovely values on the model of the nineteenth-century utopias that Marx himself despised: ethical possibilities for societies and individuals are both constrained and created by social and economic structures. Within that framework, socialists do not want to dictate individual morality but to create a world in which the range of options for people is much greater than ever before, in which lives are no longer programmed by the accident of birth in a class or race or gender, but are the creation of free men and women. Such personal freedom, socialists understand, can be achieved only on the basis of social justice.

With these qualifications, a few words about the values and morality of the new socialism.

Historically, capitalism was characterized by, among many other things, a fundamental change in the way in which human beings related to one another.* In the worldview of an Aquinas, God was in His heaven and had not only revealed Himself in scripture but was knowable by natural reason as it ascended through the hierarchies of matter and spirit to the first cause. Like everything else in the universe, economic life was under the domain of both natural and divine law, and prices were to be determined by the demands of justice rather than the play of the market. It was immoral and sinful to profiteer simply because supply was scarce and demand vigorous. This was admittedly an idealized version of a feudalism that even in Thomas's own thirteenth century was becoming more and more capitalistic. But it was an idealization with some relation to reality.

In the writings of Luther, Calvin, Pascal, and Hobbes there is a common and much darker view of humanity than in Aquinas. For the theologians, God is distant, known primarily through His own word and not through the very fallible reason of fallen beings. Human nature is corrupted in its essence by original sin and is not, as in both Aristotle and Thomas, inclined toward reason.

---

*In what follows, I develop an analysis made at much greater length in *The Politics at God's Funeral*. I should note that the discussion of the history of ethics in Alisdair MacIntyre's *After Virtue* stimulated me in reconsidering that earlier work.

Society, far from being a "perfect community," as Aristotle said and Thomas repeated, must discipline sinful citizens who, as Hobbes put it, were engaged in a war of each against all. Even in John Locke's much less pessimistic version of the origins of the state, authority is necessary or else every individual would have the right, with chaotic results, to enforce the natural law by force against every other individual. This profound change in the way influential thinkers viewed social life refracted the new forces at work in that life.

The expansion of the market principle was shattering traditional society. Max Weber wrote:

> Money is the most abstract and "impersonal" element that exists in human life. The more the world of the modern capitalist economy follows its own immanent laws, the less accessible it is to any imaginable religion with a religious ethic of brotherliness. The more rational, and the more impersonal, capitalism becomes, the more is this the case. In the past it was possible to regulate ethically the personal relations between master and slave because they were personal relations. But it is not possible to regulate . . . the relations between the shifting holders of mortgages and the shifting debtors of the banks that issue the mortgages; for in this case, no personal bonds of any sort exist.

Small wonder that, as this kind of a social world came into being, God was driven out of daily life and became a *deus Absconditus*, a hidden god, brooding over his fallen creation.

For Marx, who had anticipated much of Weber's analysis, this moment was profoundly ambiguous. The individual had been liberated from the stifling limitations of personal dependence in traditional society, and no romanticizing of the "organic" past should be allowed to disguise this fact. Moreover, the subjectivity and creativity that were thus set in motion were one of the sources of an unprecedented growth in productivity and wealth. The ancient world, which produced for the needs of men and women, he wrote in the *Grundrisse*, might *seem* nobler than capitalism, but it was in fact a parochial, limited, underdeveloped form of society. Marx even chided David Ricardo for attacking "production for production's sake," arguing against him that this seemingly base goal facilitated the development of new human needs and the power to satisfy them. But while dependence was no longer personal and the individual was "free," that same individual was now the creature of a social class identity and the puppet of impersonal forces.

Still, Marx infinitely preferred capitalism to feudalism and interpreted the breakdown of traditional society as a progress, even though it gave rise to new forms of alienation. There was another paradox in all this, and it touched directly on religion and morality.* Protestantism and Deism, Marx said, were the preferred religions of the bourgeoisie since each emphasized the independence of the individual in relationship to God and thus became the theological complement to the self-interest of the marketplace. And yet, though capitalism was created by pious burghers giving glory to the Almighty, it was the first socioeconomic formation that did not *need* God as an ideological support. When power was based on personal domination of the Lord over the serf, it was essential to legitimate that inequality by declaring it the will of God. Now that that power was allocated by the invisible hand of the secular market, there was a "rational" case for injustice and no need to sprinkle it with holy water. An atheistic or agnostic feudalism is all but unthinkable — but not an atheistic or agnostic capitalism.

This is not to say that there is *a* capitalist ethic. There have been many such ethics, and they refract national differences as well as different stages of economic development. Veblen's "conspicuous consumption," with its waste and luxury, is every bit as bourgeois as the "this worldly asceticism" of a Puritan entrepreneur described by Max Weber. But whatever the varieties of capitalist ideology, practically every one of these assumes that humans live, as Kant put it, in an "unsocial society" of egoistic individuals.

So it was that humankind lost the ancient concept, dating back at least to the Greeks in the Western tradition, that society has a

---

*Unfortunately, the document in which Marx most clearly stated this case is his essay "On the Jewish Question," an analysis that is marked by the use of anti-Semitic language. That does not change the value and profundity of much that is said there, nor does it even prove that Marx was an anti-Semite, but it understandably has caused many to react only to the anti-Semitic phrases. For a discussion of these complexities, see *The Politics at God's Funeral.*

purpose that is something more than establishing the ground rules for individual striving. Men and women, Aristotle said in *The Politics*, are "drawn together by a common interest, in proportion as each attains a share in the good life" — but people are also moved by a desire "to live a social life even when they stand in no need of mutual support." Thus, the aim of the polis (of the city, of government) "is not mere life, it is rather, a good quality of life." It is not enough that "the law becomes a mere covenant — or . . . 'a guarantor of men's rights against one another'; it should be a rule of life that will make the member of the polis good and just."

In a youthful passage that dates from his first encounter with actual workers, Marx spoke in Aristotelean accents:

> When the communist *artisans* unite, at first their purpose is propaganda, program [*Lehre*] etc. But at the same time, in uniting they acquire a new need, the need for society, and what appeared to be a means becomes an end. One can observe this practical movement in its most striking form when the French workers get together. Smoking, drinking, eating, etc. are no longer means of binding people together. . . . The society, the organization, conversation, suffice in themselves, the brotherhood of man is no longer a phrase for them, but a truth, and the nobility of humankind shines out of faces hardened by toil.

It is often true in contemporary capitalist society that the press does not understand this critical point. When a bitter strike ends, it is routinely pointed out that, if the workers had settled for the last offer and not lost pay by walking out of the job, they would have made money. But that is to assume that all strikes are only about money. In fact, they are often concerned with much deeper, more social emotions and values, with the right of men and women to have, as some of the current theorists of American labor put it, a "voice." I do not want to romanticize and will shortly qualify this analysis in the light of recent developments. But one cannot understand the history of the socialist movement if one does not realize that Marx was on to something profound in his description of the French workers.

It is worth remembering that in every country in Europe, the workers first came together not around demands for more money but in the struggle for the vote, that is, in a civil-rights rather than an economic cause. From the Chartists in England through the general strikes in Belgium and Sweden for the vote to the revolutionary abolition of unequal voting rights in Germany in 1918–19, the fight for dignity, for social rights, was often as powerful as the battles over wages and hours. This could not have happened without moral solidarity as well as rational economic calculation.

Edward Bernstein, the arch-revisionist, was more genuinely Marxist than most of his critics when he brilliantly analyzed the notion that the workers were driven by self-interest to socialist conclusions. Bernstein wrote:

> But if this interest is to be an impulse toward participation in a movement, the individual must have an "idea" of that interest, it must be *known* as such. . . . It is an interest that goes beyond that of the work group, it is a *class* interest and its maintenance requires, for a period of time at least, a sacrifice of *personal* advantage. Thus the interest which Marxist socialism assumes is bound up from the very beginning with a *social* and *ethical* element and is to that degree not only an *intellectual* but a *moral* interest.

So it was that the emergent working-class movement of the nineteenth century, we have seen, fought for community and meaningful work. It realized, in practice and sometimes in theory, that the "life world" of the middle and bottom of the society was under attack. But one of the many consequences of the transformations that took place in advanced capitalism after World War II was to subvert much, but by no means all, of that class solidarity. The Keynesian ethic of the fifties and sixties, particularly in the United States but also in Europe, was profoundly bourgeois, that is, it proposed to stimulate the economy primarily through *individual* consumption. That is why the contrast, brilliantly captured by John Kenneth Galbraith, between private affluence and public squalor became so marked. This psychology was also a source of that indifference to the degradation of the environment that accompanied the rising GNP.

This process led to social fragmentation, subverting many of the informal institutions of working-class life — the neighborhoods and pubs and local sporting teams. In an unfortunately large number of cases, unionism became, in the phrase of the English sociologists, a matter of "instrumental collectivism" in which Marx's insight was stood on its head and the forms of community were used primarily for private and individual purposes. This is one of the many reasons why a commitment to a rebirth of practical idealism, of values rooted in programs that actually change the conditions of life, is so important to the new socialism.

Another reason is tactical as well as ethical. It can be shown that all of the heterogeneous constituencies of modern capitalist society need a full-employment economy. Chronic joblessness is a menace to the traditional working class *and* to the women, minorities, and immigrant workers who, in almost every country, tend to have higher unemployment rates than anyone else. If there is to be a serious commitment to ecology, enterprises — public as well as private — have to be deprived of the argument that competition forces them to degrade the environment. The problem is, such connections are not immediately obvious, nor are they charged with the kind of emotion that gives rise to political and social movements.

Therefore, the language of a common idealism that transcends mere material interest becomes all the more important. And, contrary to the stereotypes, statistical evidence abounds that blue-collar workers are as open to such appeals as the supposedly postmaterialist — and often very materialistic — college graduates, *so long as these blue-collar workers do not perceive the idealists as people who don't care about their jobs and welfare.* In terms of the debate in the classic Marxist movement before World War I, what is being proposed here would have been contemptuously dismissed as "only" ethical socialism. So be it. The new socialism, I maintain, must understand that this ethic is both true and a source of mobilizing power.

Gramsci understood this point from a Marxist perspective; R. H. Tawney, the British socialist, grasped it just as brilliantly from the standpoint of a religiously inspired humanism. For Tawney, "fellowship" — which is a sort of translation of *fraternité* from the French revolutionary tradition — was critical to the new society. Power had to be dispersed; some would no longer "lord it over" others. Equality was seen to be not simply a matter of justice for the individual but a means of establishing the very moral atmosphere of the nation as a whole. Solidaristic values were basic and so was communication. That vision, I think, can be found in *every* serious socialist thinker, even in those, like Marx and Kautsky, who shunned the language of morality out of a contempt for moralizing. Now, in our fragmented world — and that was another Tawney theme — these values are not simply ethical imperatives; they are also strategic and tactical elements of a socialism that will unite, within nations and throughout the world, forces more disparate than those dreamed of by the founders of the movement.

First and foremost, there is the need for a global solidarity, a sense of world citizenship. I am under no illusion that such a consciousness is the work of a year, or even a decade. Its emergence, if in fact it is to be achieved, will take place during a historic epoch. And it will not come into existence simply through exhortation. The politics of international economic and social solidarity must be presented as a practical solution to immediate problems as well as a recognition of that oneness of humankind celebrated in the biblical account of the common parents of all human beings. That said, it is important that the commitment to the abolition of world poverty not be presented *simply* as an act of enlightened self-interest. The Scandinavian socialists have already succeeded in emphasizing the moral dimensions of such a politics. When, for instance, the Swedish conservatives took over from the socialists in the mid-seventies, there was no great shift in this sphere, not the least because there was a shared ethical consciousness of global solidarity.

In the domestic politics of socialism in the advanced countries, the urban planners long ago urged the development of new cities and towns that would respect the environment and create structures conducive to the rearing of children. Another aspect of that commitment should be made quite explicit: to create space for community and individual freedom. If the design of a machine in the workplace is, among other things, the incarnation of an attitude toward human beings, so is the way a house or an apartment building is constructed. In Aristotelean terms, the point is not simply the promotion of life, but the creation of possibilities for the good life.

There is a danger here clearly identified by Irving Howe in his fine book, *Socialism in America*. Howe asked: "Who does not feel the continued poignancy in the yearning for community which seems so widespread in our time? Who does not respond, in our society, to the cry that life is poor in shared experiences, vital communities, free brother- and sister-hoods?" Then he voiced an important qualification: "Yet precisely the pertinence and power of this attack upon traditional liberalism must leave one somewhat uneasy. For we live in a time when the yearning for community has been misshaped into a gross denial of personal integrity, when the desire for the warmth of social bonds — marching together, living together, huddling together, complaining in concert — has helped to betray a portion of the world into the shame of the total state."

We must not forget that the Promethean Marxist dream of a "new socialist man," of people who naturally and easily cooperated with one another, became the rationale for the totalitarian conformity of Joseph Stalin. More prosaically, in the West, in some of the new towns and cities, no one remembered to create informal communal spaces like pubs or Laundromats. Some of the gigantic apartment complexes are indeed "living machines" filled with strangers who happen to live next to one another.

These trends are the source of a surprising convergence: between the most avant-garde, anarchistic Left opponents of the bureaucratic state and the revived religious fundamentalism in the United States and the various antitax movements throughout the West. The militant conservatives, it should be remembered, are often responding to the aspects of the welfare state that turn the person into a client. And the answer to the reactionary "populism" that is part of the appeal of a Reagan or a Thatcher — or even of a racist demagogue like Le Pen in France — is a genuine and progressive populism. That is one more reason why the German socialists' critique of the bureaucratization of some of their own programs — and their search for decentralist alternatives — is so important.

How, then, do we balance the communal and the personal? The utterly privatized consumers of the Keynesian ethic in the 1960s — passive individuals who fulfilled their social obligations by buying more — are inimical to the notion of citizenship and solidarity. So is mass society with its concentrated electronic communications and, with all the best intentions, demeaning ways of delivering utterly necessary human services.

As the socialist political philosopher Michael Walzer put the problem:

> I find myself increasingly uneasy about the triumph of liberal individualism. Consider: every new census shows more Americans living alone (in "single-person households"); the divorce rate is now 50% for first marriages (considerably higher for second and third marriages) and rising; no-fault divorce has virtually ended child support payments and as a result there has been a significant shift in social resources from children to single adults; rates of suicide, mental illness, alcoholism and drug addiction are all higher among adults living alone, etc., etc. . . . I don't know what the alternative to liberal individualism is, but it's not, it doesn't have to be, a Rousseauian communitarianism; it might have more to do with such old socialist values as cooperation, mutuality, communal provision, public life, and so on.

There is a name for that mean which Howe and Walzer seek to define: it is the ancient republican ideal of the citizen in which private and public harmoniously reinforce one another. It was no accident that, in the late 1930s and early '40s, socialists and authentic Marxists began to realize that the Athenian vision of a participatory, nonbureaucratic democracy was relevant to the future. What is needed, Max Horkheimer said in a 1942 essay, is "the Greek polis without slaves."*

The participatory democracy of the polis was erected on the basis of the unfreedom of slaves and of women and of contempt for even the free manual laborer. "The best state," Aristotle had said on that last count, "will not make the manual worker a citizen." Marx commented that this greatest of Greek philosophers almost developed his own theory of value but could not because his society's prejudices would not let him even consider the notion that labor, the activity of inferiors, defined the essential value of wealth. The psyche of democratic Greece, then, was permeated by antidemocratic assumptions.

But why look back to such a tarnished ideal? Because the Greeks, at their best, built a political system in which there was

---

*As I pointed out in the last chapter, Aristotle himself had defined such a possibility in his discussion of the "states of Daedalus." It would come into existence with automation.

no bureaucracy, no state looming over the citizen, but a culture of participatory and social commitment — resting, it is true, on that immoral foundation. If one reads Marx's rather ideological description of the Paris Commune in *The Civil War in France*, it is something like an account of an Athens without slaves under the direction of the plebes rather than of the privileged. The forms of Athenian politics, in short, have a value that can be detached from their shameful historical base, particularly when technological revolution obviates the economic necessity of subordination and exploitation.

Socialists rediscovered that ideal when, as Edward Bernstein understood, it was no longer politically possible — or even desirable — to see socialism as a society in which the overwhelming majority consisted of proletarians. If it was no longer plausible that capitalism was working toward a majority working class, it made sense to project socialism as citizenship for the proletarians rather than as the proletarianization of the citizens. A similar perspective followed from Gramsci's Marxist revisionism in which the socialist working class would play a key role in a "moral and intellectual reformation" that would embrace many classes and strata. Such a new "historic bloc" would have to be united on the basis of ethical values and not simply in terms of the material interests of a single class.

At the same time, the reality of Stalinism and the growing danger of mass society led disparate thinkers of the Left to realize the importance of those "little Republics," the American town-meeting version of the Athenian ideal, which Thomas Jefferson thought indispensable to democracy.* In the early twentieth century, the great American socialist Eugene Victor Debs interpreted his own movement in precisely those terms. As Nick Salvatore summarized the attitude of Debs and his followers,

---

* There is a significant scholarly literature in America reinterpreting Jefferson in this context. A great deal of the impetus for this focus came from Hannah Arendt's *On Revolution*, a book that linked the Jeffersonian concept to Marx on the Paris Commune and Lenin's utopian vision of "Soviet" democracy. American historians, like David Montgomery, Sean Wilentz, and Leon Fink, documented the existence of this ideal in the nineteenth-century labor movement. In England, E. P. Thompson's work inspired similar concerns. Small wonder, then, that Gavin Kitchin's 1983 book, *Rethinking Socialism*, proposed that the British Labour Party focus on "the restoration of the old 'republican' virtues, of the concept of a truly human life as a public as well as a private."

"They took the republican tradition seriously and stressed the individual dignity and power inherent in the concept of citizenship. While frequently vague over exactly how to transform their society, these men and women had no doubt but that, if the people united, the vitality of that tradition would point the way."

I am not trying to make a case for one or another scholarly interpretation of the republican heritage. But I insist that the political, social, and economic development of modern society points socialism toward an ethical, multiclass, and decentralized conception of its goal based on the democratization of the workplace and the creation of new forms of community, both within the nation and throughout the world. That vision has a remarkable continuity with the basic republican values that derive from both the French and the American revolutions. It will not, of course, simply happen and it runs counter to some of the most profound currents of the age, against the elitist tendencies of the knowledge economy and the privitized conformism of mass society. It therefore requires new structures — the democratization of information and education, the vesting of real power in decentralized institutions that give the citizen a pragmatic reason for participation.

Is such a socialist republicanism possible? Can we really create a space for personal and community freedom in a modern society? No one can be sure. All we can say with confidence is that if such freedom is to come into existence, it will be the result of new global structures of solidarity and justice. Which is to say, of socialism.

V

I END WHERE I began, but hopeful and with my meanings deepened by the intervening analysis. I have been brutally critical of my own tradition because such candor is a prerequisite for its revitalization.

I write at the end of a right-wing era that resulted from the crisis of the Keynesian welfare state — and on the eve of a new move toward the Left in the West, and perhaps in the Communist East and the Third World. That means that many people, still under the spell of the recent past, will find my futurism quixotic because it is so much at odds with the age of Reagan and Thatcher and Kohl. But it should be remembered that these conservatives proved once again that their ideology is a contradiction in terms. It provides eighteenth-century rationales for twenty-first-century authoritarianism, myths of the invisible hand that justify the elitist maneuvers of the visible hand, idylls of the organic community that facilitate the growth of mass society and create both a new poverty and a vacuous hedonism.

And socialism? More than a hundred years ago, it understood the basic tendency of capitalist society, that drive toward an unsocial socialization. And it counterposed a vision of democratic socialization, one that has in fact inspired almost every gain in human freedom in modern times. But when socialism tried to implement that concept of a new civilization that went beyond simple reform, it was sometimes disastrously wrong or else vague and merely rhetorical. The question is: Can socialism learn from the defeats and betrayals that resulted from its flawed understanding of its own profound truths?

If not, socialism will turn out to have been humankind's most noble and useful political illusion, and its demise may well be followed by a scientifically organized unfreedom. But if it can learn from its own past about how to create the future, then there is hope for freedom, solidarity, and justice. And perhaps there will be a visionary gradualism equal to the challenge of the "slow apocalypse" in which we live.[4]

Notes

1 · Hypotheses

1. It is my intention to keep these notes to that minimum required for scholars to ascertain the sources of, and documentation for, my statements. Where I refer to standard texts or historical facts, for example, the Federalist Papers or the Chapelier law, both cited in this section, I will not give a reference. In my account of socialist history, I have relied in particular upon:

Julius Braunthal, *Geschichte der Internationale*, 3 vols. (Hannover: Dietz Verlag, 1961-1971);

G. D. H. Cole, *A History of Socialist Thought*, 5 vols. (New York: St. Martin's Press, 1965);

Iring Fetscher, Helga Grebing, and Gunter Dill, eds., *Sozialismus*, (Munich: Verlag Kurt Desch, 1968);

Carl A. Landauer, *European Socialism*, 2 vols. (Berkeley: University of California Press, 1959);

George Lichtheim, *Marxism: An Historical and Critical Study* (New York: Frederick Praeger, 1961);

———, *The Origins of Socialism* (New York: Frederick Praeger, 1969);

———, *A Short History of Socialism* (New York: Frederick Praeger, 1970);

Albert S. Lindeman, *A History of European Socialism* (New Haven: Yale University Press, 1983);

William E. Paterson and Alastair H. Thomas, *Social Democratic Parties in Western Europe* (New York: St. Martin's Press, 1971);

———, *The Future of Social Democracy* (Oxford: Clarendon Press, 1986).

In this section of the text:

Werner Sombart on "the Internationale": Landauer, *European Socialism*, Vol. I, p. 1095, n. 6.

2. Marx's comments on the "negation of the negation": *Marx-Engels Werke* [hereafter cited as *MEW*] (Berlin: Dietz Verlag, 1957–67), Vol. 23,

pp. 770–73. [*Capital* (Moscow: Progress Publishers: 1971), Vol. I, pp. 713–16.]

technology and capitalism in Marx: see Michael Harrington, *The Twilight of Capitalism* (New York: Simon and Schuster, 1976), p. 94ff.

the "visible hand" of the corporation: Alfred A. Chandler, Jr., *The Visible Hand: The Managerial Revolution in American Business* (Cambridge, Mass.: Belknap Press of Harvard University Press, 1977).

Lash and Urry: *The End of Organized Capitalism* (Cambridge and Oxford: Polity Press in association with Basil Blackwell, 1987).

U.S. Congress, Office of Technology Assessment: *Technology and the American Economic Transition: Choices for the Future*, OTA-TET-283 (Washington, D.C.: U.S. Government Printing Office, March 1988), p. 3.

Shoshana Zuboff, *In the Age of the Smart Machine* (New York: Basic Books, 1988).

3. Engels on capitalist nationalization: *MEW* XX, p. 259.

Engels on capitalist nationalization: *MEW* XX, pp. 259, 618.

Engels's 1881 letter: *MEW* XXXV, p. 170.

Lafontaine: *Die Gesellschaft der Zukunft* (Hamburg: Hoffmann und Campe, 1988), p. 111.

Hilferding: W. S. Woytinsky, *Stormy Passage* (New York: Vanguard Press, 1961), p. 471.

Theories of Surplus Value, *MEW* XXVI-1, pp. 145–46, 171, 189–90, 274; XXVI-2, p. 576. Although the *Theories* are often called the "fourth volume" of *Das Kapital*, the manuscripts were written long before Marx did his final work on Volume I. He was thus aware of the changes in capitalist class structure in the 1860s, a good twenty years before he died, but he never really integrated that critical revision into the writings of the next two decades.

Michels: *Political Parties* (New York: Dover Publications, n.d.).

Gramsci: *Quaderni del Carcere* (Turin: Einaudi, 1966), Vol. I, p. 13.

Kautsky: A. M. and May Wood Simons, trans., *The Social Revolution* (Chicago: Charles Kerr, 1902 [1902]), p. 20.

2 · Socialisms

1. Martin Buber, *Paths in Utopia* (Boston: Beacon Press, 1958), p. 80.

Saint-Simon: C. Bouglie and Elie Halevey, eds., *Doctrine de Saint-Simon, Exposition, Première Année, 1829* (Paris: Marcel Rivière, 1924), pp. 203, n. 91, 235.

Fourier on love: Jonathan Beecher and Richard Bienvenu, eds., *The Utopian Vision of Charles Fourier* (London: Jonathan Cape, 1971), p. 172; Introduction, pp. 60, 62.

feminism, Flora Tristain: George Lichtheim, *The Origins of Socialism* (New York: Frederick Praeger, 1969), pp. 54, 59, 69.

Owenites: E. P. Thompson, *The Making of the English Working Class* (New York: Vintage Books, 1963), p. 789ff.

Owen and marriage: Barbara Taylor, *Eve and the New Jerusalem: Socialism and Feminism in the Nineteenth Century* (New York: Pantheon Books, 1983), pp. 42, 45–46.

artisans in the United States: David Montgomery, *Workers' Control in America* (Cambridge: Cambridge University Press, 1979); ———, *Beyond Equality: Labor and the Liberal Republicans, 1862–1872* (Urbana: University of Illinois Press, 1981); see also David M. Gordon, Richard Edwards, and Michael Reich, *Segmented Work* (Cambridge: Cambridge University Press, 1981).

2. Buber: *Paths in Utopia*, p. 82ff.

Marx's utopianism: *Grundrisse der Kritik der politischen Ökonomie* (Berlin: Dietz Verlag, 1953), p. 592ff [*Grundrisse*, Penguin edition (Hammondsworth, Middlesex: Penguin, 1973), p. 704ff]; *Das Kapital, MEW* XXV, p. 828 [*Capital* (Moscow: Progress Publishers, 1971), p. 820]

"from each . . .": *MEW* XIX, p. 21 ("The Critique of the Gotha Program")

state and education: Ibid., p. 30.

"socialized man": *MEW* XXV, p. 828.

Manifesto: MEW IV, p. 481.

Marx and utopians: Richard Hunt, *The Political Ideas of Marx and Engels*, Vol. I, *Marxism and Totalitarian Democracy* (Pittsburgh: University of Pittsburgh Press, 1974), pp. 147ff, 171ff.

Marx on irrelevance of utopian tradition: *MEW* XIV, p. 439 [*Herr Vogt*].

Ernst Bloch, *Das Prinzip Hoffnung*, Vol. II (Frankfurt: Suhrkamp Verlag, 1959), p. 1410; Paul Ricoeur, *Lectures on Ideology and Utopia* (Chicago: University of Chicago Press, 1986), pp. 16, 61.

Proudhon polemic [original in French]: *Proudhon/Marx: Misère de la Philosophie/Philosophie de la Misère* (Paris: 10/18, 1964), p. 487ff.

The History of the Communist Party of the Soviet Union (Bolshevik) (New York: International Publishers, 1939), pp. 73ff, 184–85; Hal Draper, *The "Dictatorship of the Proletariat"* (New York: Monthly Review Press, 1986); Hunt, *Marxism*, p. 184ff.

Engels in 1891: *MEW* XXII, p. 509ff.

American Marxists: Paul Buhle, *Marxism in the USA* (London: Verson, 1987).

Ernst Bloch: *Das Prinzip Hoffnung* (Frankfurt: Suhrkamp Verlag, 1959), Vol. II, pp. 1620–21.

Thomas Meyer, *Bernstein's konstruktiver Sozialismus* (Berlin–Bonn–Bad Godesberg: Dietz Verlag, 1977), p. 38ff; Jean Cohen, *Class and Civil Society* (Amherst: University of Massachusetts Press, 1982), passim. Alvin Gouldner's *The Two Marxisms* (New York: Oxford University Press, 1980) makes a similar point but mutes the contradiction within Marx by making it part of a higher unity.

3. Kautsky and Luxemburg: Gary Steenson, *Karl Kautsky: 1854–1938* (Pittsburgh: University of Pittsburgh Press, 1978), p. 141.

"ignoramuses and intriguers": Victor Adler, *Briefwechsel mit August Bebel und Karl Kautsky* (Vienna: Verlag der Wiener Volksbuchhandlung, 1954), p. 464.

Engels on fossils: *MEW* XVI, p. 67.

Revolution of 1848: *MEW* VI, p. 397.

armed proletariat and liberals: *MEW* VII, p. 248.

1860s: Arthur Rosenberg, *Socialism and Democracy* (New York: Knopf, 1939), pp. 154–64, 297ff; Gustave Mayer, *Radikalismus, Sozialismus und burgerliche Demokratie* (Frankfurt: Suhrkamp Verlag, 1969), p. 141ff; Franz Mehring, *Geschichte der Deutschen Sozialdemokratie* (Berlin: Dietz Verlag, 1960), Vol. II, Book 3; Geoffrey Barraclough, *The Origins of Modern Germany* (New York: Norton, 1984), p. 425ff.

Lassalle and Bismarck: Hunt, *The Political Ideas of Marx and Engels*, Vol. II, *Classical Marxism, 1850–1895*, p. 167; Boris Nickolaevsky and Otto Menchen-Helfen, *Karl Marx, Man and Fighter*, (Hammondsworth, Middlesex: Penguin, 1977), p. 175; Isaiah Berlin, *Karl Marx* (London: Oxford University Press, 1950), p. 155ff.

Marx and Engels on Lassalle: *MEW* XVI, pp. 70, 76, 79; *MEW* XXX, p. 340; *MEW* XXXII, pp. 53, 55, 69, 446, 451; *MEW* XXXII, pp. 568–70.

Engels on bourgeois liberties: *MEW* XVI, p. 77.

social structure and Hitler: Barrington Moore, *Social Origins of Dictatorship and Democracy* (Boston: Beacon Press, 1966), pp. 184, 435, and passim.

conservatives and King of Prussia: Carl E. Schorske, *German Social Democracy, 1905–1917* (Cambridge, Mass.: Harvard University Press, 1955), p. 168.

negative integration: Gunther Roth, *The Social Democrats in Imperial Germany: A Study in Workingclass Isolation and National Integration* (Totowa, N.J.: Bedminster Press, 1963). For a critique of Roth, see Vernon Lidtke, *The Alternative Culture: Socialist Labor in Imperial Germany* (New York: Oxford University Press, 1985).

social democrats outside of Germany: John D. Stephens, "Democratic Transition and Breakdown in Europe, 1870–1939: A Test of the Moore Thesis," Working Paper #101, Helen Kellog Institute for International Studies, University of Notre Dame, 1987.

Jaurès at the 1904 Congress: *Comte Rendu Analytique* (Paris: Socialist International, 1904), pp. 132–34, 180ff.

Engels on middle strata: *MEW* XXII, p. 525.

On the puzzle of why Engels did not object to Kautsky's formulations, see Arthur Rosenberg, *Socialism and Democracy*, p. 293ff.

Kautsky and unemployment: A. M. and May Wood Simons, trans., *The Social Revolution* (Chicago: Charles Kerr, 1902), p. 111.

tactical coalitions: Massimo Salvadori, *Karl Kautsky and the Socialist Revolution* (London: New Left Books, 1979), p. 151ff.

Kautsky on Erfurt Program: Ibid., pp. 43, 51.

Engels in 1891: *MEW* XXII, p. 23.

Kautsky on Revolution: Salvadori, *Karl Kautsky*, p. 24.

Erfurt Program: Meyer, *Bernstein's konstruktiver Sozialismus*, pp. 391–92.

Bebel at Erfurt: Rosa Luxemburg, *Gesammelte Werke* (Berlin: Dietz Verlag, 1974), Vol. II, p. 284.

Braunthal: *Geschichte der Internationale*, Vol. I (Hannover: Dietz Verlag, 1961), p. 272.

Gramsci: *Quaderni del Carcere* (Turin: Einaudi, 1966), Vol. I, p. 13.

Lenin on Kautsky: *Collected Works* (Moscow: Progress Publishers, 1964), Vol. V, p. 383ff.

IWA Congresses and socialization: Braunthal, *Geschichte*, pp. 142–49.

Kautsky and state: *Das Erfurter Programm* (Stuttgart: Dietz Verlag, 1892), p. 130.

Engels on state socialism in Java: *MEW* XXXVI, p. 109.

Kautsky on state exploitation: *Das Erfurter Programm*, pp. 129–30.

freedom of labor: Ibid., pp. 167–69.

Kautsky and reality of party: Adler, *Briefwechsel*, pp. 501, 531, 582–83.

history and detour: Ernesto Laclau and Chantal Mouffe, *Hegemony and Socialist Strategy* (London: Verso, 1985), p. 19ff.

Jaurès quoted: Michael Harrington, *Socialism* (New York: Saturday Review, 1972), p. 200.

4. Schumpeter: Otto Bauer, *Die Oster-Reichische Revolution* (Vienna: Verlag der Wiener Volksbuchhandlung, 1965 [1923]), pp. 175–76.

Bauer description: Ibid., p. 199.

Party organ in 1918: Salvadori, *Karl Kautsky*, p. 235.

Korsch: *Schriften zu Sozialisierung* (Frankfurt: Europäische Verlagsanstalt, 1969), p. 25.

Lange: *Die Arbeiterfrage* (Winterthur: Bleuler-Hausheer, 1879), p. 370.

Carl Landauer: *European Socialism* (Berkeley: University of California Press, 1958), Vol. II, p. 1405.

Hilferding: *Das Finanzkapital* (Berlin: Dietz Verlag, 1947 [1910]).

Hilferding on socialism in the twenties: *Die Aufgaben der Sozial Demokratie in der Republik, Parteitag, 1927, Kiel* (Berlin: SPD, 1927), pp. 168–69.

Hilferding in 1932: W. S. Woytinsky, *Stormy Passage* (New York: Vanguard Press, 1961), p. 471.

British Labour in the twenties: Harrington, *Socialism*, p. 193ff.

Keynes as a "socialist": Elizabeth Durbin, *New Jerusalems* (London: Routledge and Kegan Paul, 1985), p. 65.

3 · Authoritarian Collectivisms

1. Lubomir Sochor: "Contribution to an Analysis of the Conservative Features of the Idealogy of 'Real Socialism'," (Munich: Research Project, Crises in Soviet-Type Systems, 1984), p. 5.

"false brothers": letter, Karl Marx to Joseph Wedemeyer, Jan. 1, 1859, *MEW* XXIX, p. 573.

Karl Kautsky and Lenin's seizure of power: Karl Kautsky; John H. Kautsky, ed., *The Dictatorship of the Proletariat* (Ann Arbor: University of Michigan Press, 1964), p. 61.

Guild Socialism: G. D. H. Cole, *History of Socialist Thought* (New York: St. Martin's Press, 1967), Vol. III-1, p. 246ff.

Lenin on revolution from below: "Can the Bolsheviks Retain State Power?" (October 1917), *Collected Works* [hereafter *CW*] (Moscow: Progress Publishers, 1964–68), Vol. XXVI, pp. 101–03, 112–13.

socialization of poverty: *MEW* III, pp. 34–35.

Kautsky's agreement with Trotsky and Lenin: Leon Trotsky, *1905* (New York: Random House, 1971), p. 21.

Lenin in 1920: *CW* XXXI, p. 21.

"declassed" proletariat: Lenin, *CW* XXXIII, p. 69; see also p. 310.

Trotsky on "substitutionism": Norman Geras, "Classical Marxism and Proletarian Representation" in *Literature of Revolution* (London: Verso, 1986).

Lenin on unions, 1920: "The Trade Unions, The Present Situation and Trotsky's Errors," *CW* XXXII, p. 20.

Lenin on social-democratic illusion: *CW* XXX, p. 266.

Luxemburg on Lenin, 1905: *Gesammelte Werke* (Berlin: Dietz Verlag, 1974), Vol. I-2, p. 440.

Luxemburg on bourgeois democracy: Ibid., Vol. IV, p. 359ff.

2. Lenin in 1918 on nationalization and state capitalism: *CW* XXVII, pp. 333, 334–35, 337, 339–40.

Taylorism: Ibid., p. 259.

Bukharin during War Communism: *Oekonomie der Transformationsperiode* (Hamburg: Rowohlt, 1970), pp. 77, 127; see also Stephen Cohen, "Bolshevism and Stalinism" in *Stalinism*, Robert Tucker, ed. (New York: Norton, 1977), pp. 20–21.

discontent in 1921: Robert Vincent Daniels, *Conscience of the Revolution* (New York: Simon and Schuster, 1969).

Lenin's last articles: *CW* XXXIII, pp. 462ff, 467ff, 476ff, 481ff, 487ff.

Bukharin on the "world city": Stephen Cohen, *Bukharin and the Bolshevik Revolution* (New York: Knopf, 1973), p. 253.

3. "revolution from above": *The History of the Communist Party of the Soviet Union (Bolshevik)* (New York: International Publishers, 1939), p. 305. This book was written under Stalin's personal direction.

Hannah Arendt: *Origins of Totalitarianism* (Cleveland and New York: World, 1958), revised edition, p. 318.

1925–26 situation: Cohen, *Bukharin*, p. 271; E. H. Carr, *Socialism in One Country* (Baltimore: Penguin, 1979), Vol. II, p. 389.

On the problem of investment: Alexander Erlich, *The Soviet Industrialization Debate* (Cambridge, Mass.: Harvard University Press, 1967), pp. 24–25.

Erlich on polemics: Robert Tucker, ed., "Stalinism and Marxian Growth Models" in *Stalinism*.

Preobrazhensky on "primitive socialist accumulation": Brian Pearce, trans., *The New Economics* (Oxford: Clarendon Press, 1961), Part II, "The Law of Primitive Socialist Accumulation."

Preobrazhensky's last articles: Alec Nove, *An Economic History of the USSR* (Hammondsworth, Middlesex: Penguin, 1982), revised edition, p. 127; see also Erlich, *Soviet Industrialization Debate*, p. 59.

the scholarly debates on Stalin: see Tucker, "Stalinism as Revolution from Above" in *Stalinism*, Tucker, ed.; Alec Nove, *Economic History*, p. 186; ———, *Socialism, Economics and Development* (London: Allen and Unwin, 1986), p. 80ff; Alexander Gerschenkron, *Economic Back-*

wardness in Historical Perspective (Cambridge, Mass., Belknap Press of Harvard University Press, 1966), p. 144ff; Isaac Deutscher, *Stalin: A Political Biography* (New York, Vintage Books, 1960), p. 295.

1929 and 1934: Nove, *Economic History*. Unless otherwise noted, the source for the history of Stalinism in the thirties narrated in the following pages is this volume by Nove.

comment to Churchill: Ibid., p. 177.

Nove on standard of living: Ibid., p. 108.

secret session: Ibid., p. 220.

genuine enthusiasm: Ibid., p. 191.

Stalin on "equality mongering": Collected Works (Moscow: Foreign Language Publishing House, 1954), XIII, p. 121.

Arendt: *Origins of Totalitarianism*, passim.

Deutscher: *Stalin*, p. 565ff.

4. Myrdal, *Asian Drama* (New York: Pantheon Books, 1968), Vol. II, pp. 799ff, 808, 722.

Indian socialism: Ibid., p. 808.

Sartre in *The Wretched of the Earth*, by Frantz Fanon (New York: Grove Press, 1963), p. 11.

Fanon: Ibid., pp. 82–83.

lumpenproletariat: Ibid., p. 104.

Chinese national bank: Theda Skocpol, *States and Social Revolutions* (Cambridge: Cambridge University Press, 1979), p. 243.

first years leading up to 1935: Harrington, *Socialism* (New York: Saturday Review, 1972), p. 222ff. In general, the sources for the Chinese history outlined in the next few pages are found in this volume and its notes.

Mao and the blank page: Quoted by Charles Johnson in "The Chinese Revolution," *China Quarterly* 39 (July–September 1965): 22–23. For a very similar statement by Mao, see *Selected Works* (Peking: Foreign Language Publishing House, 1977), Vol. V, p. 306.

Chinese industrial percentages: Skocpol, *States*, p. 247.

5. Rostow: *The Stages of Economic Growth* (Cambridge: Cambridge University Press, 1960). See also Myrdal, *Asian Drama*, Vol. II, p. 1847ff; and Alain Lipietz, "Marx and Rostow," *New Left Review* 132 (March–April 1982).

Rostow on Russian sequence: *Stages*, p. 93ff.

central "fact": Ibid., p. 126.

Kissinger: Michael Harrington, *The Vast Majority* (New York: Simon and Schuster, 1977), p. 40.

Barrington Moore, *Social Origins of Dictatorship and Democracy*

(Boston: Beacon Press, 1966). See also, Theda Skocpol, *States;* John D. Stephens, "Democratic Transition and Breakdown in Europe, 1870–1939: A Test of the Moore Thesis," Working Paper #101, Helen Kellog Institute for International Studies, University of Notre Dame, 1987.

Alexander Gerschenkron: *Economic Backwardness,* p. 353ff.

Myrdal on India and railroad: *Asian Drama,* pp. 456–57.

South Korea and Four Dragons: "Standing Tall: A Survey of South Korea," *London Economist,* May 28, 1988.

Marx on India: Shlomo Avineri, ed., *Karl Marx on Colonialism and Modernization* (New York: Doubleday, 1968), p. 132ff (original in English); on genetic and ethical justification, see also Frantz Mehring, "Die Neukantianer" in *Marxismus und Ethik,* Hans Jorg Sandkuhler and Rafeal de la Vega, eds. (Frankfurt: Suhrkamp Verlag, 1974), p. 363.

4 · *The* Realpolitik *of Utopia*

1. Bauer: *Zwischen Zweier Weltkriegen? Die Krise der Weltwirtschaft, der Demokratie und des Sozialismus* (Bratislava: Prager, 1936), p. 17.

Woytinsky: *Stormy Passage* (New York: Vanguard, 1961), p. 464; Mario Telo, *La Socialdemocrazia European nella Crisis Degli Anni Trenta* (Milan: Franco Angeli, 1985), p. 80.

Keynes and ILO: Telo, *La Socialdemocrazia,* p. 37.

De Man: Ibid., p. 90ff.

Blum on De Man: *L'Oeuvre de Leon Blum* (Paris: Albin Michel, 1972), Vol. III-2, pp. 543–44; see also Jean Lacouture, *Leon Blum* (New York: Holmes and Meier, 1982), p. 300.

Roosevelt in thirties: Kenneth Davis, *FDR: The New Deal Years, 1933–1937* (New York: Random House, 1986), p. 320.

Piore and Sabel: *The Second Industrial Divide* (New York: Basic Books, 1984), p. 96.

Blum and Roosevelt: Blum, *L'Oeuvre,* pp. 552, 587–91.

British Fabians: Elizabeth Durbin, *New Jerusalems: The Labour Party and the Economics of Democratic Socialism* (London: Routledge and Kegan Paul, 1985).

Crosland: *The Future of Socialism* (London: Jonathan Cape, 1961 [1955]), p. 59.

Swedish social-democratic history is drawn from Walter Korpi, *The Working Class in Welfare Capitalism* (London: Routledge and Kegan Paul, 1978); and John D. Stephens, *The Transition from Capitalism to Socialism* (London: Macmillan, 1979).

288 · Socialism

Stephens on 1920: *Transition*, p. 133.

Schumpeter on Wicksell: *History of Economic Doctrines* (New York: Oxford University Press, 1954), pp. 1117, 863n.

Myrdal: quoted in Telo, *La Socialdemocrazia*, p. 321, n. 104; see also p. 319, n. 96.

functional socialization: Ibid., p. 273.

2. Therborn: "Labour's High Plateau," *New Left Review* 145 (May–June 1984): 27 and passim.

Swedish income: *Social Indicators, 1976* (Washington: U.S. Department of Commerce, December 1977), p. 478.

3. Crosland and mass abundance: *Future of Socialism*, p. 515.

end of poverty: Ibid., p. 155.

nationalization: Ibid., Chapter 22.

Marx and ownership: Ibid., p. 69.

Harry Braverman, *Labor and Monopoly Capital* (New York: Monthly Review Press, 1975).

Crosland and industrial democracy: *Future of Socialism*, Chapter 16.

production for profit: Ibid., p. 92.

government influence: Ibid., p. 27.

Przeworski: *Capitalism and Social Democracy* (Cambridge: Cambridge University Press, 1985), p. 102ff.

Christine Bucci Glucksman and Goran Therborn: *Le Defi Social Democrate* (Paris: Maspero, 1981), p. 129.

4. on moral breakdown: Michael Harrington, *The Politics at God's Funeral* (New York: Holt, Rinehart and Winston, 1984).

Marcuse and Hilferding: Douglas Kellner, *Herbert Marcuse and the Crisis of Marxism* (Berkeley: University of California Press, 1984), pp. 233, 441, n. 5; Marcuse, *One-Dimensional Man* (Boston: Beacon Press, 1964).

Kolakowski on Marcuse: *Main Currents of Marxism* (New York: Oxford University Press, 1978), p. 96ff.

1967 Conference: *La Fin de l'Utopie* (Paris: Seuil, 1968), p. 87.

Kellner on Kolakowski and "totalitarianism": *Herbert Marcuse*, p. 479, n. 9.

one-dimensional society: Marcuse, *One-Dimensional Man*.

Marcuse on Marx and *Grundrisse:* Ibid., p. 35ff.

Marcuse coalition: Ibid., p. 2.

Harrod on Keynes: *The Life of John Maynard Keynes* (New York: St. Martin's Press, 1964), p. 333.

Minsky: *John Maynard Keynes* (New York: Columbia, 1978), p. 147.

"doctrinaire state socialism": John Maynard Keynes, *General Theory of Employment, Interest and Money* (New York: Harcourt Brace and World, 1964), p. 378.

1926 essay: John Maynard Keynes, *Essays in Persuasion* (New York: Norton, 1963), p. 341.

"social customs and economic practices": Ibid., p. 369.

G. E. Moore and Keynes: Alasdair MacIntyre, *After Virtue* (South Bend, Ind.: University of Notre Dame Press, 1981), pp. 14–15.

toast: Harrod, *The Life*, p. 194.

5 · *The End of Socialism?*

1. Peter Jenkins, *Mrs. Thatcher's Revolution: The Ending of the Socialist Era* (Cambridge, Mass.: Harvard University Press, 1988), p. 335; "Croslandite socialism," Ibid., p. 167.

Gordon, Edwards, and Reich: *Segmented Work, Divided Workers*, (Cambridge: Cambridge University Press, 1986 [1982]), p. 22ff.

Summary of conservative theories of the crisis: Chistrian Barrere, Gerard Kebadjian, and Olivier Weinstein, *Lire la Crise* (Paris: PUF, 1983).

Callaghan quote: Patrick Seyd, *The Rise and Fall of the Labour Left* (New York: St. Martin's Press, 1987), p. 23.

Keynes on inflation: *General Theory* (New York: Harcourt Brace and World, 1964), p. 303ff.

OECD: *Social Expenditures, 1960–1990* (Paris: OECD, 1983), p. 15.

five countries: Goran Therborn, *Why Some Peoples Are More Unemployed than Others* (London: Verso, 1986).

social expenditure timing: OECD, *Social Expenditures*, p. 14.

David Cameron, "Does Government Cause Inflation? Taxes, Spending and Deficits," in *The Politics of Inflation and Economic Stagnation*, Leon M. Lindberg and Charles S. Maier, eds. (Washington, D.C.: Brookings Institution, 1985), pp. 229–31.

Therborn on Japan: *Why Some Peoples*, p. 122.

character of transfer payments: OECD, *Social Expenditures*, pp. 57–58.

2. on the "regulation" of capitalism: see Gordon, Edwards, and Reich, *Segmented Work;* Michel Aglietta, *A Theory of Capitalist Regulation* (London: New Left Books, 1979 [1976]); Alain Lipietz, *L'Audace ou l'enlisement* (Paris: Editions de la Decouverte, 1983); Michael Piore and Charles Sabel, *The Second Industrial Divide* (New York: Basic Books, 1984); Michael Harrington, *The Next Left* (New York: Henry Holt, 1987).

law of gravity: *MEW* XXIII, p. 89 [*Capital* (Moscow: Progress Publishers, 1971), p. 80].

Fabians on socialization: "Industrial" by William Clarke in *Fabian Essays in Socialism*, Bernard Shaw, ed. (Gloucester, Mass.: Peter Smith, 1967).

Fordism: Harrington, *The Next Left*; Christine Bucci Glucksman and Goran Therborn, *Le Defi Social Democrate* (Paris: Maspero, 1981).

Brody: *Workers in Industrial America* (New York: Oxford University Press, 1980), Chapter 2.

Gramsci: *Quaderni del Carcere* (Turin: Einaudi, 1961), Vol. III, pp. 70–71, 106, 157; Vol. IV, "Americanismo e Fordismo," p. 309ff [*Selections from the Prison Notebooks*, Quinton Hoare and Geoffrey Nowell Smith, eds. and trans. (New York: International Publishers, 1971), pp. 118ff, 277ff].

France in the eighties: Michel Beaud, *La Politique Economique de la Gauche*, Vol. I: *Le Mirage de la Croissance* (Paris: Syros, 1983); Vol. 2: *Le Grand Ecart* (Paris: Syros, 1985).

3. social costs: James O'Connor, *The Fiscal Crisis of the State* (New York: St. Martin's Press, 1973).

Piore and Sabel: *Second Industrial Divide*, p. 184.

Keynes, capital and boom: *General Theory*, pp. 315, 323, 372.

French and British export percentages: Alain Lipietz, "Toward Global Fordism?," *New Left Review* 132 (March–April 1982): 36; see also, Piore and Sabel, *Second Industrial Divide*, p. 139.

Postwar trade patterns: David Gordon, "The Global Economy," *New Left Review* 168 (March–April 1988).

Mihelick: Louis Uchitelle, "As Output Gains, Wages Lag," *New York Times*, June 4, 1987.

Stephen Cohen and John Zysman: *Manufacturing Matters* (New York: Basic Books, 1987), p. 156.

Japanese cars: Ibid., p. 168.

Denmark and health: John Logue, "Will Success Spoil the Welfare State?," *Dissent* (Winter 1985): 87.

Fred Siegel: "Dependent Individualism," *Dissent* (Fall 1988): 437.

4. Martin Neil Baily and Alok K. Chakrabarti, *Innovation and the Productivity Crisis* (Washington, D.C.: Brookings Institution, 1988), p. 1.

Edward F. Denison, *Accounting for Slower Economic Growth* (Washington, D.C.: Brookings Institution, 1979), p. 4.

Lester Thurow, *The Zero Sum Solution* (New York: Simon and Schuster, 1985), pp. 57–58, 72, 78–79.

Baily and Chakrabarti on Thurow: *Innovation*, pp. 24–25.

Baily and Chakrabarti on new technology and business sector: Ibid., p. 101.

U.S. and Europe employment comparison: "America's Next Jobless," *The Economists* [London] (February 6, 1988).

Business Week on part-time jobs: December 15, 1986. See also interview with Sar Levitan, *New York Times*, August 14, 1988.

Congressional Research Service: *Children in Poverty*, Committee on Ways and Means, May 22, 1985, p. 10.

demand and innovation: Baily and Chakrabarti, *Innovation*, p. 108.

Barbara Timan, "Tory Paradox: In Thatcher's Britain, Free Enterprise Leads to More State Control," *Wall Street Journal*, October 6, 1988.

The New Spartans: Samuel Brittan, *A Restatement of Economic Liberalism* (London: Macmillan, 1988), p. 241.

Susan MacGregor, *The Poll Tax and the Enterprise Culture* (Manchester: CLES Reports, 1988), p. 14.

Council of Economic Advisors: *Economic Report of the President Together with the Annual Report of the Council of Economic Advisors, 1982* (Washington, D.C.: Government Printing Office, February 1982), pp. 116, 117.

government expenditures: Britain: Samuel Brittan, *Restatement*, pp. 245–46; United States: Tim W. Ferguson, "So Who Will Cut Federal Spending?" *Wall Street Journal*, July 17, 1988.

taxes in Britain: Peter Jenkins, *Mrs. Thatcher's Revolution*, p. 321.

United States income distribution: Lawrence Mishel and Jacqueline Simon, *The State of Working America* (Washington, D.C.: Economic Policy Institute, 1988), p. 6, Table 11, p. 9, Table 17.

North Sea and government assets: Andrew Gamble, *The Free Economy and the Strong State: The Politics of Thatcherism* (Durham, N.C.: Duke University Press, 1988), p. 123.

"good" jobs in the United States: Mishel and Simon, *State of Working America*, p. 285; Britain: Gamble, *Free Economy*, p. 234.

"darker side" of Thatcherism: Brittan, quoted, *Restatement*, p. 266.

5. Cohen and Zysman, *Manufacturing Matters*, passim.

Karl Mannheim, *Ideology and Utopia* (New York: Harcourt Brace, n.d.), p. 263. The German original was published in 1929, and the English translation of an expanded version of the text appeared in 1936.

6 · The Third Creation of the World

1. American Natural Resources Planning Board: Fred L. Block, *The Origins of International Economic Disorder* (Berkeley: University of California Press, 1977), p. 232, n. 16

Harry Dexter White: Ibid., p. 43.

Keynes: Ibid., p. 48.

Taft and Conservatives: Harry Wachtel, *The Money Mandarins* (New York: Pantheon Books, 1986), pp. 42–43; see also, Block, *Origins*, pp. 50–55, 71; Michael Piore and Charles Sabel, *The Second Industrial Divide* (New York: Basic Books, 1984), pp. 107–10.

Morganthau: Wachtel, *Money Mandarins*, p. 43.

1947 and Marshall Plan: Block, *Origins*, p. 82.

4.5 percent of GNP: Harold Lever and Christopher Huhne, *Debt and Danger* (Boston: Atlantic Monthly Press, 1986), p. 125.

"economic bonanza": Wachtel, *Money Mandarins*, p. 53.

Arthur Schlesinger, Jr.: *A Thousand Days* (Boston: Houghton Mifflin, 1965), pp. 649–50, 652, 654.

"Gold War": Wachtel, *Money Mandarins*, p. 76.

New York Stock Exchange: *U.S. International Competitiveness: Perception and Reality* (New York: NYSE, 1984), p. 16, Table 4.

transnationals' internal trade: Raymond Vernon, "Global Interdependence in a Historical Perspective," in *Interdependence and Co-Operation in Tomorrow's World* (Paris: OECD, 1987), p. 25.

trade and Pacific Rim: Robert Reich, "The Trade Gap" *New York Times*, February 12, 1988.

IMF strategy: Giovanni Andrea Cornia, Richard Jolly, and Frances Stephens, eds. *Adjustment with a Human Face, Volume I, Protecting the Vulnerable and Promoting Growth* (Oxford: Clarendon Press, 1987), pp. 52, 60, 66.

Lever and Huhne: *Debt and Danger*, p. 6.

nature of Third World Debt: *World Debt Tables, 1987–8, Volume I, Analysis and Summary Tables* (Washington, D.C.: World Bank, 1988), p. xi.

transfer of funds "worked": Lever and Huhne, *Debt and Danger*, p. 53.

terms of trade and Latin America: Enreique Iglesias, "The Impact of OECD Economic Policies on LDCs: A Comment," in *Interdependence and Co-Operation*, p. 107.

Keynes: *General Theory* (New York: Harcourt Brace and World, 1964), pp. 158–59.

"The Casino Society," *Business Week*, September 16, 1985.

Koren, "Longer Term Aspects of International Financial Flows," in *Interdependence and Co-Operation*, pp. 59–60.

Joint Economic Committee study: "The Impact of the Latin American Debt Crisis on the American Economy," May 10, 1986.

Bill Bradley: Quoted in Susan George, *A Fate Worse than Debt* (New York: Grove Press, 1988), p. 193.

World Bank on rescheduled debt: *World Debt Tables*, pp. xii–xiii.

World Bank 1988 estimates: Clyde H. Farnsworth, "Money Loss Grows for Poorer Lands, World Bank Finds," *New York Times*, December 19, 1988.

State of the World's Children Report: "Children Bear Third World Debt Burden, says UNICEF," *Financial Times*, December 21, 1988.

CEO of American Express: James D. Robinson III, "It's Time to Plan a Third World Revival." *New York Times*, August 28, 1988.

conservative think tank: William B. Johnston, *Workforce 2000* (Indianapolis: Hudson Institute, 1987), p. xxii.

2. population vs. wealth figures: Maurice Bertrand, *Refaire L'ONU* (Geneva: Editions Zoe, 1986), pp. 78–79.

manufactured exports of Third World: Kenneth Dadzie, "LDC Growth and Development: A Record of Diverse Experiences," in *Interdependence and Co-Operation in Tomorrow's World*, p. 49 and Table 3.

Gorz: *Paths to Paradise* (Boston: South End Press, 1985 [1983]), pp. 3–4.

South Korea and Taiwan: "Anything Japan Can Do," *Economist* (February 24, 1988); "Transition on Trial," *Economist* (March 5, 1988); "Stand Tall: A Survey of South Korea," *Economist* (May 21, 1988); "Korea Seeks to Develop Seven High-Tech Industries," *Wall Street Journal*, August 24, 1988; Giovanni Andrea Cornia, "Economic Development and Human Welfare in the First Half of the 1980s," in *Adjustment with a Human Face*, p. 27.

Latin America: *Economic Development in Latin America and the Debt Problem*, Joint Economic Committee (Washington: GPO, 1987), passim.

Kolm: *La Transition Socialiste* (Paris: Editions du Cerf, 1977); see also Alec Nove, *Socialism, Economics and Development* (Boston: Allen and Unwin, 1986), chapter 1.

Pinochet: Mayio, in *Economic Development in Latin America*, p. 283.

Michael Manley, *Global Challenge* (London: Pan, 1985), p. 147ff.

World Bank on African debt: *World Bank Tables*, Vol. I, p. xix.

Susan George: *A Fate Worse than Debt*, p. 87.

African agriculture: Manley, *Global Challenge*, pp. 146–47, 157.

Chakravarty: *Development Policies and the Crisis of the 1980s*, Louis Emmerij, ed. (Paris: OECD, 1987), p. 88.

Evelyne Huber Stephens and John Stephens: *Democratic Socialism in Jamaica* (Princeton: Princeton University Press, 1986), passim.

3. Brazil's trade policy: Ivo Daway, "Brazil switches to new trade strategy," *Financial Times*, April 7, 1988.

Maurice Bertrand: *Refaire L'ONU*, p. 93ff; "Some Reflections on Reform of the United Nations (Geneva: UN, 1985).

South-South trade: Manley, *Global Challenge*, p. 27.

Otto Bauer: *Die Nationalitatenfrage und die Sozialdemokratie* in *Werkeausgabe* (Wien: Europaverlag, 1975), Vol. I, p. 575.
comparative advantage: Ibid., p. 562ff.

7 · Socialization Revisited

1. Thomas Meyer, "Die Diskussion um das neue Grundsatzprogramm und die politischen Kulturen der Linke," Friedrich Ebert Stiftung, mimeo, June 16, 1986.

U.S. Congress, Office of Technology Assessment, *Technology and the American Economic Transition: Choices for the Future* (Washington, D.C.: U.S. Government Printing Office, May 1988), p. 3.

Wierton case: "Has Wierton's ESOP Worked Too Well?," *Business Week*, January 23, 1989.

Zuboff: *In the Age of the Smart Machine* (New York: Basic Books, 1988).

managerial expertise: Ibid., Part Two, "The Spiritual Dimensions of Authority."

The Accidental Century (New York: Macmillan, 1965).

psychology of managers: Zuboff, *Smart Machine*, p. 245ff.

Marx: *Grundrisse der Kritik der politischen Okonomie* (Berlin: Dietz Verlag, 1953), p. 592ff.

Technology, Economic Growth and the Labour Process: Phil Blackburn, Red Coombs, Kenneth Green (New York: St. Martin's Press, 1985).

2. postwar nationalization debate: Horst Heiman, "Das Sozialismusverstandnis des Godesberger Programms und seine parteioffentliche sowie offentliche Resonanz," in *Braucht die SPD ein neues Grundsatzprogramm?*, Sven Papcke and Karl Tehodor Schuon, eds. (Berlin: Verlag und Versansbuchhandlung Europäische Perspektiven, 1985); Patrick Seyd, *The Rise and Fall of the Labour Left* (New York: St. Martin's Press, 1987), p. 12.

on criteria for nationalization: see Alec Nove, *The Economics of Feasible Socialism* (London: Allen and Unwin, 1983), p. 167ff.

left-wing French socialist: quoted in Michel Beaud, *La Politique Economique de la Gauche*, Vol. II, *Le Grand Ecart* (Paris: Syros, 1985), p. 90.

Swedish wage-earner funds: Rudolf Meidner and Anna Hedborg, *Model Schweden* (Frankfurt: Campus Verlag, 1984), passim.

Northern Italy: Charles Sabel, *Work and Politics* (Cambridge: Cambridge University Press, 1984 [1982]), p. 219ff; see also Dieter Otten, "Die Aktualitat der Genossenschaftsidee für die Bewaltigung der dritte industrieller Revolution," *Neue Gesellschaft*, December 1984.

critics of small machine shops: Joanne Barkan, *Visions of Emancipation* (New York: Praeger, 1984).

ESOPs: "Revolution or Ripoff," *Business Week*, April 25, 1985.

Wall Street Journal on General Motors modernization: Jacob M. Schlesinger and Paul Ingrassia, "GM Woos Employees . . . ," *Wall Street Journal*, January 12, 1989.

Home work: Ranier Wagner, "Wie fortschittliche sind die neuer Technologien?," *Neue Gesellschaft/Frankfurter Hefte*, January 1985.

Auroux laws: Michel Beaud, *Le Grand Ecart*, p. 206.

Gorz: *Farewell to the Workingclass* (Boston: South End Press, 1982 [1980]); see also *Paths to Paradise* (Boston: South End Press, 1985).

3. François Mitterrand, "Lettre a tous les Français," Paris, 1988, pp. 21–22.

Kaufman: quoted in Harry Magdoff and Paul M. Sweezy, *Stagnation and the Financial Explosion* (New York: Monthly Review, 1987), p. 22. I am indebted to this volume for many of the ideas in this section of the chapter.

debt and GNP: Ibid., p. 15.

Keynes: *General Theory* (New York: Harcourt Brace and World, 1964), p. 373.

"rewards of success and punishments of failure": Christopher Jecks, *Inequality* (New York: Basic Books, 1972), p. 218.

Drucker: *The Unseen Revolution* (New York: Harper and Row, 1976).

Swedish pension funds: John D. Stephens, *The Transition from Capitalism to Socialism* (London: Macmillan, 1979), p. 178.

Kuttner: "Blue Collar Board Room," *New Republic*, June 17, 1985.

Business Week, September 19, 1988.

Office of Technology Assessment, *Technology*, p. 53.

Stephen S. Cohen and John Zysman, *Manufacturing Matters* (New York: Basic Books, 1987).

Richard Lowenthal: "Godesberg und die gesellschaftliche Situation unserer Zeit," in *Braucht die SPD ein neues Grundsatzprogramm?*

8 · *Market and Plan*

1. Ten Hours Law: *MEW* XXIII, pp. 275–321 [*Capital*, Progress Publishers, ed., I, pp. 252–87].

"absolute" and "relative" surplus value: Ibid., Sections 3, 4, and 5.

"modest Magna Carta": Ibid., p. 320 [Progress, p. 286].

"triumph of the political economy . . .": *MEW* XVI, p. 11.

"historic tendency": *MEW* XXIII, Chapter 24, Section 7 [Progress, Chapter 32].

Selucky: *Marxism, Socialism and Freedom* (New York: St. Martin's Press, 1979), p. xi.

2. Bukharin's 1924 polemic: "Une nouvelle revelation sur l'economique Sovietiste . . . ," in *Le Debat Sovietique Sur La Loi de Valeur* (Paris: Maspero, 1972), pp. 197–98.

Bukharin on Lenin's last essays: "La Nouvelle Politique Economique et nos Taches," in *La Question Paysanne en U.R.S.S. (1924–1929)* (Paris: Maspero, 1973), pp. 147–48, 155.

Trotsky: "The Soviet Economy in Danger," in *Writings of Leon Trotsky (1932)* (New York: Pathfinder, 1973), pp. 277–78; *The Revolution Betrayed* (New York: Merit, 1965), p. 75. See also Alec Nove, "Trotsky, Collectivization and the Five Year Plan," in *Socialism, Economics and Development* (London: Allen and Unwin, 1986).

Stalin's economic policies in late thirties: Alec Nove, *An Economic History of the U.S.S.R.* (Hammondsworth, Middlesex: Penguin, 1982 [revised ed.]), p. 261.

Arendt: *Origins of Totalitarianism* (Cleveland and New York: World Publishing Company, 1958 [revised ed.]), p. 495.

second edition: Ibid., "Reflections on the Hungarian Revolution."

Arendt on Khrushchev: Ibid., p. 493.

anti-Stalinist campaign lasted until 1964: Serewyn Bialer, *The Soviet Paradox* (New York: Vintage, 1986), p. 9.

Khrushchev the last true believer: Ibid., p. 12.

Brezhnev raised living standard: Ibid., p. 46.

Zaslavskaya: Ibid., p. 134.

Brezhnev and problems: M. Elizabeth Denton, "Soviet Perceptions of Economic Problems, in *Soviet Economy in the 1980s: Problems and Prospects* (Washington, D.C.: Joint Economic Committee, Government Printing Office, December 31, 1982), pp. 32–33. Denton wrote her analysis as an employee of the Central Intelligence Agency, but there is no reason to think that it is anything but a scholarly account.

1979 "avalanche": Martin J. Kohn, "Overview," in *Soviet Economy in the 1980s*, p. 4. Kohn was also employed by the CIA when he authored this essay.

Deng reforms: Harry Harding, *China's Second Revolution: Reform after Mao* (Washington, D.C.: Brookings Institution, 1987), passim.

Reformers and Four Tigers: Ibid., pp. 78–79.

Safire: Ibid., p. 128.

China's output sectors: Ibid., p. 129, Table 5–2.

John King Fairbank, *The Great Chinese Revolution, 1800–1985* (New York: Harper and Row, 1987), pp. 348, 350.

French analysts: Denis Clerc, Alain Lipietz, and J. Satre-Buisson, *La Crise* (Paris: Syros, 1985), pp. 111–12.

Gorbachev: *Political Report of the CPSU Central Committee to the 27th Party Congress* (Moscow: Novosti Press Agency Publishing House, 1986), p. 42.

3. Swedish labor-market policy: Walter Korpi, *The Working Class and Welfare Capitalism* (London: Routledge and Kegan Paul, 1978); Rudolf Meidner and Anna Hedborg, *Model Schweden* (Frankfurt: Campus Verlag, 1984); John D. Stephens, *The Transition from Capitalism to Socialism* (London: Macmillan, 1979).

Attali: *La Nouvelle Economie Française* (Paris: Flammarion, 1978), p. 188.

Grundrisse: (Berlin: Dietz Verlag, 1953), p. 593 [*Grundrisse*, Hammondsworth, Middlesex: Penguin, 1973, p. 705].

Nove on Marx: *The Economics of Feasible Socialism* (London: Allen and Unwin, 1982), pp. 15–16.

Daniel Callaghan, *Setting Limits* (New York: Simon and Schuster, 1987), p. 184.

Neighborhood Health Centers: Paul Starr, "Health Care for the Poor," in *Fighting Poverty: What Works and What Doesn't*, Sheldon Danziger and D. H. Weinberg, eds. (Cambridge, Mass.: Harvard University Press, 1986); Lisbeth Schorr with Daniel Schorr, *Within Our Reach* (New York: Doubleday, 1988), p. 130.

German long-range program: Thomas Meyer, "Die Diskussion um das neue Grundsatzprogramm." Friedrich Ebert Stiftung mimeo, June 16, 1986.

alternative movements in Germany: *Lern- und Arbeitsbuch deutsche Arbeiterbewegung*, Meyer, Miller, and Rohlfes, eds. (Bonn: Verlag Neue Gesellschaft, 1988), p. 18.

Oskar Lafontaine, *Die Gesellschaft der Zukunft* (Hamburg: Hoffmann und Campe, 1988), pp. 123, 119.

Nove: *The Economics of Feasible Socialism*, pp. 19–30; "Market Socialism," *NLR* 161 (January–February 1987); Mandel, "In Defense of Socialist Planning," *NLR* 159 (September–October 1986).

Stojanovic: Svetozar Stojanovic, *Between Ideals and Reality* (New York: Oxford University Press, 1973), pp. 127, 132.

Attali and failure: *La Nouvelle Economie Française*, p. 207.

Crosland: *The Future of Socialism* (London: Jonathan Cape, 1956), p. 92.

"socialized markets": Diane Elson, "Socialization of the Market," *New Left Review* (November–December 1988).

9 · *Visionary Gradualism*

1. A recent book, quite interesting in some of its insights but excessively "orthodox" in its framework, relates contemporary revisions of Marxist doctrine to the True Socialists: Ellen Meiksins Wood, *The Retreat from Class* (London: Verso, 1986).

The Communist Manifesto: MEW IV, p. 473 [*Selected Works in One Volume* (New York: International Publishers, 1986), p. 45].

The Theories of Surplus Value: MEW XXVI-2, p. 576 [Chapter 18].

history of "classical Marxism": I found the comments on this subject in *Hegemony and Socialist Strategy* by Chantal Mouffe and Ernesto Laclau (London: Verso, 1985) quite stimulating even though I share Jeff Issac's criticism of that book in *Power and Marxist Theory* (Ithaca, N.Y.: Cornell University Press, 1987).

Luxemburg on 1905: *Gesammelte Werke* (Berlin: Dietz Verlag, 1974), I-2, pp. 487ff; II, p. 9.

Bernstein: *Die Voraussetzungen der Sozialismus* (Berlin: Dietz Verlag, 1923), pp. 183, 246.

popularity of Gramsci: See Chantal Mouffe, ed., *Gramsci and Marxist Theory* (London: Routledge and Kegan Paul, 1979).

"Western" Marxism: Perry Anderson, *Considerations on Western Marxism* (London: New Left Books, 1976).

Scholars have called attention to similarities between Gramsci and Otto Bauer as well as between Gramsci and Bernstein. See Detlev Albers, Josef Hindels, and Lucio Lombardo Radice, *Otto Bauer und die "Dritte" Weg* (Frankfurt: Campus Verlag, 1979).

2. blacks in the United States and "guest workers" in Europe: See my discussion of these phenomena in *The New American Poverty* (New York: Holt, Rinehart and Winston, 1984).

funding of welfare-state programs for the aging: *Social Expenditure, 1960–1990* (Paris: OECD, 1985), p. 30, Table 5 ("Pensions") and pp. 57–58, 61.

European peasants and American blacks: Michael Piore and Charles Sabel, *The Second Industrial Divide* (New York: Basic Books, 1984), pp. 167–68.

working-class militancy in late sixties: Robert J. Flanagan, David W. Soskice, and Lloyd Ulman, *Unions, Economic Stabilization, and Income Policies: European Experience* (Washington, D.C.: Brookings Institution, 1983), pp. 8, 371–73, 650.

French workers in 1968: Ibid., p. 579.

3. trends in U.S. working class: *Statistical Abstract of the United States, 1987* (Washington, D.C.: Bureau of the Census, 1986), p. 389, Table 661.

Robert Blauner: *Alienation and Freedom* (Chicago: University of Chicago Press, 1964).

annual meeting of American Economic Association: quoted in Richard B. Freeman and James L. Medoff, *What Do Unions Do?* (New York: Basic Books, 1984), pp. 243–44.

Hine: "Leaders and Followers: Democracy and Manageability in the Social Democratic Parties of Western Europe" in *The Future of Social Democracy*, William E. Paterson and Alastair H. Thomas, eds. (Oxford: Clarendon Press, 1986), p. 277.

Mallet: *La Nouvelle Classe Ouvrière* (Paris: Seuil, 1969).

Middle managers: "Caught in the Middle," *Business Week*, September 12, 1988.

Engels's 1894 letter [to W. Borgius]: *MEW XXXIX*, p. 205 (*Selected Works*, p. 704). This document was mistaken for a long time as a letter to Heinz Starkenberg, who published it, and is cited under this incorrect rubric by Lukacs in *Geschichte und Klassenbewustssein*.

Georg Lukacs: "Der Functionwechsel des historischen Materialismus," in *Geschichte und Klassenbewustssein* (Berlin: Malik Verlag, 1923 ["The Changing Function of Historical Materialism" in *History and Class Consciousness*, Rodney Livingstone, trans. (Cambridge, Mass.: MIT Press, 1968].

Habermas: *Theorie des kommunikativen Handelns* (Frankfurt: Surhkamp Verlag, 1981).

4. On Marxism and ethics, see my essay, "Preliminary Thoughts for a Prolegomena to a Future Analysis of Marxism and Ethics," in *Darwin, Marx and Freud*, Austin L. Caplan and Bruce Jennings, eds. (New York and London: Plenum Press, 1984).

The Politics at God's Funeral (New York: Holt, Rinehart and Winston, 1983); *After Virtue* (Notre Dame, Ind.: University of Notre Dame Press, 1980).

Weber: *From Max Weber: Essays in Sociology*, H. H. Gerth and C. Wright Mills, trans. and eds. (London: Routledge and Kegan Paul, 1948), p. 331.

Marx on capital in *Grundrisse: Grundrisse der Kritik des politischen Okonomie* (Berlin: Dietz Verlag, 1953), p. 387 [*Grundrisse*, (Hammondsworth, Middlesex: Penguin, 1973), p. 487].

"On the Jewish Question": "Zur Judenfrage," *MEW* I, p. 347ff.

Aristotle: *The Politics*, Vol. III, *Aristotle in Twenty-three Volumes*, with an English translation by H. Rockmann, M.A. (Cambridge, Mass.: Harvard University Press, 1972), pp. 216–17.

young Marx and workers: *MEW* I, pp. 553–54 [*Karl Marx Economic and Philosophic Manuscripts of 1844* (Moscow: Foreign Language Publishing House, n.d. [1956?], pp. 124–25].

"instrumental collectivism": John H. Goldthorpe, David Lockwood, Frank Bechhofer, and Jennifer Platt, *The Affluent Worker in the Class Structure* (Cambridge: Cambridge University Press, 1969), pp. 26, 170, 187.

Bernstein on ethics: quoted, Meyer, *Bernstein's Konstruktive Sozialismus*, pp. 254–55.

Tawney: see R. H. Tawney, *Equality* (New York: Harcourt, Brace and Company, 1931), passim; and Ross Terrill, *R. H. Tawney and His Times* (Cambridge, Mass.: Harvard University Press, 1973), p. 210.

Irving Howe: *Socialism in America* (New York: Harcourt Brace Jovanovich, 1985), pp. 162–63.

convergence of Left and Right: Habermas, *Theorie*, Vol. II, p. 578.

Walzer, in Howe, *Socialism*, pp. 163–65.

Horkheimer: Martin Jay, *The Dialectical Imagination* (Boston: Little, Brown, 1973), p. 119.

Marx on Aristotle: *Das Kapital*, Vol. I, *MEW* XXIII, pp. 73–74 [*Capital* (Moscow: Progress Publishers, 1971), pp. 60–65].

Bernstein: *Die Voraussetzungen*, pp. 183, 246.

Arendt: *On Revolution* (New York: Viking Press, 1963).

Kitchin: *Rethinking Socialism* (London: Methuen, 1983), p. 33.

Salvatore: *Eugene Victor Debs, Citizen and Socialist* (Urbana: University of Illinois Press, 1982), p. 148.

Index